D0545399

Other books by the author:

Theatre Language
William Shakespeare: Writing for Performance
New Sites for Shakespeare: Theatre, the Audience and
  Asia
Shakespeare: The Tragedies
The Oxford Illustrated History of Theatre (*editor*)

Shakespeare
and
the Theatrical Event

John Russell Brown

palgrave
macmillan

First published 2002 by
PALGRAVE MACMILLAN
Houndmills, Basingstoke, Hampshire RG21 6XS and
175 Fifth Avenue, New York, N.Y. 10010
Companies and representatives throughout the world.

PALGRAVE MACMILLAN is the global academic imprint of the Palgrave
Macmillan division of St Martin's Press, LLC and of Palgrave Macmillan Ltd.
Macmillan® is a registered trademark in the United States, United Kingdom
and other countries. Palgrave is a registered trademark in the European
Union and other countries.

ISBN 0–333–80131–8 hardcover
ISBN 0–333–80132–6 paperback

This book is printed on paper suitable for recycling and
made from fully managed and sustained forest sources.

A catalogue record for this book is available
from the British Library.

Library of Congress Cataloging-in-Publication Data

Brown, John Russell.
Shakespeare and the theatrical event / John Russell Brown.
   p. cm
Includes bibliographical references and index.
ISBN 0–333–80131–8 – ISBN 0–333–80132–6 (pbk.)
  1. Shakespeare, William, 1564–1616–Dramatic production.
2. Theater–Production and direction. 3. Theater audiences. I. Title

PR3091 .B727 2002
792.9'5–dc21   2002074800

10   9   8   7   6   5   4   3   2   1
11   10   09   08   07   06   05   04   03   02

Printed in China

Contents

Preface   vii

Introduction: Theatrical Events   1

PART I: AUDIENCES

1   Playgoing and Participation   7
2   Functions   30
3   Responses   41

PART II: ACTORS

4   Texts and Techniques   65
5   Persons in a Play   84
6   Parts to Perform   100
7   Actions and Reactions   117
8   Visual Interplay   137
9   Improvisation   150

PART III: CONTEXTS

10   Stage Space   165
11   Off-Stage Space   180
12   Time   197

PART IV: PLAYS IN PRINT

13   Reading   207
14   Study and Criticism   211

Index   232

Preface

To describe, analyse and assess a single performance of one of Shakespeare's plays as an event taking place through the active co-operation of many people and for the pleasure of many others is a formidable task. To define the potential of any one play in a number of such events is still more difficult. Yet these are necessary steps towards an understanding of Shakespeare's achievements that this book sets out to describe and exemplify. Elements of a theatrical event are considered one at a time, starting with the gathering of an audience, the contribution of author and actors, and the response of audiences. The next section discusses what an actor does on stage in response to a text, the performances of other actors, and an audience's reactions. A third section proceeds to the context of performance, both on stage and in a social and historical environment. In conclusion, a fourth section considers how theatrical events can be taken into account when reading and studying the printed texts.

Although its subject is large, this is a short book, offering not an account of any one play but an introduction to phenomena that need to be taken into account if we are to respond to any of the plays in a manner appropriate to the experience they were intended to give. I have had in mind readers already interested in Shakespeare, hoping to encourage independent study of the plays and to suggest new ways of staging them. Readers who have had little opportunity to see them in performance are offered ways of extending that experience in relation to other plays.

I have tested some of my arguments in conference papers and published articles before developing them here and my indebtedness to those opportunities are acknowledged in endnotes to individual chapters. I have benefited from membership of a working party on 'The Theatrical Event' sponsored by the International Federation for Theatre Research; discussions with fellow members have greatly increased my awareness of the scope of this enterprise. When the book began to take shape, research grants from Middlesex University supported my travel and supplied funds for workshops in which I was able to explore acting techniques that are no longer in common use.

I have been indebted continually to colleagues and students at Michigan, Middlesex, and Columbia Universities and to actors, directors, and producers with whom I have worked over the last dozen or so years; the contributions of these colleagues have been so pervasive and, by now, so thoroughly digested that I have been quite unable to keep track of them. In chapter endnotes I am able to acknowledge particular debts to printed works but I must ask my many close associates to accept this general acknowledgement by way of thanks; its brevity should not hide the fact that this book could not have been written without their help. Four friends I can thank for the very particular assistance of reading and commenting on the first draft of this book: Dennis Kennedy, Randall Martin, Robert Shaughnessy, and Tony Thorlby. I have tried to benefit from their insights and recommendations without which the book would have been much the poorer; its remaining faults are entirely my own.

At Palgrave Macmillan, Anna Sandeman has guided and encouraged the book's progress and Judy Marshall has been its attentive copy-editor. I am most grateful for all they have done on my behalf.

Unless otherwise stated, quotations and references to Shakespeare's plays are from the edition by Peter Alexander (London: Collins, 1951, and many times reprinted into the present century).

Introduction: Theatrical Events

On leaving a theatre and being asked what was most remarkable in a performance of *Hamlet*, most people will be likely to speak about one person in the play. Among many different answers, they may remember Hamlet when he swore revenge or first saw Ophelia, the Ghost on his entry, or the First Player weeping for Hecuba. Encounters, too, may be remembered: Hamlet seeing the Ghost and then listening to him, or seeing Claudius and deciding not to kill him; the long meeting with his mother in her closet; his encounter with Yorick's skull, his struggle with Laertes in Ophelia's grave or their final fight together. A few memories may concern figures isolated among others: Gertrude sitting and wringing her hands, the Polish Captain remaining on stage to answer Hamlet, Osric flourishing his hat, Fortinbras entering to face the on-stage carnage. The odds are high that these memories will not be concerned with verbal statements or arguments, or the meaning of the play: the primary memory will be of performance, of an actor's presence and what he or she does.[1] The words of the playtext may not have registered at all.

Even when a few words are securely held in the memory, the manner of speaking them, the situation in which they were spoken, and the speaker's commitment to them are inseparable from those words and tend to dominate their effect. Performance can turn familiar words into extraordinary expressions of deep and exact feeling as, for example, 'My father's spirit in arms!' or 'I loved Ophelia'. When words are used to define an intellectual dilemma or belief – as in 'To be or not to be ...' or 'The readiness is all' – the posing of the idea, the tone, phrasing and timing of speech, together with the physical and emotional state of the speaker, are all inextricably part of what an audience experiences at that moment. In a theatre, words are not encountered as in a book, all the same size and neatly marshalled, awaiting the moment of reception and understanding; they come to life with sudden vividness or simplicity, tension or passion, with a form and pressure that seem entirely necessary to the speaker.

What words can do when they are part of a theatre performance is too complicated and variable for the reader of a text to comprehend easily and yet Shakespeare's plays were written for this kind of presentation. He worked in a theatre, had a share in its ownership, and was a member of its resident acting company: through repeated and close experience, he knew how theatrical performances come about and how the effect of his words would change every time they were acted on a stage. He was aware of a whole theatre of spectators responding instinctively – without second thoughts – to a happening that might send them away wanting to return for another play or for the same one over again. He must also have known that his writing served this audience and that their pleasure was essential for the well-being of the theatre; he was his company's leading playwright and, more frequently than other poets writing for them, he could fill its auditorium and various others around the country and at court.

Words and Sensations

Every one who is prepared to seek out meanings and suggestions in the text of one of Shakespeare's plays will know how far this study can lead, even before any attention has been paid to its performative possibilities. Shakespeare took great pleasure in the use of words and also wrestled with them so that he could set down his thoughts for others to understand and to communicate feelings that would otherwise remain lost forever. For all these reasons, the plays have been studied as literature, writings that have meanings to enrich and exercise the keenest intelligence. They have become storehouses of subtle arguments and amazing verbal images, specimens to be carefully dissected and analysed. Poets and philosophers echo these words and wonder at them. No library is without a copy of all 36 or 37 plays and new editions are published year after year. Shakespeare's words are popular, too: quotations are to be found everywhere, on advertisements and greeting cards, in political debate and exhortation, in journalism, sermons, lovemaking, and day-dreaming. We can meet a phrase or two of Shakespeare's at almost any time in almost any circumstance.

But all this does a disservice to the words, because it misuses them. Shakespeare's texts were not written to be read, either silently or aloud; they were meant to be part of entire plays performed by actors on a stage before audiences, events that are almost as complicated as life itself, and more able to give pleasure. Memory, emotion, sensation, sound, physical presence, movement in space, and nervous tension are all part of the illusory world they were written to set in motion. Shakespeare thought of words as they would be embodied by actors with the assistance of producers, managers, technicians, dressmakers, carpenters, all contributing according to their own skills and individual identities, shaped by their life-stories and social backgrounds. He must have known that each time a play was performed it would be different, revealing new possibilities, as performers and audiences changed and as accident and fresh invention played their parts. When we try to understand Shakespeare's texts as a part of plays in performance, little is indisputable. We are faced with elements that are temporary and local as well as those that are permanent and generally viable. We should be ready to venture into territory where we may well lose our bearings.

Considering Shakespeare's plays as they become part of a theatrical event, each one different from all previous ones, will lead us to think about the ways in which Shakespeare thought about theatre, how he responded to his life and times, what he imagined might become of himself and others, what pleasures he discovered, what warnings he felt impelled to give. Feelings, sensations, and physical presence will be taken into account, as well as words and their meanings; the time and place of performance and the people who create and share in it are also involved. This book investigates one aspect of the theatrical event at a time, seeking what is common to all performances as well as particular to a single one, and taking into account the conditions of performance in Shakespeare's day and our own. Various approaches are used, sometimes with regard to a single play, sometimes moving rapidly between several.

Notes

1. Commenting on his own thoroughly documented research into audience-responses, Willmar Sauter concluded that, for most spectators, 'How something is performed is obviously more important than *what* is performed': and this did not seem to vary with choice of play (*The Theatrical Event: Dynamics of Performance and Perception* [Iowa City: University of Iowa Press, 2000], pp. 46–7).

PART I : AUDIENCES

1

Playgoing and Participation

When a play becomes part of a theatrical event, anything that happens on stage will have meaning, give pleasure, or cause uncertainty according to how the audience receives it.[1] In one way, this makes judging its effect easier because we can all be members of an audience and use our own experiences to elucidate what happens on any one occasion, but our experiences will differ and we have little means of holding on to passing impressions. In trying to understand a play's effect on an audience, the best way to start is to stand back and observe other people's behaviour as well as our own, and to start at the beginning.

How we come to the theatre and take our places in the auditorium and how we relate to the actors on stage provide the basis for every other experience, and these factors differ greatly from one theatre to another and from one age to another. For us, theatre-going to see a play by Shakespeare is an experience very unlike anything he might have envisaged and so our understanding of the theatrical event has to be qualified by theatre history and by the present-day practices of theatres that satisfy their audiences with very different repertoires.

Elizabethan and Present-day Playgoers

Playgoing in Shakespeare's day was a lengthy, complicated, and unpredictable business, not to be conveniently fitted in after a long day's work, other diversions, or an evening meal. To get to the Globe, you probably had to walk through the tangle of narrow city streets and then cross the single bridge over the Thames or pay a water-man to ferry you across – the latter option not always an easy trip with the quick-flowing tide. Or you might travel on horseback, finding a boy to take care of your mount during the show; if very wealthy, you could use a coach and its attendants. Performance started at two o'clock in the afternoon but, for a popular attraction or on a holiday, you would be well advised to arrive much earlier to secure a good seat or be sure of admission to standing room in the yard. At the Boar's Head, we know that doors were shut to the inn's regular customers at eleven in the morning when the business of theatre began to take over for the afternoon's performance.[2]

In winter, at the height of the theatrical season, a play would end at half-past four or five, in twilight or, perhaps, darkness, and then you would have to make your way home through unlit streets. In Spain at the end of the seventeenth century, performance time in the open-air courtyard theatres was brought forward in winter by up to two hours so that playgoers could be home before dark,[3] even though their theatres, being much nearer to the Equator, enjoyed longer winter daylight. In London, the enjoyment of a play could take five or six hours of your time and a good deal of effort and ingenuity as well. If you stayed on for a jig – a comic diversion after the main attraction – you would need still more time. Refreshments were necessary in such conditions and so drinks and snacks were on sale during performances.

Not everyone could be kept happy all the time, and those who had expended a good deal of energy to stand and see what they hoped to enjoy could well become rest-less and sometimes disorderly if they were disappointed. Scuffles and general lawlessness were not uncommon and pickpockets thrived in the crowds. Only in comparatively recent years has theatre-going become peaceable, com-fortable, and convenient; well into the eighteenth century, two armed grenadiers were posted at either side of the stage as a reminder that the audience had to be kept under some measure of control.[4] A notorious example of theatre rioting occurred in New York in 1849 when William Charles Macready was assaulted on stage with eggs, apples, potatoes, wood, and at least one bottle of drink; the performance of *Macbeth* had to stop and the actor escorted to his lodgings before rioting spread to the streets and numerous people were killed.[5] Although these Astor Place riots were fired by nationalistic as well as theatrical rivalries, the fact that a theatre audience could be manipulated to such an effect marks how far playgoing in comparatively recent times was more volatile than in our own.

At the end of the nineteenth century, a visit to the theatre could still be a lengthy and uncertain business. Seats were unreserved and, for a popular attraction, queues would form before doors opened in late afternoon. To secure a good seat for the first night of Henry Irving's *Hamlet* in 1874, you would have to arrive some hours early or send someone else to stand in line for you. When the audience was settled into its places, a farce was performed before the play itself could begin and then the production took its own time. You would not leave the theatre until five and a half hours later, well after midnight, and then you had to get home; the streets were better lit and policed by this time but, since the city was now more widespread, the journey might well take longer. To be sure of seeing this performance of *Hamlet*, you would have had to set aside some six or seven hours of one day and at least one of the next.[6]

Today, in a more prearranged world, playgoing is much easier. Access is comparatively easy, either by public transport or by using convenient and subsidized carparks. Promotion and sales have benefited from modern technology so that we always know what is showing and what seats are available. We can phone or e-mail to reserve a seat and pay by credit card. In some countries, we can buy a subscription for a whole theatre season and take whatever is on offer, month by month, assured of the same excellent seat on every occasion. If we decide to go at the last minute and fail to get a ticket on arrival at the theatre, we can always go off to some other play or enjoy some other entertainment that is available: a film, concert, or sports event; or we could go home to watch television or videos. Once in the theatre, we expect to sit comfortably in undisturbed darkness while the actors play to our respectful attention; we are likely to be hushed by other playgoers if we start to talk or make the slightest disturbance, such as rustling sweetpapers. Our day-by-day lives will be very little disturbed as theatre occupies a few predictable hours.

At best, our theatre-going is a minority enthusiasm, not a popular and communal event. Educational initiatives, tourism, and state subsidies have turned it into an accredited leisure activity and journalists tell us what to expect. Perhaps the greatest change has come with the arrival of television, video cassettes, and film libraries that offer new ways of viewing Shakespeare in performance. Our experience of these is dominated by visual images that have been chosen for us by the director, cameraman, and editor. Our responses are continuously guided by frequent change of location and focus, highly controlled use of colour and light, sudden cuts from one point of view to another, and an all-pervasive soundtrack. Moreover the actors' performances never vary in the slightest detail from one viewing to the next. With the arrival of inexpensive videos, most of us can see performances at home and at our own convenience: we can be on our own or in chosen company, and we are in charge of the occasion; a favourite scene can be repeated as often as we wish; we can stop the show to make notes and skip what begins to bore us. None of this is possible in a theatre and none of the versions seen on a screen, whether large or small, provides an equivalent experience. Seeing Shakespeare on video is like feeding ourselves on convenience foods, the plays packaged and reliable, easily consumed but falling short in nourishment when compared with a specially prepared product. We should hesitate before assuming that we know what reception Shakespeare expected for his plays.

Audience Behaviour

Changes that time has brought are just as striking once a performance has begun. Seldom today can it be said of an audience that

> Within one square a thousand heads are laid
> So close, that all of heads, the room seems made.[7]

We do not suppose that the theatre building might 'crack' with the vigorous response of a 'full-stuff'd audience', as John Marston imagined in *What You Will* (1601), III.ii, or that it might actually 'shake when shrill claps' greet the performers, as Michael Drayton claimed in his poem, 'The Sacrifice to Apollo' (1606). We are seldom part of an audience so continuously active that the theatre resounds with 'shouts and claps at ev'ry little pause'[8] and we will not have experienced the 'rare silence' that, according to Thomas Dekker, sometimes took possession of such an unbridled crowd.[9]

Also gone is the assumption that the audience belongs to the same world as the actors, separated according to their roles of watchers or performers but sharing the same light under the same sky. That is not possible when a stage faces the audience, and is not surrounded by it, and when productions are augmented by sound and lighting effects that have been developed for large-scale and fantastic musicals. Some of the audience in an Elizabethan theatre would have sat in galleries immediately adjacent to the acting area and favoured members were accommodated on the stage itself. Reports tell of audience members talking to the actors during a performance or leaving their places to take part in the action. When a person in the play was threatened in a fight, spectators might run onto the stage in order to 'save the blow'.[10] The loss of this immediate contact between actors and playgoers is probably the most fundamental difference between our theatres and those of Shakespeare's day.

We can build Elizabethan-type theatres, with thrust stages and encircling galleries, and use Elizabethan-type settings that provide an unchanging and structured background for the whole performance but audiences will still be entirely modern and will usually be kept in what is now considered to be its place, in the dark and in allotted seats. Safety regulations are partly responsible for resistance to Elizabethan tradition in these respects, insisting on fixed seating, clear gangways of regulation size, illuminated exit signs, and no more than a maximum number of spectators. A darkened auditorium is the preferred choice of theatre producers and directors because it enhances the effect of stage lighting and strengthens the visual impact of performances. It is also liked by audiences because it enhances privacy and encourages quiet behaviour: going to a theatre has become a serious business that requires an unrestricted view of the stage and the peace of mind to respond as each individual wishes. Occasions do occur when an entire audience is moved to respond vigorously but very different expectations are signalled everywhere in the carpeted and capacious foyers, the stalls selling playtexts and souvenirs, and programmes setting out the artists' biographies, photographs of the production, and informative and critical essays. Elizabethan playgoing was riskier than ours because an audience would not know what to expect and liked it that way. Account books of the Rose theatre at the turn of the sixteenth century show that plays were very seldom repeated within a week and that an average of 17 new plays were performed each year by that company.[11] In 1633 Thomas Heywood said that he had 'had either an entire hand, or at the least main finger' in 220 plays;[12] that gives him an average of more than five plays a year in a career of 40 years. Elizabethan audiences seem to have had an insatiable appetite for new plays whereas we wait for reviews or word of mouth about a new play before paying to see it, even when we have enjoyed earlier work by the same author and the same actors and director.

In the nineteen-nineties, a brand new Globe theatre on Bankside in London brought physical conditions much closer to those of original performances, but safety considerations have dictated that some 30 ushers are employed to watch over the audience, especially those members who are standing in the pit around the stage. Admission tickets can be booked in advance and audiences are well briefed on how to behave in the replica theatre. Vocal response to performances tends to have a self-conscious air, as if spectators were in some privileged and good-humoured charade, playing their parts as 'groundlings' with stereotypical behaviour. Despite the best intentions, any 'reconstruction' of Elizabethan audiences is bound to be incomplete, because it is impossible to change minds and habitual responses, but at the new Globe resistance to older procedures is also evident in the work of producers, directors, and actors. The management has not attempted to produce a large Elizabethan repertoire with one company of actors presenting a different play every day, with 20 or 30 in a single season and a good number of them entirely new. Its actors perform in a very few parts in the same plays day after day and, inevitably, the words they speak have lost most of their previous relationship to everyday speech.

Going to the original Globe put an audience in touch with the present moment and, through the created illusions of the drama, gave a unique view of the world in which everyone lived. In those days men and women lived in their own small circles since they were without newspapers or a cheap and regular postal service and, of course, without radio or television. It might well be that only at a theatre could they gain a fuller perspective on their lives, encounter other opinions, and hear and see the consequences of actions not entirely dissimilar from their own. Sermons, official publications and proclamations, occasional single-page broadsheets, ballads, and word of mouth were the only other means of mass communication, all less engaging and most of them giving only a single viewpoint. Books were still comparatively expensive and literacy far from universal. Theatre, in contrast, was accessible to almost everyone and always up to the minute; no wonder it was carefully censored by the authoritarian state. Actors were, as Shakespeare's Hamlet said:

> the abstract and brief chronicles of the time; after your death you were better have a bad epitaph than their ill report while you live.
>
> (*Hamlet*, II.ii.517–20)

In an often closed and divided world, one of the attractions of theatre was that its 'players cannot keep counsel; they'll tell all' (ibid., III.ii.136–41).

The experience that playgoers enjoyed was more varied, as well as more communicative, than their usual lives, because they would find themselves among a crowd more mixed in status and wealth than any other company with which they were familiar. Some public occasions, like a royal visit, the return of a victorious general, or some acts of religious worship, would also draw a wide range of people but they would expect to be segregated according to class. By seeing a play, Shakespeare's contemporaries shared an entertainment with almost every kind of person in town, except those who disapproved of theatre on moral or political grounds. For a new play, it was said that a theatre could so 'swarm' with spectators that 'gentles mix'd with grooms', against the decorum in force elsewhere.[13] The Merchant Tailors' Company of the City of London decided to ban the use of its hall for the performance of plays on the grounds that:

> at our common plays ... every lewd person thinketh himself (for his penny) worthy of the chief and most commodious place without respect of any other, either for age or estimation in the common weal; which bringeth the youth to such an impudent familiarity with their betters that often times great contempt of masters, parents, and magistrates followeth thereof.[14]

Today we visit a theatre with people very like ourselves. Everyone tends to be in the same salary group, the price differential between the most expensive and the cheapest seats having shrunk during the last few decades. Some theatres have a single ticket price, others sell a high proportion of seats to season-ticket holders or to registered and paid-up patrons who are thereby assured of sitting among other regulars every time they go to the theatre. By closing the galleries in our older theatres, with their wooden benches and restricted view of the stage, managements have lost a previously significant and often vocal part of the audience, packed close together and positively enjoying its freedom from supposedly superior company. Audiences have become less diverse and more predictable.

Actors in Contact with their Audience

Remembering that Hamlet respected the censure of a single 'judicious' auditor more than the reactions of a 'whole theatre of others' (*Hamlet*, III.ii.28), we might suppose that Shakespeare was not concerned with the 'fool multitude that choose by show' (*Merchant of Venice*, II.ix.26). But his individual characters do not speak for him; if they did, he would have held many strange and contradictory beliefs. Given the behaviour of Elizabethan audiences, we can see that a prince might care little for a crowded theatre while an author would have a quite different opinion. Shakespeare could not be guided by any single person's view of his plays, not even the monarch's before whom they were likely to be played, because unless the public endorses performances by its attendance and attention, the theatre loses money and the actors lose confidence. Even in these days of tamed and well-behaved playgoers, a theatre company has no more demoralizing experience than playing to an empty or indifferent house; everyone in the theatre senses the rejection, like a smell permeating the entire building. While Hamlet castigated audiences as incapable of anything but 'inexplicable dumb shows and noise' (III.ii.12), Shakespeare, for his own peace of mind and that of the players, could not neglect those customers. His task was to please the public and, at the same time, write the plays he wanted to write.

To experience the kind of demands that audiences made upon Shakespeare and so understand his need to respond to them, we can go to see those companies that perform today in streets and public places. They will not be using Shakespeare's texts and are likely to be small in size and poorly equipped, but they work in conditions much closer to those of Elizabethan theatres than those enjoyed by more established companies. Their actors can draw mixed and active audiences and engage with them on their own terms; much in their performances is improvised, introducing new words and new business when they see the need; sometimes offering new twists in the story-line or new interpretations of character as they see opportunity. Welfare State company, for example, has developed a strong public following for its open-air performances so that its actors speak from long and varied experience:

> You're waiting for the energy of your audience. ... If you're one end of a square it's quite hard to relate to the other end, but if you're in a circle, you can run round the edges and you're all together ... [then] the audience puts in 50% of the energy. ...
>
> On the street, the performer must take power and charge the space, so that no matter how many trucks drive past, or jets fly over, the audience's attention is seized. That does not necessarily mean belting it out to drown the surrounding din ... It can mean a performance so totally still, controlled and concentrated, that no one can walk away from it. ...
>
> Eye contact is vital – sharing with the audience. It is a vibrant communication. They can, after all, reach out and touch you if they want to ... You are there – it is not the telly – it is really happening live before them. It may go wrong, it may be marvellous. The tensions are real, and that bond is what the performer works with, and must be awake to. ... [15]

The structure and content of their plays, the effect of words and actions, and the use of the stage are spoken of here in the same breath as contact with an audience and that audience's reactions. These elements are all inextricably mixed in such theatres, as they are likely to have been in Shakespeare's.

John McGrath has described the work of the 7:84 Theatre Company which he founded and directed in the nineteen-seventies and eighties. Performing in Working Men's Clubs in the North of England where audiences were free to move around, drink, talk, and respond in any way they chose, this company developed its own kind of theatre. McGrath, who wrote the plays, as well as directing and acting, was forthright about audiences:

> If a writer in theatre does not love his or her audience, he or she will die. It can be a critical love, an aggressive love, but if it turns to indifference, cynicism, hate, or simply exploitation, then the theatre-maker will turn into a solipsist or a psychopath. ...

He judged any play in relation to its appropriate audience: it could 'completely change its meaning, given the wrong theatre, or wrong publicity, or even the wrong ticket prices'.[16]

Theatres whose audiences are in close contact with the stage and encouraged to respond freely, will have their own rules for performance. They might start with the advice of Bim Mason who founded the Mummer and Dada Theatre Company in 1985 and proceeded to conduct many experiments to find ways of drawing and holding an audience. For a 'stationary show', as opposed to mobile performances, he believed that:

> the most important aspect of performance [is] timing. Timing cannot be fixed as in a musical score, it has to be gauged according to the mood of the audience. If they are with you then the act can be slowed down and played for all it is worth and more, by improvisation, inventing and extending the movements. If they are getting bored

or restless, then pace will need to be quickened, but not rushed, otherwise control is lost and it looks desperate. ...

Expectation and tension can be built into each section of the show but must also be built into the whole structure. A show with a narrative can set up situations that set the public wondering how they will be resolved. ... Surprise is a key element to any show. It keeps the audience alert and maintains expectation because after one surprise who knows what others might be concealed ... ?

To a good performer most interruptions are not a problem, on the contrary they are a gift. Because they present a situation that could not have been rehearsed, the audience is fascinated to see what will happen and how well it is handled. ... Audiences will give warm sympathetic support if it is well handled. Aggression always looks bad but so does indecisive weakness. ...

Since society has become so fractured into sub-cultures, it is necessary to use stories and archetypes that transcend divisions of age, sex and class.[17]

The work of all such theatres is very specific to the location and time of performance, current political and moral issues, and the talents of the performers. In so far as Shakespeare worked for a similar audience–stage relationship, he is likely to have followed much the same rules, modified according to time and place, and the participants in each theatrical event.

These ways of performing are not those of the highly regarded theatres that stage Shakespeare today, but they are common elsewhere: in the highly efficient Jatra theatres of Bengal, Orissa, and Bangladesh, for example, or the long-running Marathi productions in and around Mumbai, and in many small-scale touring companies throughout Asia. Around the world popular theatres thrive by contact between actors and audiences: it brings a sense of shared achievement at the close of a play and ensures that a theatrical event is a truly public and social occasion, often becoming an irreplaceable feature in the year's calendar or a necessary ingredient of communal celebrations.

Actors Speaking to their Audience

A recurrent and basic feature of Shakespeare's playtexts is the use of asides, a frequent sign that they were written to be played in open contact with an audience. Modern editions usually mark the most obvious of these with '*Aside*' or '*They speak aside*,' but the device was so common in Elizabethan performances, so constantly to be expected, that authors, scribes, and printers seldom bothered with stage-directions. Editors add them today for readers and actors who are not familiar with performances that are open to an audience and might miss the comparatively few occasions where speaking aside is necessary for making sense. If contemporary actors start looking for further opportunities to speak directly to their audience, they will find them everywhere in Shakespeare's plays. Many lines in the longer soliloquies can be acted in this way, the audience becoming another self or *confidante* for the speaker to address, or some persons, alive or ageless, who are sharing in the situation that is being confronted. An alternation between self-communion and communication, with appropriate changes in projection or phrasing of the words, encourages a mental and emotional dynamic that contributes to that energy in performance by which the actors of Welfare State hold the attention of their audiences. Sensitively timed according to the mood of the moment, direct address can also spring surprises, sharpen focus or raise questions. By the manner in which an address to the audience is phrased, a speaker can share a sense of desperation, confidence, or ease, or a search for some new initiative or understanding.

If the actor of Hamlet frequently changes to whom he speaks in soliloquy, he is likely to keep attention and be better able to develop his own interpretation of the role. The first time he is alone, 'But two months dead!' can be directed to the audience, sharing an outright anger or disbelief; or he might speak the phrase to himself either tenderly or in bitter recollection, not addressing the audience until 'Nay, not so much, not two', as if he now wants to be sure that he understands rightly what had happened. This qualification can be spoken in one phrase or in two or, even, three, all addressed to the audience, or only the first or last, the weight of each word changing with each choice the actor makes. Similarly, the following lines can be spoken either to himself, in self-reproach for forgetfulness, or to the audience, in anger or disbelief. When he speaks of the wind touching the skin of his mother's face, he can become more remote, caught up in his own memories and sensations:

> Nay, not so much, not two.
> So excellent a king that was to this
> Hyperion to a satyr; so loving to my mother,
> That he might not beteem the winds of heaven
> Visit her face too roughly.

Feelings can now break out of conscious control with 'Heaven and earth!', spoken neither to himself nor to the audience. Then two very different impulses lie behind the question and exclamations that follow, either one dominant: specific memories of his mother and father together in intimacy and a larger vision of the natural course of life pulled awry and destroyed by 'woman':

> Heaven and earth!
> Must I remember? Why, she would hang on him
> As if increase of appetite had grown
> By what it fed on; and yet, within a month –
> Let me not think on't. Frailty, thy name is woman! –
> A little month, or ere those shoes were old …
> *(Hamlet,* I.ii.137ff.)

When memories are uppermost in his mind, Hamlet is likely to speak to himself; when his sense of betrayal and disaster is stronger, he may speak out to the audience as if demanding its belief and support. 'Let me not think on't' can suggest that a sexual obsession has taken hold of him, after which, in contrast, 'Frailty, thy name is woman' is likely to be a sudden accusation, perhaps directed out to the audience and spoken violently, as if he is accusing the women who are watching the play. Or it can be spoken to himself, in the bitterness of experience and with a precise and profound sense of loss. Then Hamlet changes again, remembering his mother on the day of her new marriage, even to the shoes that she wore.

Somehow the actor must manage and shape the great range of feeling and consciousness that this speech implies and expresses. No regular exposition or sustained argument can order its delivery: syntax and phrasing, as well as words, require many changes of consciousness. Repetition calls for certain key issues to register forcefully with varying emphasis: 'two months ... not two ... within a month ... a little month' and, a little later, 'must I remember? ... let me not think on't'. Delivery that is sensitive to Hamlet's conscious and half-conscious thoughts, both driven and held back by overwhelming feelings, can make an audience uneasy by many different appeals for its attention: sometimes told what to think, sometimes left to itself to be amazed at the force of feeling or puzzled by Hamlet's uncertainties. When an actor is in contact with his audience on an open stage and gives a strong dynamic to this soliloquy by changing the direction in which it is spoken, his hearers may feel the emotional pressures within Hamlet's mind; they may even share the sensations that he experiences.

Longer speeches addressed to a whole court, army, family, or other assembly can be spoken to include a theatre audience so that it tends to merge with the on-stage audience. By acknowledging the presence of this wider public, an actor can gain both a sounding board and a visible, if not vocal, response. Audience members can be drawn together or divisions marked among them, for instance between the young and old, privileged and disadvantaged, conservative and radical, according to the issues involved. They can be wooed by both sides in an argument; in *Julius Caesar*, III.ii, the two very different funeral orations that follow each other are an obvious example of this: by addressing both to the theatre audience, these political rivals can each make his own pitch and directly invoke a positive response. A particularly close focus of attention will be achieved by addressing only one person in the crowd of spectators, personalizing an appeal or giving point to a joke.

Everywhere in Shakespeare's dialogue actors can find opportunities for direct address to their audience. The Fools do so most of the time, commenting on other persons and their attitudes, sharing jokes or undermining assumptions or presumption. Some characters who more directly drive the action of the play forward have a similar freedom: Richard the Third, Iago, and Edmund; Beatrice, Rosalind, and Falstaff; Brutus and Cassius. Affected by the apparent openness, in which words seem to be spoken only for them to hear, an audience will be drawn to these persons and may identify with them, even when what they are saying or doing seems improbable, reprehensible, or downright wrong. By these means direct address plays a prominent part in Shakespeare's handling of story and argument, as well as in the relationship between audiences and individual actors and the persons they present.

Some actors in major parts have been given comparatively few opportunities to address the audience, but these are carefully placed and occur at vital points in the narrative. For example, in the first scene of *King Lear*, when the king addresses the entire court, the actor can choose whether he includes the theatre audience in his formal pronouncements. Later scenes have more obvious opportunities to address the audience, as if it were an actual witness of his misfortune:

> Does any here know me? This is not Lear.
> Does Lear walk thus? speak thus? Where are his eyes?
> Either his notion weakens, or his discernings
> Are lethargied. – Ha! waking? 'tis not so. –
> Who is it that can tell me who I am?
>
> (I.iv.225–9)

Some 50 lines on, when Lear calls on Nature to hear his sustained curse, the king's isolation will be more apparent if he now turns away, not only from Albany and

Goneril, but also from the audience to whom he had previously addressed his words.

All this time, while other persons in the play have had numerous calls to address the audience in soliloquy or asides, Edmund and the Fool particularly, Shakespeare has not given Lear a single soliloquy with which to establish contact, only some passing and optional opportunities for direct address. In his next scene, however, Lear does come closer to a sustained soliloquy during his encounter with Regan and Goneril:

> Those wicked creatures yet do look well-favour'd
> When others are more wicked; not being the worst
> Stands in some rank of praise.

Soon after this, he may soliloquize with greater passion:

> You think I'll weep.
> No, I'll not weep. *Storm and tempest.*
> I have full cause of weeping; but this heart
> Shall break into a hundred thousand flaws
> Or ere I'll weep.

> (II.iv.255–7, 281–5)

Contact with an audience remains intermittent. Alone with the Fool on the heath, Lear addresses the storm, then himself, and only then, perhaps, the audience: 'No, I will be the pattern of all patience; / I will say nothing' (III.ii.37–8). Soon he speaks to specific persons whom he imagines to be somewhere within call: the 'perjur'd', the 'simular man of virtue / That art incestuous', the 'caitiff' who would practise on a man's life (III.ii.51–9). Having addressed 'poor naked wretches, wheresoe'er you are', he may turn to the audience to confess: 'O, I have ta'en / Too little care of this!' (III.iv.28–33). As madness takes progressive hold and he meets with the blind Gloucester, opportunities to speak to the audience grow more frequent and less reserved: 'They told me I was everything; 'tis a lie – I am not ague-proof'. Speaking of Gloucester, he calls all who hear him to witness: 'see how the subject quakes'. He seems to see persons he knows and asks the theatre audience to see them too: 'Behold yond simp'ring dame ... See how yond justice rails upon yond simple thief ... Thou rascal beadle ... Why dost thou lash that whore?' (IV.vi.103–61).

In the last scene of all, when Lear speaks rarely, many of his words can be addressed to the theatre audience as if to a wider court of appeal. By this means, direct access is given to his sense of what is happening, his conflicting feelings, and the continuing exertion of his will:

> This feather stirs; she lives. If it be so,
> It is a chance which does redeem all sorrows
> That ever I have felt. ...
> I might have sav'd her; now she's gone for ever. ...
> Do you see this? Look on her. Look, her lips.
> Look there, look there!
>
> (V.iii.265–7, 270, 310–11)

As Lear draws close to death, those on stage know that 'vain is it / That we present us to him' and that, finally, they must obey the 'weight of this sad time' (V.iii. 293–4, 323). If direct address involves them in this death, a theatre audience may also feel powerless, neither moving nor making a sound in response. Careful manipulation of the contact between actor and spectators has progressively encouraged a sensitive perception of the hero's suffering and powers of endurance.

The manner of Lear's death can be seen as a development of Shakespeare's continuous experiment with presentation and the engagement of the audience in a theatrical event. His very last moments exist in two different versions, that in the Quarto of 1608 and a longer version in the Folio of 1623; these show many small changes that are typical of the fine tuning that a dramatist will attempt when intent on achieving exceptional effects in the performance of his script. They should encourage us, as well as actors, to study the text with every possible care.

Audience Response

The various ways in which Shakespeare encouraged audiences and actors to interact can both charge performance with energy and accentuate the seeming reality and immediate relevance of a play. While present-day modes of staging seldom allow actors to take advantage of this, some non-theatrical events of our own times offer better parallels to playgoing at the original Globe: for example, political meetings when the issue is of immediate concern to the crowd, mass religious observances that are not strictly prescribed in order or form of words, popular music concerts, especially those in the open air, and many spectator sports. Some audiences are now so huge that other factors intrude but the way in which crucial games between a few skilled opponents are watched, the audience sharing in the excitement and relating to individual participants, provides a revealing contrast to the self-absorption of theatre audiences seated comfortably in a darkened auditorium and watching a self-contained, well-rehearsed performance of a play.

When players are close at hand and known to us as individuals, we can be caught up 'in the play' as audiences might have been at the Globe or the more intimate Blackfriars theatre. Verbal accounts of a final of the Men's Singles Championship at Wimbledon some years ago, before television influenced other forms of commentary, can suggest the close attention of the crowd, its expectations and critical attitudes, and the gradual build-up of excitement that might have been experienced at early performances of Shakespeare. In the London *Times* of 8 July 1991, David Miller reported on a match between Boris Becker, an established favourite with the crowd, and Michael Stich, the latest in a series of German players whose serves and volleys had proved devastatingly effective:

> As the second set began to go the way of the first, Becker's nerves, extraordinarily, disintegrated. As he cursed, shouted and shook his fists at the heavens, the

front row of Royal ladies smiled tolerantly like school parents watching someone misbehave on junior sports day. Becker was warned for time abuse; it was his reputation that was more threatened. ...

Now came, for [Becker], the agony of the third set ... The executioner at the other end was unrelenting; and served to love for 5–4. As they changed ends, you could sense that Becker's intolerance of his decline had forfeited the crowd's sympathy. In that harsh way of the sporting public, they were ready for symbolic death.

The match finished with Stich's 'remorseless forehand return', and then:

As the two young men embraced, you could sense the crowd's sudden forgiveness for the fallen champion's frenzy. He looked about 30. This modern game strips you bare. How long can Stich last in the goldfish bowl?

When we want to know the nature of the event in which Shakespeare imagined his plays being performed, a tennis audience offers a useful point of reference. The swift and complete changes of mood, exemplified in this *Times* report, warn against assuming that a drama awakens a single or constant response. The spectators' instinct to move ahead of the play, to identify with one player at a time, to mix emotional and moral judgements, to be harsh and pitiless, and, at certain moments, to become united in reaction, all indicate how a knowledgeable audience, in close contact with the actors, might be transformed when keyed up with expectation. And the players' responses suggest the competitive energy and intensified playing that might arise among members of the King's Men during each unprecedented and, as we shall see, largely unrehearsed performance.[18] While actors and some of their audience will know ahead of time who will die and who survive or which two persons will go off stage together and at peace, neither party will know exactly how the end will be achieved, what passions, what access of power, or what revaluations will be involved in the conclusion.

When we try to assess what the plays do in performance, rather than what is said on-stage, we should give
attention to expectation and anticipation, to delay and
speed of fulfilment, to repetition of incidents as well as
the clarification and understanding that derive directly
from words. Forms of combat and chase should be carefully noted as basic structural devices that quicken attention and concentrate issues. On-stage transformations,
either inward or outward, moments of bonding, efforts
to contain irreconcilable differences, and the settling of
accounts are all actions that give spectators special satisfaction. Although momentary actions and the presence
of an actor are more immediately memorable and the
means by which an audience is drawn into a play, the
entire action of the play as its story unfolds is what trans-
mits the greatest charge and holds an audience, even
though few of them will realize that this is so. This part of
a theatrical event is the hardest to evaluate.

Shakespeare could not have envisaged what the plays
offer to audiences today, both playgoing and participation having changed so much. The elaborate scenery,
complicated lighting, and carefully rehearsed performances to which we have become accustomed were
unthinkable in earlier times. Yet present-day productions have originated, at least in part, from a study of
the printed plays and can reveal new aspects of
Shakespeare's artistry. Audiences are led to give concentrated attention to particularly significant words by
finely tuned speech. Alterations of location or mood
that are indicated in the text are reinforced by swiftly
changing and impressive stage effects. A director's distinctive production that reveals a new 'reading' of the
text is made possible by the same qualities in the
writing that fostered the open and improvised performances of earlier times: as later chapters will show, a
huge hinterland of meanings and sensations lies
behind Shakespeare's texts and it contains many paths
to explore with many different intentions.[19]

The most successful Shakespeare productions in our theatres are renowned for clarity of meaning and argument, efficient and elaborate showmanship, and finesse in performance, virtues which are now prized more than those of early performances. But they have limitations too. Most obviously, they no longer draw audiences from a wide spectrum of society or occupy a dominant place in popular culture. Secondly, the companies presenting Shakespeare are no longer part of a profession that is confident of its own future and financially self-supporting. Thirdly, performances cannot respond readily to the changing concerns of the public, being set in one form by means of long rehearsals and careful direction. Whether any of these shortcomings could be eradicated is an underlying concern throughout the following chapters and one that sharpens awareness of what the texts demand of actors, directors, and readers.

Notes

1. The earlier parts of this chapter draw upon 'Shakespeare's Plays and Traditions of Playgoing', in *Shakespeare and Cultural Traditions: The Selected Proceedings of the International Shakespeare Association World Congress, Tokyo, 1991*, ed. Tetsuo Kishi, Roger Pringle and Stanley Wells (Newark: University of Delaware Press; London and Toronto: Associated University Presses, 1994), pp. 253–65.

    The subject of this chapter has been treated in an Elizabethan and Jacobean context by Andrew Gurr in *Playgoing in Shakespeare's London* (Cambridge: Cambridge University Press, second edition, 1996).

2. See C. J. Sisson, *The Boar's Head Theatre; An Innyard Theatre of the Elizabethan Age*, ed. Stanley Wells (London: Routledge & Kegan Paul, 1972), p. 37.

3. See N. D. Shergold, *A History of the Spanish Stage from the Medieval Times until the end of the Seventeenth Century* (Oxford: Clarendon Press, 1967), pp. 519–20.

4. See Allardyce Nicoll, *The Garrick Stage: Theatres and Audience in the Eighteenth Century*, ed. Sybil Rosenfeld (Athens, GA: University of Georgia Press, 1980), pp. 97–8.

5. See W. C. Macready, *Journal*, ed. J. C. Trewin (London: Longmans, 1967), pp. 261–2.

6. See Laurence Irving, *Henry Irving: The Actor and His World, by His Grandson* (New York: Macmillan, 1951), pp. 248–9.

7. Thomas Middleton and Thomas Dekker, *The Roaring Girl, or Moll Cut Purse* (1612), I.ii.

8. Michael Drayton, *Idea* (c. 1612), Sonnet 47.

9. Thomas Dekker, *If It Be Not a Good Play, the Devil is in It* (1612), Prologue.

10. Verses prefixed to Francis Beaumont and John Fletcher, *Comedies and Tragedies* (1647).

11. The statistics that can be gathered from the Rose accounts, usually referred to as *Henslowe's Diary*, have been thoughtfully analysed in Peter Thomson, *Shakespeare's Theatre* (Routledge & Kegan Paul: London, 1983), pp. 55–7. At that time it was thought that plays were marked 'ne' in the 'diary' to signify a new or newly revised playscript that had not been previously performed in its present state. More recently, however, in *Notes and Queries*, ccxxxvi (1991), 34–54, Winifred Frazer showed that 'ne' signified a performance in the theatre at Newington Butts; the actors probably moved there when the Rose was being used for bear-baiting or some other purpose.

12. Thomas Heywood, *The English Traveller* (1633), Epistle.

13. *Pimlico, or Run Red-Cap* (1609). sig. C1r.

14. Charles M. Clode, *The Early History of the Guild of Merchant Tailors* (London: Harrison, 1888), p. 235.

15. Tony Coult and Baz Kershaw (eds), *Engineers of the Imagination: The Welfare State Handbook* (London: Methuen, 1983), pp. 28–9, 34–6.

16. John McGrath, *A Good Night Out: Popular Theatre – Audience, Class, and Form* (London: Eyre Methuen, 1981), pp. 116 and 6–7.

17. *Street Theatre and Other Outdoor Performance* (London and New York: Routledge, 1992), pp. 98, 99, 101, 117.

18. See below, pp. 90–1.

19· See, especially, Chapter 4, below, pp. 71–6.

2

Functions

An author will usually deliver a more or less finished script to a theatre, but no play is complete – not seen and heard in its full life – until many other very different people have contributed to what has been written.[1] Nor is any single production the one necessary form in which it reaches an audience. Change the actors, staging, audience, or theatre building and vary the infinite number of choices and accidents that occur during rehearsals and performance, and the life of a play is bound to change, often quite radically. While the words may remain the same, their effect depends on how they are spoken and on everything else that happens on stage and in the auditorium. The author will often be surprised when a play becomes part of a theatrical event and will come to think differently about the script he had handed to the players. In the less controlled productions of Elizabethan theatres a play would vary far more in performance than it does today and, until the last century or so, the same was true of productions in most other theatres. What Shakespeare wrote about the processes of writing and performance in his own time provides a first step towards understanding what was, and still may be, involved.

How Plays Come to Life

Near the end of *A Midsummer Night's Dream,* Shakespeare inserted an account of the threefold relationship between author, actors, and audience. While the 'tedious brief scene' of *Pyramus and Thisbe* is being performed, time is allowed for Duke Theseus and his warrior bride, Hippolyta, to comment:

HIPPOLYTA   This is the silliest stuff that ever I heard.
THESEUS   The best in this kind are but shadows: and
    the worst are no worse, if imagination amend them.
HIPPOLYTA   It must be your imagination then, and not
    theirs.
THESEUS   If we imagine no worse of them than they of
    themselves, they may pass for excellent men.

                                        (V.i.209–14)

Opinions expressed by persons in a play do not represent what their author thought on his own account but Theseus distinguishes separate elements of a theatrical event and so provides us with categories in which Shakespeare thought about performance and his own art. In calling actors 'shadows', he implied that they were imitations, reflections, portraits, or shapes, as if they were not creatures of real and substantial life; they could also be like phantoms, for that was another current meaning of the word. The 'best' of the persons appearing in a play are changing, fleeting, insubstantial beings who need to be 'amended' and given substance and credibility by an audience's imagination. None of the technical means of Elizabethan theatre production are mentioned here, neither costume, stage-property, sound, nor music, as if they were not essential for success. On the other hand, Theseus holds members of an audience responsible, at least in part, for bringing the play to life, perhaps the 'best' of it. The underlying assumption is that only in the imaginations of its audience can a play seem to be full of 'excellent men'.

A few years later, the Chorus to *Henry the Fifth* showed that very much the same distinctions were still in Shakespeare's mind. Actors are 'ciphers' on which the audience should let their 'imaginary forces work' and, in doing so, 'piece out' the imperfections of performance in their minds (Prol. 17–18, 23). He rallies his hearers, with 'Work, work your thoughts', so that what is presented is converted into immediate and actual activity: as they 'sit and see', members of an audience will be 'Minding true things by what their mock'ries be' (IV, Prol. 52–3) and the author's play takes on a true life in their own imaginations. After the first two Acts, the Chorus assumes that his audience will create the play themselves when nothing is taking place on stage:

> Play with your fancies; and in them behold
> Upon the hempen tackle ship-boys climbing;
> Hear the shrill whistle ...
>   ... behold the threaden sails, ...

He asks spectators to 'eke our performance with your minds' (III, Prol. 7–8, 25, 35).

In *A Midsummer Night's Dream*, Theseus speaks of a poet in much the same terms:

> The lunatic, the lover, and the poet,
> Are of imagination all compact ...
> The poet's eye, in a fine frenzy rolling,
> Doth glance from heaven to earth, from earth to
>   heaven;
> And as imagination bodies forth
> The forms of things unknown, the poet's pen
> Turns them to shapes and gives to airy nothing
> A local habitation and a name.
>
>   (V.i.4–22)

In his imagination the poet sees visions and then, by what his pen sets down, he gives them a place and means of identification. Neither 'local habitation' nor 'name' involves the giving of actual life, but both are the means whereby the life he envisioned may be re-created in the minds of readers. *Shapes* was in those days close in meaning to *shadows*, the word Theseus uses of actors in a play; in some contexts the two words were interchangeable. He implies that the words of a poem need readers with their own imaginations before an 'airy nothing' is given lively substance, in much the same way as a play needs both actors and audience before it can come to a convincing and imaginatively charged life.

In the *Sonnets* Shakespeare wrote in his own person about poetry using much the same terms. The concluding couplet of Sonnet 107 tells his young friend:

> Now with the drops of this most balmy time
> My love looks fresh, and Death to me subscribes,
> Since, spite of him, I'll live in this poor rhyme,
> While he insults o'er dull and speechless tribes:
> And thou in this shalt find thy monument,
> When tyrants' crests and tombs of brass are spent.

The transformation of 'rhyme' to 'monument' only happens when some other person than the poet 'finds' it and converts the words on paper into an enduring representation of a living person.[2] Again, a reader is said to fulfil the function that Theseus gave to an audience. Sonnet 81 varies the idea:

> The earth can yield me but a common grave,
> When you entombed in men's eyes shall lie.
> Your monument shall be my gentle verse,
> Which eyes not yet created shall o'er-read,
> And tongues to be your being shall rehearse
> When all the breathers of this world are dead.
> You still shall live – such virtue hath my pen –
> Where breath most breathes, even in the mouths of
>   men.

The 'monument' of the poem can 'live' only when its words are read and spoken by a living person.

Re-creating Life

Imagination, a process of the mind, has always been difficult to define. Today, our response to the word is likely to be coloured by the criticism and poetry of Samuel Taylor Coleridge and by later usages in the English romantic tradition. For Coleridge, exemplifying his definition by references to Shakespeare's non-dramatic poetry, the 'esemplastic power' of imagination was the prime gift of all great poets, enabling them to draw together many diverse visual images, together with mythological and literary references, 'affecting incidents, just thoughts, interesting personal or domestic feelings', and to draw all these into a 'unity of effect'.[3] In operation, imagination is 'both passionate & tranquil', acting upon us as Nature does 'when we open our eyes upon an extended prospect'.[4] Although Shakespeare's non-dramatic poetry provided Coleridge with examples of these effects and *imagination* in his sense applies equally to the poetry of the plays, the word was, in Elizabethan days, used in other, less loaded senses. For Shakespeare it usually implied any mental illusion, as opposed to a substantial reality: a 'seeming', 'fancy', 'dream', or hallucination, that could give expression to strong feelings or unexpected fantasies. Such *imaginations* could contain and sustain an overflow of sensation or pleasure: they were imaginary versions of the actual world that could be wonderful, unexpected, irrational, or terrible and special to the person who was experiencing them.

While Coleridge distinguished *fancy* from *imagination*, the two words, and also *fantasy*, had previously been close in meaning and often used indifferently. Common to all three for Shakespeare was a totally convincing ability to transform ordinary behaviour and everyday phenomena. Malvolio, thinking that he will marry Olivia, is physically altered: 'Look how imagination blows him,' comments Fabian, 'Contemplation makes a rare turkey-cock of him; how he jets under his advanc'd plumes!' (*Twelfth Night*, II.v.39–40 and 28–9). When Prospero orders a masque to be played before Ferdinand and Miranda in order to 'enact my present fancies', the vision that materializes is like a 'paradise' and far from any ordinary reality (*Tempest*, IV.i.122–4). The shapes created by imagination or fancy can also be horrifying, especially when they remain hidden within the mind: Macbeth's 'present fears / Are less than horrible imaginings'; Lady Macbeth has 'thick-coming fancies / That keep her from her rest' (*Macbeth*, I.iii.137–8 and V.iii.38–9); Hamlet fears his 'imaginations are as foul / As Vulcan's stithy' (*Hamlet*, III.ii.81–2). Boundaries between imaginary and real experience can become confused: Theseus knows that a bush is only 'suppos'd a bear' but, after waking from a dream, Hermia still thinks a 'crawling serpent' has to be plucked away from her breast (*Dream*, II.ii.145–6; V.i.22).

While ghosts and other supernatural phenomena were commonly thought to be real, they were also considered no more than 'tricks' of the imagination (*Dream*, V.i.18). Horatio believes the Ghost of Hamlet's father is 'but our fantasy' and that Hamlet 'waxes desperate with imagination' when he follows it off stage (*Hamlet*. I.i.23; I.iv.87). In Plutarch's *Lives of the Greeks and Romans*, as translated by Sir Thomas North in 1579, Cassius argues that the Ghost of Caesar is a fabrication of Brutus's own mind:

> we do not always feel, or see, that which we suppose we do both see and feel: but that our senses (being credulous, and therefore easily abused, when they are idle and unoccupied in their own objects) are induced to imagine they see and conjecture that which they in truth do not. For our mind is quick and cunning to work (without either cause or matter) any thing in the imagination whatsoever. And therefore the imagination is resembled to clay and the mind to the potter; who, without any other cause than his fancy and pleasure, changeth it in what fashion and form he will.[5]

Shakespeare had read this Epicurean 'opinion' about the seeming reality that imagination can produce when he was preparing to write *The Tragedy of Julius Caesar* and shortly before turning to *Hamlet*. It was a common belief: in his *Anatomy of Melancholy* (1621 etc.), Robert Burton lists many authorities, ancient and modern, for whom all manner of 'witches' progresses, ... transformations, ... chimeras, antics, golden mountains, and

castles in the air' were created by 'the force of imagination'.[6] Like Theseus, Burton argues that imagination
can give an impression of reality that escapes from the
limitations of ordinary and substantial experiences.

All this has far-reaching consequences for an understanding of a theatrical event. Shakespeare's Hamlet and
many scholars before him confidently asserted that the
task of actors was to 'imitate humanity' and that 'the
purpose [and] end of playing ... [was] to hold, as 'twere,
the mirror up to nature' (III.ii.17–37) but, when imagination is at work, these priorities must change or be understood in a very special sense. Theseus implies that the
primary task of a poet-dramatist is not to imitate everyday
experience, in the sense of copying it; it is to change
nature, to re-create it and set out upon a stage an
amazing and unprecedented world with shapes or
shadows that express what North's Plutarch would call
the author's own 'fancy and pleasure'. Actors become
vehicles for this re-vision or re-creation of the world and
they respond to its challenge by embodying it in their
performances, using their own imaginations and skills. In
its turn, an audience can take pleasure in the marvellous
transformation and, by exercise of its own imaginations,
re-create yet again the stage performance to suit its own
individual and very various minds. A theatrical event does
not merely 'hold a mirror' up to nature but re-creates it
three times over. In doing so, the crucial functions are
the imagination of an author in the first place and, then,
those of both actors and audience.

Imagination at Work

For Coleridge, it was the images expressed in the words of
Venus and Adonis and *The Rape of Lucrece* that showed
Shakespeare to be a 'myriad-minded' poet[7] and the verbal
richness of the dialogue most readily reveals the imaginative nature of his plays, in prose as well as verse. Rosalind's
speeches in *As You Like It* mix direct sensations drawn from
everyday experiences with far-fetched ideas as her mind

changes. No person in real life thinks or speaks like this, only such a 'shadow' that may be found in a play:

> dost thou think, though I am comparison'd like a man, I have a doublet and hose in my disposition? One inch of delay more is a South Sea of discovery. I prithee tell me who is it quickly, and speak apace. I would thou couldst stammer, that thou mightst pour this conceal'd man out of thy mouth, as wine comes out of a narrow-mouth'd bottle – either too much at once or none at all. I prithee take the cork out of thy mouth that I may drink thy tidings.
>
> (III.ii.181–9)

In *All's Well that Ends Well*, Helena's longing for Bertram brings together images of combat, simple domestic chores, flowing waters, and physical surrender:

> I know I love in vain, strive against hope;
> Yet in this captious and intenible sieve
> I still pour in the waters of my love,
> And lack not to lose still.

The end of this surge and eddy of ideas is simple, as if Helena is about to be forced back into silent thought. Her next words introduce a different tone and rhythm, and yet another image that is awesome and universal in reference:

> Thus, Indian-like,
> Religious in mine error, I adore
> The sun that looks upon his worshipper
> But knows of him no more.
>
> (I.iii.192-8)

Her thoughts have come back to earth and her words express that experience with a further flight of imagination.

Each successive play brings changes in verbal style, but always with amazingly varied verbal images that express lively sensations and rapidly changing thoughts. Suddenly confronted with a frightened messenger, Macbeth adds a rapid string of metaphors to his simple curse: 'The devil damn thee black, thou cream-fac'd loon! / Where got'st thou that goose look?' (V.iii.11–12). Walking in her sleep, Lady Macbeth invokes other persons and then speaks, with a sudden self-awareness, of her own hands and, then, of her husband: her attention shifts abruptly, as if responding to thoughts and feelings at the very moment they surface into consciousness:

> The Thane of Fife had a wife; where is she now? What, will these hands ne'er be clean? No more o' that, my lord, no more o' that; you mar all with this starting.

Her terrible vision calls for physical actions as it awakens sensations of smell, sight, and touch, and only then does she express the pressures exerted by her imagination in a far-fetched verbal image followed by an inarticulate cry:

> Here's the smell of the blood still. All the perfumes of Arabia will not sweeten this little hand. Oh, oh, oh!
>
> (V.i.40–50)

Images seem to grow out of each other and overreach each other, sometimes mingling with inexpressible feelings or necessary practicalities of action. Their swiftly succeeding verbal impressions set a pace with which actors and audience will often fail to keep up. Shakespeare, as playwright, did not lay out all his imaginary visions in broad perspectives and careful detail, like Edmund Spenser in the narrative of *The Faerie Queen,* nor did he draw disparate reactions together in tightly organized networks of metaphors and images, like John Donne in his *Songs and Sonnets.* At his most commanding, Shakespeare's images seem to stream forth in the dialogue wherever a wilful imagination led him: as his contemporaries said, his writing 'flow'd with that facility' that it seems to 'be nature', his head and hand moving together.[8] So confident the writing appears to be that, when failing to catch individual images and allusions, or even the sense of what is being said, the attention of audience members can be held merely by the energy of speech, its speed, weight, rhythms and variations of sound; their imaginations may then 'amend' what is spoken with responses drawn from their subconscious and so, ultimately, from their own life-experiences.

While incidental verbal images show the range, sensuality, and subtlety of Shakespeare's imagination, he gave 'local habitation' to more than could be spoken and to all kinds of actions and interactions between people. The persons of the plays make entries and exits, engage in various business and change in appearance with the passage of time; a succession of different locations and situations are presented. Some feelings are too instinctive, terrible, or rapturous to be fully presented in words. A play's action often involves unspoken conflicts in families, classes, or political groups, the processes of history and the effects of chance; individuals are unconsciously drawn towards mutual affection, sexual satisfaction, or peace of mind. In all these matters, much is not presented in the author's words and it is the inarticulate, wider but, often, more sustained elements of a drama – the movement of the play at the deeper level of its shape, structure, and 'inner' life – that enables the most considered and deeply-felt experiences to be 'shadowed forth'. In all this, as well as in the plays' verbal poetry, the esemplastic power of the author's imagination is at work and, in all these respects, the actors and audiences are called upon to respond with their individual imaginations. The theatrical event of a Shakespeare performance invites the same kind of imaginative response as his non-dramatic poetry: intuitive, sensuous, and emotional, as well as intellectual; subconsciously drawing upon individual life-experiences and re-creating them through the agency of the performers.

Notes

1. This chapter develops a paper written for a symposium of the Connotations Society for Critical Debate at Halberstat, Germany, in 1999; a version called 'Cold Monuments' was published in *Connotations*, 9 (1999/2000), No. 1, 34–42.
2. In this context, *monument* could mean either an effigy, a physical representation of some person, or, more simply, a verbal document or testimony.
3. S. T. Coleridge, *Biographica Literaria*, ed. J. Shawcross (Oxford: Oxford University Press, 1907), ii. 14; see also, i. 202.
4. S. T. Coleridge, *Lectures 1808-1819: On Literature*, ed. R. A. Foakes (Princeton, NJ: Princeton University Press, 1987), i. 81.
5. See Geoffrey Bullough, *Narrative and Dramatic Sources of Shakespeare*, v (London: Routledge & Kegan Paul and New York: Columbia University Press, 1964), pp. 116–17.
6. Robert Burton, *Anatomy of Melancholy* (1621), ed. 1932 (London: Dent), i. 254 etc.
7. Coleridge, *Biographica Literaria*, ii. 13.
8. See 'To the great Variety of Readers', by John Hemming and Henry Condell, prefaced to the 1623 first edition of Shakespeare's collected works, and Ben Jonson, *Timbers; or Discoveries* (1623–37); Folio (ed., 1642), p. 37; quoted in E. K. Chambers, *William Shakespeare: a Study of Facts and Problems* (1930), ii. 210.

3

Responses

The physical staging of Shakespeare's plays calls for much the same active imagination as their dialogue.[1] For the histories, actors and audience must travel to the 'vasty fields of France', the battle grounds of England, and the great palaces of earlier ages. They must also settle into places of rural calm and familiar domesticity that might be on their own doorsteps and in their own time. The comedies are usually more confined in location and it is their variety of mood that taxes the actors' versatility and stretches an audience's imagination. *Much Ado About Nothing* takes place in and around Leonato's house but its action involves an army returning from battle, a masked ball, a religious ceremony, and a night-time conspiracy; these scenes are interspersed with leisured talk in an orchard, ladies dressing for a wedding, and men challenging each other to a duel and keeping vigil in a tomb. Modern production, design, technology and expert stage-management have lessened the physical difficulties of staging but personal appearances continue to make exceptional demands. In the comedies, some people should look amazingly beautiful or be able to disguise their identity and gender completely. In the tragedies the most famous lovers of all time must be shown on the stage, a hero who 'could drink hot blood' and a king who is more than 80 years old and goes to the brink of insanity. In every one of the plays audiences are expected to believe in at least one threat of death. What is supposed to happen repeatedly goes beyond any actor's or audience's real-life experiences and only the active imagination of both, together with the actors' skill, can ensure that the persons represented are not, to some degree, unbelievable or laughable.

To understand how the plays carried belief in performance and were the basis of theatrical events that Elizabethan spectators enjoyed in their thousands, clues must be sought in the words that are the only detailed evidence that survives about what physically happened on stage. Implicit in Shakespeare's dialogue are speakers and listeners, human beings who journey through time and to various places while progressively revealing their innermost natures and the consequences of their actions. How Shakespeare put so much into words and how actors can bring these persons and actions to life will be the principal concern of later chapters; here the main focus is on the function of an audience in re-creating an impression of life. A start will be made by considering an Elizabethan practice that goes against almost all that is acceptable today: the casting of young male actors to play the women's roles. Why were audiences satisfied with this travesty of life?

Representing Sexuality on Stage

The women in Shakespeare's plays present difficulties for any actor, male or female. Many of them call for such exceptional intelligence, sentiment, and sexuality that it is hard to believe that credible performances could be given by actors young enough to be called 'boy actors'. Contemporary references to them squeaking their lines and posturing their greatness have added to modern incredulity and given rise to various explanations. Some scholars have argued that the androgynous sexual attraction and pert wit of these boys compensated for the absence of an appropriate physical presence and sensibility. That might be granted with regard to the earliest comedies, but it does not explain how under-age intelligence and immature physicality could present the sensitive and passionate heroines who drive the action of the major tragedies.

The word *sexuality* was not used by Shakespeare's contemporaries but in life and art sexual desire would have been as common as it ever is and theatre's ability to represent it on stage was usually taken for granted. The first theatrical event in the world was said to have been invented by Danaus, the son of Belus, when he wanted to celebrate a wedding and give pleasure to the lovers.[2] Marriage, love-making and sexual pleasure were frequent themes in popular Elizabethan plays: Rosalind in *As You Like It* is remarkable in being conscious of what is happening, not in the experience of being 'many fathoms deep' in love (IV.i.185–6). The young John Donne was said to have been 'a great visitor of ladies, a great frequenter of plays, a great writer of conceited verses',[3] as if his early love poems were the outcome of these three associated activities. Young men were reported to have gone to the theatre for a supply of amorous and enticing phrases that they could recycle for their own use.[4]

The mating of man and woman has central importance in the action of Shakespeare's comedies and without some way of representing sexual arousal performances could not have been credible. The principal characters in *Romeo and Juliet*, *Othello*, and *Antony and Cleopatra* face death because of their committal or enthralment to sexual passion. The action of *Measure for Measure* is said to be driven by 'concupiscible intemperate lust' (V.i.98): Angelo gives his 'sensual race the rein' and releases a destructive force in himself that is called 'sharp appetite' and a 'prompture of the blood' that produces 'a pond as deep as hell', 'a momentary trick', 'dark deeds', 'a game of tick-tack' (II.iv.160, 161 and 178; III.i.95 and 115; III.ii.167; I.ii.184–5). Sexual passion is not central to *Hamlet, Lear,* or *Macbeth* but contributes powerfully to these tragedies and, at times, is crucial for the motivation of their principal characters and the outcome of their actions. In the histories, it plays a less central but still vital part: the Lady Margaret is 'enthrall'd' to the Earl of

Suffolk (*I, Henry VI*, V.iii.101); in the presence of Richard the Third, Lady Anne forgets her undying hatred and, subsequently, marries him; the Princess of France seems to have a 'witchcraft' in her lips that charms King Henry silent and renders him complaisant (*Henry V*, V.ii.275).

Love-making would have raised special difficulties in Elizabethan theatres whoever the actors had been because it was a strictly private activity unsuitable for daylight performance on an open stage almost surrounded by a potentially unruly audience. Reliance on the audience's imagination to 'amend' the staged illusion would have been crucial in meeting this challenge, as it was for much else in the plays. One of Shakespeare's methods was to curtail speech so that spectators would want to fill out the tongue-tied silence of a sexually charged engagement in their own imagination. When Rosalind approaches Orlando at their first meeting in *As You Like It* and gives him a gift, he says nothing in reply and, in that silence, many in an audience will be ready to imagine what he is feeling; only after Rosalind has left the stage, does he speak of the 'passion [that] hangs these weights upon my tongue' (I.ii.224–67). In early encounters with Edmund in *King Lear*, Goneril says almost nothing to express her feelings but, as Regan says later, she gives him 'strange oeillades and most speaking looks' (IV.v.25–6). Sometimes two lovers are held motionless, gazing at one another, while another person speaks of them: 'at first sight / They have chang'd eyes', says Prospero of the silent Ferdinand and Miranda in *The Tempest* (I.ii.440–1).

In his first encounter with Isabella in *Measure for Measure*, Angelo has a sequence of silences which grow in length and awkwardness until the sexual content of the scene is unmissable by being almost unbearably stifled. Lucio and the Provost fill in the gaps with comment and, towards the close, Angelo twice speaks to himself, as if in a trance; when he does address Isabella it is so briefly that he seems to be struggling to hide his true feelings. The awkwardness of this encounter develops until everyone except Angelo has left the stage and then he acknowl-

edges his sexual compulsions, at first in short exclamations and bitter questions. He is more coherent and
sustained in speech only when he tries to dismiss all that
has happened as if it were a dream (see, especially,
II.ii.173, 179).

Although Shakespeare became progressively more
skilled at finding words to express the varying processes
and growth of sexual desire, he still left the audience's
imagination to complete the task. In the Nunnery Scene,
Hamlet speaks very simply to Ophelia of his love and yet
his stumbling and lurching prevarications most strongly
express the frightening effects of his passion: speech
buckles and breaks down into silence. So strained are
syntax and sense that multiple readings have found their
way into the original editions, as if no one was quite sure
what should be printed:

> OPHELIA How does your honour for this many a day?
> HAMLET I humbly thank you, well.
> > or ... *thank you, well, well, well.*
> OPHELIA My lord, I have remembrances of yours
> That I have longed long to redeliver.
> I pray you now receive them.
> > or *I pray you now, receive them.*
> > or *I pray you, now receive them.*
> HAMLET   No, not I;
> > or *No, no.*
> I never gave you aught.
> OPHELIA My honour'd lord, you know right well you
> did, ...
> > or ... *I know right well you did, ...*
> > > (*Hamlet,* III.i.91–7)

Hamlet's 'I never gave you aught' and the half-line
silence that follows can seem to shudder with passion and
pain or become tense with the effort of concealment.
Moments later, he acknowledges 'I did love you once'
and almost immediately seems to abandon belief in what
he has said with the contradictory, 'I loved you not'
(ll.115, 119). Words and silences together imply a rift

deep within his consciousness and feelings more powerful than anything of which he can speak. In whatever way
an actor performs this scene, the audience's experience
of its drama will depend on following very closely and
sensing in its own imaginations what Hamlet has not fully
expressed. Ophelia's reply, although coherent and understated, will seem scarcely less fraught with memories and
emotion: 'I did love you once' – 'Indeed, my lord, you
made me believe so' (ll. 116–17). An audience is drawn
into the play, not so much in comprehension as in imagination, so that it shares and half-creates both his pain
and hers, their sexual longings and instinctive reactions –
the sensations of both in this delayed moment of
confrontation.

Othello is the most directly and repeatedly passionate
play. Terrible disjunctions of sexually driven speech
render words almost useless, even as they are being used.
A convulsive fit eventually stops the lacerating flow:

> It is not words that shakes me thus – pish! – noses, ears,
> and lips. Is't possible? Confess! Handkerchief! O devil!
>
> (IV.i.41–3)

Later in the same scene, in front of the official messenger
from Venice, Othello's passion breaks out repeatedly in
cries disconnected from other speech: 'Fire and brim-
stone! ... Devil! ... Goats and monkeys!' (ll. 228–60).
Here, in imagination, an audience may be able to share
his incomprehension, compulsion, and almost speechless
pain or, more likely, it will be so repelled by his cruelty
that its response is centred on the speechless Desdemona
and shares in her bewilderment and horror.

In the comedies, in opposite and lighter vein, sexual
desire often provokes a kind of madness. Rosalind recognizes very early on that 'Love is merely a madness' and,
later, exemplifies its waywardness (*As You Like It*,
III.ii.370–5, and see IV.i.124–95). The lovers of *A
Midsummer Night's Dream* know that they are 'wood [mad]
within this wood' (II.i.192); in *Twelfth Night*, Sebastian
that either 'I am mad / Or else the lady's mad'

(IV.iii.15–16); in *Much Ado,* Benedict can summon only stupid and babbling rhymes to express his feelings (V.ii.22–37). Petruchio and Katharine both learn the truth about themselves when it seems that 'being mad herself, she's madly mated' (*Taming of the Shrew,* III.ii.240). Audiences are called to follow as best they can and, in doing so, imagine the underlying feelings that give unusual energy to speech and strangeness to behaviour.

In representing sexual involvement verbally, Shakespeare would often use bawdy talk and indecent puns so that an audience finds itself straining to catch the possible meanings and so, once more, is caught up in the speaker's inner consciousness. A run of *doubles entendres* can show where a mind is going, as if by compulsion: in *Much Ado About Nothing,* when Benedick and Beatrice spar with each other in public, sexual allusion often gallops ahead of the ostensible subject of their talk, whether that happens to be warfare, wit, each other, other people, or an unruly 'jade' (I.i.123). Even at cross-purposes, these speakers ride willingly together on sexual submeanings. When Rosalind talks about love to Orlando, or to Celia or Touchstone, bawdiness seems to come unbidden; and so it does when Viola and Feste talk together about Orsino or Hamlet talks to almost anyone about almost anything. In Ophelia's presence at the performance of 'The Mousetrap', Hamlet's obscenities will either seem a calculated and public affront or an outward sign of feelings so unmanageable that they turn into unthinking aggression. Bawdiness in Shakespeare can also be benign, an easing of other troubles, as in the 'sweetest morsel of the night' that Doll Tearsheet and Falstaff promise each other (*II. Henry IV,* II.iv.33–6) or in the talk between Florizel and Perdita at the shepherds' feast in *The Winter's Tale* when bawdy allusions are at one with tenderness and reverence (IV.iv.127–53).

Perhaps Shakespeare's most extraordinary use of words to awaken an audience's imagination to the power of sexuality is the introduction, through metaphor and simile, of references to the everyday processes of living. A shift away from abstract description and avowal to well-remembered and familiar sensations brings a sense of physical actuality to longing and fantasy so that everyone in an audience may be able to appreciate verbal images of love-making. Examples are everywhere, from early plays to the very last. A suckling child comes to the Earl of Suffolk's mind as he painfully parts from his mistress:

> Here could I breathe my soul into the air
> As mild and gentle as the cradle-babe
> Dying with mother's dug between its lips; ...
>   (*II, Henry VI*, III.ii.391–3)

When Olivia's eyes fasten on Cesario's mouth, her mind at once races on to think of a guilty criminal before she comes to the heart of her message:

> O, what a deal of scorn looks beautiful
> In the contempt and anger of his lip!
> A murd'rous guilt shows not itself more soon
> Than love that would seem hid: love's night is noon.
> Cesario, by the roses of the spring,
> By maidhood, honour, truth, and every thing,
> I love thee so ...
>   (*Twelfth Night*, III.i.142–7)

Seeing the youth to whom she is so strangely attracted, her recollection of more mundane experiences – of night and high noon, roses and springtime – gives her speech substance, or a 'body', as Shakespeare might have called it.[5] In the images of Olivia's imagination, members of an audience might subconsciously awaken their own memories and find their own feelings kindled.

In *Antony and Cleopatra*, the lovers on their first entry speak with exaggeration and airy playfulness that observant Roman soldiers take as signs of weakness and triviality. Yet the mundane references to boundaries of land, beggars, and bills of reckoning (as in a shop or tavern) are all immediately recognizable and together suggest the sexual nature of their relationship while grounding it in everyday actuality. Talk of a new heaven and earth is grand, mythic and, even, religious in reference but it would also have reminded Shakespeare's audience of that new-found land across the Atlantic from which, standing close to the Globe theatre, one might see ships returning laden with long-absent sailors and, if fortunate, with treasure:

> CLEOPATRA If it be love indeed, tell me how much.
> ANTONY There's beggary in the love that can be
>   reckon'd.
> CLEOPATRA I'll set a bourn how far to be belov'd.
> ANTONY Then must thou needs find out new heaven,
>   new earth.
>
> (I.i.14–17)

Ordinary tactile images are often used so that they give access to the strangest and most unsettling experiences of sexual arousal, as when a lover vows 'to *weep* seas, live in *fire, eat* rocks, *tame* tigers ...' (*Troilus and Cressida*, III.ii.76–7).

All these strategies rely, to some degree, on an audience making good what can only partially and imperfectly be achieved by words and actions on a stage; each person watching the play will be led to complete the illusion of sexual encounter in his or her own mind and to do so freely, according to whatever has entered their subconscious through individual and everyday experience. An incomplete verbal depiction of sexuality enabled Shakespeare to give it a large role in the plays and goes far to explain why it carries conviction in such variety and gives such widespread pleasure. The Elizabethan practice of using young male actors to play the women's roles suited this way of writing because their lack of feminine sexuality was another factor that could bring an audience's imagination into play. Too many actresses have triumphed as Shakespeare's women for us to believe that this practice limited his imaginative input or that modern productions should follow Elizabethan precedent in this matter. Being so dependent on suggestion, the texts in performance can draw an audience, instinctively and subconsciously, to contribute its own fantasies to what is presented on stage, whether the actors are male or female.

It might be objected that imaginative collusion is too sophisticated and too mental an activity for Elizabethan audiences that were drawn from a wide social range and included many with little education. But other popular theatres have used all-male casts and a considerable number of them still do despite competition with productions that have mixed casts and with the more accessible entertainment of film and television. The Jatra theatres in Bengal, Bangladesh, and Orissa, for example, draw audiences of thousands for night-long performances.[6] In Japan, a modernized and well-established Kabuki theatre has retained the male Onnagata performers for female roles from its more popular past. Fantasizing about sex is not a rare gift and need not be a sophisticated one; by exploiting its potential, theatre can give reliable and popular pleasure.

An Audience's Contribution to On-stage Illusion

Questions raised by the use of cross-gender casting highlight a dramatic strategy that is at work in all of Shakespeare's plays. Although its use varies from play to play, according to the persons of the play, its story, setting, argument, and verbal style, reliance on the imagination of audiences is found throughout his career and is not exclusive to any one kind of encounter. As a boy or young man could be accepted as an accomplished and attractive woman, so the presence of any actor, in the context of a performance, could awaken an audience's individual fantasies and imaginations and the play seem to be as immediate and credible as life itself, however exceptional the actions and persons presented. This creation of an illusion of reality is able to give pleasure, even when the play's action is painful, terrifying, perplexing, or provocative: members of an audience escape into an experience that is welcoming because they have helped to create it; and it is mysteriously attractive because it speaks to their senses and subconscious memories, as well as to their conscious minds.

Shakespeare well understood that imagination can endow a performer's very presence with many extraordinary and fictive qualities. In *Much Ado About Nothing*, Benedick spies 'marks of love' in Beatrice when, to anyone else's eyes, she is being abrupt and unco-operative towards him, perhaps even contemptuous. As Theseus predicated in *A Midsummer Night's Dream*, his active imagination sees only a 'fair lady' with a loving 'double meaning' in her simple words and so he resolves to take pity on her (II.iii.204ff.). In *Othello*, Iago activates his master's imagination and so turns Desdemona's 'virtue into pitch' and drives the action towards violence and tragedy: in Othello's mind, Desdemona has become a 'public commoner, ... [an] impudent strumpet ... : that cunning whore of Venice / That married with Othello' (II.iii.349; III.iii.326–8; IV.ii.71–91). While this transformation seems appallingly real to Othello, an audience sees only a faithful and cruelly misused wife. 'There is nothing either good or bad, but thinking makes it so', as Hamlet says (II.ii.248–50) and so the innocent Miranda, faced with a gathering of traitors and would-be murderers, sees only 'many goodly creatures' and exclaims in wonder: 'How beauteous mankind is! O brave new world / That has such people in't' (*Tempest*, V.i.182–4).

An audience's ability to half-create what they see can be demonstrated most convincingly in theatres where what is performed is far from anything in real life. Puppets, masks, stilts, elaborate facial make-up, unnatural and bizarre gestures, or dances calling for extraordinary expertise can be seen in the minds of audiences as living realities that exceed the physical bounds of ordinary existence. By use of music, dance, a narrator, strange make-up, and costumes that almost conceal the human form, a centuries-old Kabuki play, known in English as *The Bone Gathering of Iwafuji*, can present horrendous stage battles in which a single warrior slays dozens of opponents; by the same means, it presents intimate sexual longing leading to violence and yet comes nowhere near an enactment of it. While Kabuki is an exceptional example, a degree of contrived deception is present in all theatre and is essential for creating its most marvellous effects. When Peter Stein was directing Ibsen's *Peer Gynt* at the Schaubühne in Berlin in 1972, a play not written with the practicalities of performance in mind, he scornfully turned down a proposal that real horses should be brought on stage: he wanted the horses to be 'completely fake' because 'everything that is used, or let's rather say quoted, creates an illusion to a certain extent'. A live horse could not share 'the game' that actors and audience would be playing together; it would draw attention to its own reality and that would not serve the illusory one in the minds of the audience.[7]

For Shakespeare, words were a primary means of creating an illusion of physical reality on stage. He used them to awaken an audience's expectation and alert its senses to respond in particular ways, to draw attention to a revealing movement or gesture, to create atmosphere and mood, to describe what is meant to be happening off-stage, and, of course, to clarify argument and draw narrative forward. The relation between the spoken text and the physical component of performance will be considered more fully in Part II of this study where actors and acting are the main concerns; here one scene will be used to show how what is seen but not heard joins with words in awaking the imaginative response of an audience.

A Present-day Example of Audience Involvement

During the last century many theatre productions tried to come as close as possible to what happens in actual life, leaving little to the imagination. This pursuit of realism, reproducing actual living-spaces on stage and requiring actors to imitate ordinary behaviour, was encouraged by the popularity of the novel and concepts of 'character' based on popular psychology. At first, the arrival of photography, film, and television still further encouraged this trend. Theatrical realism was also in tune with the current interest in sociology and political science and, to dramatists, it offered the means for addressing new and urgent political issues in immediately recognizable situations. Before the end of the twentieth century, however, when visual technology was no longer new and more was known about the workings of the mind, prevalent fashions changed and assertion, challenge, suggestion, and shock displaced careful demonstration and argument. Many theatres turned their backs on realism: stage action became bizarre and unlikely, and seemingly impossible performances were favoured. Today audiences are frequently meant to be puzzled so that they are left to seek an underlying coherence for themselves or to accept a play that they do not fully understand. Variety in presentation is preferred to consistency, exceptional narratives rather than the recognizable and acceptable. In some ways this is a return to the past and a comparison between our modern theatre and Shakespeare's is less far-fetched than history might lead us to think. He too lived in a time of change and worked for an adventurous, innovative theatre and his plays may have been more surprising and disturbing than later opinion came to believe or a reading of their texts at first suggests. Both theatres depend on imaginative acceptance, not instant recognition of a mirror-image of life.

The Wooster Group's 1998 production of Eugene O'Neill's *Emperor Jones*, with Kate Valk in the central role, provides a useful example. Both the occasion and location of this theatrical event were very different from those of Shakespeare's plays, but its audiences, like those at the original Globe, were crowded and varied in age and wealth, if not in class or education. How did these people come to accept a cross-dressed performance? According to a *New York Times* reviewer (13 March 1998), they were 'seduced' into belief and this was the culmination of a progressive experience, not a recognition of any life-likeness. To act the Afro-American fugitive from justice who is the hero of the play, the actress blackened her face, as if with shoe polish, but kept neck and hands their natural pale colour. She made no attempt to look like any person to be found in everyday life, but created a stereotype familiar in stage-shows that were popular many years earlier. Her voice sounded like that of Al Jonson or the more recent vocalist, Pigmeat Markham. The large cast of the play was reduced to two actors, together with two chorus-members or stage-assistants. The setting was an adaptation of earlier ones used by the Wooster Group: a bare and uniformly steel-grey platform, surrounded with scaffolding, lights, TV monitors, and speakers. During the performance, nothing of this varied at all, but some parts of the set moved at times, often with a metallic clang, a throne-like chair circled around on castors, and the monitors were switched on and off.

A production less likely to hold an audience's attention with a sense of reality is hard to imagine but accounts of early performances, as well as my own experience, bear witness that this is what happened. Ben Brantley, critic of *The New York Times,* reported that:

> Her eyes rolling feverishly and her voice a brazen evocation of the dumb but crafty black figures in minstrel shows and melodramas, Ms. Valk initially registers as an obscene cartoon. Yet as the performance continues, it acquires a searing depth, a compounded feeling of entrapment. It's a performance that sucks you in just when you're feeling safely distanced from it.
>
> (13 March 1998)

Having recalled earlier productions of O'Neill's text, Michael Feingold registered a similar surprise in *Village Voice* (24 March): 'You feel for her as intensely as you might for Robeson' in an earlier production; in the last scenes 'Valk's bravura carr[ies] the show nearly alone. It hardly matters, because we're so with her by that point nothing could tear us away'. This was no ordinary illusion of reality: at times, according to Fintan O'Toole in the *Daily News* (13 March, 1998): 'The whole thing achieves a fevered, dreamlike clarity in which past and present, reality and imagination are fused.'

Much of the production would have been familiar to anyone who had seen earlier productions by the Wooster Group. Performances made no attempt to imitate ordi-

nary reality. Speech was far more varied, extremely ener-
gized and agile, and often directed towards the audience.
Voices were given extra resonance and made more striking by use of microphones and speakers. Movement was
often large, ornate, and unusual; on numerous occasions,
when two persons were engaged in talk with each other,
the actors would cross and recross the entire space of the
stage. Gestures were signs or signals, rather than those of
everyday behaviour and were often made repeatedly. The
actors made no secret of their technical accomplish-
ments: on occasion, they danced formally together and
were, for much of the time, accompanied by music or
specially devised sounds; the performances had a shapeli-
ness and finish more usual in dance productions than in
dramas. The actors had not been culled from near and
far, especially for this production, but were all members
of the company who had worked together on many previous occasions. In an interview, Kate Valk said: 'We are like
a band; each of [us] has a sixth sense about the other,
about when to step forward and when to draw back.'[8]
This production was not the product of some three-and-a-
half weeks of rehearsals, or even twice that number which
would be generous in most Euro-American theatres, but
had grown out of some years of work by a group of actors
totally familiar with each other: it was a project that had
been taken up many times in breaks between other
engagements. And the production was always changing:
the director, Elizabeth LeCompte, made almost daily
visits and called further rehearsals during the run to
develop performances and keep them ahead of whatever
had been achieved so far in the production's long life. As
Euridice Arratia reported of an earlier show: 'A word,
gesture, or sound that works today can easily be discarded tomorrow, and the search begins all over again.'[9]

In many ways, the Wooster Group's style of performance is much nearer that of Shakespeare's theatre than
those adopted by well-established theatres for staging his
plays today. An open, uncluttered platform is set against a
single and familiar background; a 'fellowship' of actors
work together for years at a time, technically expert at

speaking a verbal text, performing close to their audience, making strong gestures, and moving with 'agility'.
While Elizabethan performers were not accompanied by
almost continuous music and sound, the speaking of
verse made its own music: it was a carefully formed and
highly controlled aural accompaniment to the action that
arose out of the actors' performances to supplement and
enhance them. Eye-witnesses tell us that audiences at this
late twentieth-century theatrical event were held by the
seeming reality of performance and amazed by what they
experienced, as audiences were said to have been at the
original Globe. In both instances, actors were the centre
of attention, with no scenic changes to take eyes away and
establish subtle moods or symbols. According to the *Daily
News* critic: 'However far [the production of *Emperor
Jones*] strays from familiar conventions, it comes back to
the old virtues of actors inhabiting the stage.'

What at first had seemed grotesque and perverse was,
in the end, received as a depiction of Jones that was both
extraordinary and totally convincing, somewhat like a
very clear dream. What actually happened on stage was
not the end of the matter; the effect it had on the audience is what mattered – what the audience *thought* it was
experiencing. This was not realistic acting, but the means
of encouraging an audience to use its imagination and so
create an illusion of reality in terms of its own and very
various sense-memories and of its own prejudices and ide-
ologies. A young man playing Juliet might have com-
manded a similar belief if attention had been gripped
and imagination charged by analogous means.

Effects of Performance

The young heroine of *Romeo and Juliet* is attracted to its
hero and dies for love of him. Gender, sexuality, sensuality and a very particular sensibility are all so basic to its
action that they must have been represented in some way
on stage by the young male actors of the day. To our
minds, accustomed to gender-specific casting, this seems

almost incredible: the disguises, double-thinking, and playfulness of Shakespeare's comedy give little help to • the actor here and would seem inappropriate for presenting young persons driven to suicide. The text of this tragedy therefore provides a suitably challenging testing-ground on which to examine whether, despite the great differences in culture, the audience's acceptance of Kate Valk's Emperor Jones holds any clue towards understanding the cross-dressed performances of Shakespeare's day.

The scene in which Romeo and Juliet meet for their marriage ceremony at Friar Lawrence's cell (Act II, scene vi) includes some of the play's greatest difficulties for a male actor since, in real life and in dreams, a young girl on such an occasion can seem to shine with beauty and be filled with unusual strength, desire, and tenderness; her sexuality and femininity may seldom be more apparent. Shakespeare's Juliet enters without a word while the Friar continues from a previous speech:

> Here comes the lady. O, so light a foot
> Will ne'er wear out the everlasting flint.
> A lover may bestride the gossamer
> That idles in the wanton summer air
> And yet not fall; so light is vanity.
>
> (ll. 16–20)

A stage-direction in the first Quarto, which seems to describe an actual performance, adds a gloss to this: '*Enter Juliet somewhat fast and embraces Romeo*'. Juliet's entry for this delicate meeting is as physically alive as it is verbally silent, but any speed is offset by comment from the Friar that is quick and simple at first but then develops slower and graver phrases, while still maintaining a lightness until he has nearly finished. As if on monitors, his verbal images offer three different visions: a strangely indestructible flint, an airy, sensuous, and indulgent summer's day, and, finally, a moral comment that may give a glimpse of a figure from a morality play or allegorical sermon. With a highly active central performance to take attention, an audience's imagination would be amply fed – one might say bombarded with fragmented impressions – while Juliet herself both takes an audience's attention and remains not entirely revealed, speaking to the eyes only and not at all to the ears. Then, almost at once, her body is physically half-concealed as she embraces Romeo. Only enough has been seen to whet an audience's imagination and allow each member to endow words and visual images with whatever sensuous memories and sexual fantasies arise instinctively from the subconscious.

Juliet's first words are not to her lover. They give a fairly simple greeting to the Friar, but with wordplay on *ghostly*, as 'non-physical': 'Good even to my ghostly confessor.' The Friar deflects attention to the tongue-tied Romeo and then Juliet has one more line that is, at last, about the person she loves, although only in the third person:

> FRIAR   Romeo shall thank thee, daughter, for us
> both.
> JULIET   As much to him, else is his thanks too
> much.

Once more the response is partly playful. It may seem that Juliet has experienced a sexual thrill and an overflow of feelings, which she here expresses in a satisfied verbal merriment; or, possibly, she uses words as a deflection, as a way of shielding both growing excitement and virginal fear. The sight of Romeo and Juliet together remains the visual centre of attention while it is kept an active element of the drama by the changing physical positions that are required for the changing modes of address in the speeches. An audience will find that many quick impressions are bunching together and will unconsciously choose where to pay attention and how to fill out or go beyond the fragmented verbal messages that are being given. Again, incompleteness is an important element of Shakespeare's technique, the full emotional, intellectual, and sensual content of the encounter being neither defined nor established by words.

Next come two longer speeches of which only Juliet's last two lines sound as if they might express feeling directly:

> ROMEO   Ah, Juliet, if the measure of thy joy
> Be heap'd like mine, and that thy skill be more
> To blazon it, then sweeten with thy breath
> This neighbour air, and let rich music's tongue
> Unfold the imagin'd happiness that both
> Receive in either by this dear encounter.
> JULIET   Conceit, more rich in matter than in words,
> Brags of his substance, not of ornament.
> They are but beggars that can count their
>   worth,
> But my true love is grown to such excess
> I cannot sum up sum of half my wealth.

Even now, the 'imagin'd happiness' of the wedding day is scarcely expressed, except by indirection in talk about talking with references to music, weight, ornament, wealth, and beggars. Technically, the speeches make considerable demands if they are to be spoken clearly and musically. Physically, the actors are likely to remain close together but they speak with a self-conscious care that implies an awareness of a third person's presence. They will have to move a little to take adequate breath and deliver their sustained and musical speeches; probably, they are no longer embracing.

Despite the extended phrasing of both speeches, the emotional and mental energy of the two lovers is rising all the time; the Friar quickly concludes the scene, as if he recognizes a sexual arousal that craves fulfilment as soon as possible:

> Come, come with me, and we will make short work;
> For, by your leaves, you shall not stay alone
> Till holy church incorporate two in one.
>   *Exeunt.*

Perhaps these three lines will raise a laugh at an old man's caution. But another factor at the end of this episode is more certain: Juliet and Romeo conclude the scene silently. They may follow the Friar, taking whatever time their physical and verbal performances have dictated; or they might go before him, if he waits to keep them under his eye. The scene's last image is a short dance-like passage for two actors: an audience will supply what more is needed to complete the representation.

In none of this episode's short phases are Juliet's feelings expressed fully in words. The effect of the actor's performance must derive in large part from physical actions. Often during the short scene, Juliet gives individual expression to what she feels only by her presence or in her changing physical relationships to other persons, her meetings and greetings, her passages across the stage in her own timing and direction. These physical expressions work together with the spoken words but sometimes give a different message. The music of speech, as distinct from its often incomplete verbal expression, also contributes to the full effect and this operates constantly whoever is speaking.

In most theatres staging Shakespeare today, actresses respond to the difficulties of this text by striving to make what is verbally understated more directly convincing than it is on the page, taking time to establish Juliet's emotions and sexuality without the help of speech. Directors introduce subtle stage-business with costume or stage properties in order to illustrate what she feels. A stage setting and atmospheric lighting represent whatever physical location the designers have sensed behind Shakespeare's words. Sometimes the action is set in modern times, not Elizabethan, in order to give an impression that it is actually happening in the present time.

An alternative staging is, however, available.[10] Imitating the Wooster Group's style of production, actors could be placed on a plain platform and engage an audience by using a choreographic and open style of performance that does not attempt any direct imitation of real life. By staging the action with only a few stage properties against an unchanging background and giving continuous attention to music and the sound of speech, a company might present this delicate scene without striving to provide a recognizable 'moving picture' of any reality. The actors could hold attention and give substance to the drama and yet leave their audiences to add to what is shown, completing what is presented so that the play will seem truly alive and meaningful in their own imaginations.

Applying these perceptions to Shakespeare's plays in performance in his own times will have several consequences. Because each member of an audience would have been free to respond to a 'boy actor' by re-creating him in whatever form pleased their individual fantasies and desires, the content of the drama could have seemed more sexual and intimate than it does to us. It also implies that we should not think of a penetrating 'gaze' being brought to bear on an Elizabethan cross-dressed performer, looking for a recognizable reality. Such a response is appropriate for a film, painting, or photograph, not for an ever-changing and 'incomplete' performance in front of a theatre audience that occupies the same light as the actors. In performance, this scene from *Romeo and Juliet* is a series of various, interlocking, and constantly changing effects, at once physical, aural, and sensuous; only the words of the text are fixed and, sometimes, intellectually precise. Together these stimulate the individual imaginations of audiences and are capable, during the course of any one performance, of carrying conviction and, to the mind's eye, an exceptional lifelike *impression* of living persons in action.

The young male actors are unlikely to have performed in a style that was totally out of keeping with that of the rest of the company and so Kate Valk's Emperor Jones may persuade us to change how we read an entire play. We should not expect that the text will define or signal the entire content of any scene: that will depend on what the actors do, as well as what they say, and on what an audience is able to contribute. The purpose of Shakespeare's words was to awaken and guide performances which, in their turn, would awaken responses in the minds of audiences that have greater vitality and further repercussions than those present in either the words of the text or any attempt that might be made to achieve life-like acting.

Reality on a Shakespearean stage was, we may believe, in the imagination of the spectators. In the mind, a play became progressively more real during the course of a performance, appearing to be so in the changing presence and actions of the actors, as well as in the words they speak. To progress further in an understanding of the theatrical experience that Shakespeare's plays offer, Part II of this study considers what the texts require an actor to do.

Notes

1. Parts of this chapter draw on two articles, 'Representing Sexuality in Shakespeare's Plays' and 'Cross-dressed Actors and their Audiences: Kate Valk's Emperor Jones and William Shakespeare's Juliet', both published in *New Theatre Quarterly*, xiii (1997; *NTQ* 51), 205–13 and xv (1999; *NTQ* 59), 195–203.

2. Robert Burton, *The Anatomy of Melancholy* (1621), Partition II, ii, 3; ed. 1932, iii. 181.

3. Sir Richard Baker; quoted in R. C. Bald, *John Donne: A Life* (Oxford: Oxford University Press, 1970), p. 72.

4. See *II, Parnassus* (c. 1599), III.i.1006–55: when Gullio begins to woo a lady, Ingenioso predicts, correctly, 'We shall have nothing but pure Shakespeare and shreds of poetry that he hath gathered at the theatre.'

5. The phrase is adapted from *All's Well*, I.i.169–70.

6. For a vivid description of Jatra, see Balwant Gargi, *Folk Theater of India*, 2nd edn (Calcutta: Rupa & Co, 1991), pp. 11–36. Their similarities to Elizabethan theatre are discussed in John Russell Brown, *New Sites for Shakespeare: Theatre, the Audience and Asia* (London and New York: Routledge, 1999), pp. 8–28.

7. Quoted in Michael Patterson, *Peter Stein* (Cambridge: Cambridge University Press, 1981), p. 74.

8. Quoted in Susie Mee, 'Chekhov's *Three Sisters* and the Wooster Group's *Brace Up!*', *Drama Review*, xxxvi, iv (1992), 145.

9. 'Island Hopping: Rehearsing the Wooster Group's *Brace Up!*', *Drama Review*, xxxvi, iv (1992), 122.

10. The following description is neither detailed nor precise because it does not refer to any full-scale public production but originates in a series of workshops during 2000 and 2001 at the Nehru Centre in London and the Bremer Shakespeare Company in Germany.

PART II: ACTORS

4

Texts and Techniques

Shakespeare's playscripts are both immediately enjoyable and endlessly demanding. Their words can occupy so much attention that a reader may not wish to look further, towards the theatrical events in which they were intended to play their part. Add to the words a voice, an actor, and space on stage, an auditorium full of people drawn from various backgrounds, and the day, time, and place for consecutive performance of the entire play and then, clearly, the changes wrought on what the words on the page might communicate will, at first, baffle enquiry. Yet here is the centre of interest for anyone wishing to know how the texts can do their proper work.

We can start by limiting attention to the actor and speech. Fortunately, a great deal of study has been devoted to these subjects during the last century, first of all in acting schools and private studios and, more recently, in universities and research institutes. What actors are taught gives a baseline for understanding how Shakespeare's texts function in a theatre. While for some readers this will be unfamiliar information, for those who are actors, it may serve as a reminder of how they instinctively react to words in performance.

What a Text Requires from an Actor

While an actor's vocal task can be comprehended only in practice and as part of a theatrical event, a simple experiment will make its basic demands very clear. For this, one needs to speak out loud and have someone to whom to speak; the listener should then report if every word has been heard and understood, either by giving a visual sign or by repeating out loud what has been heard:

> *Stand some 20 metres away from the listener and try speaking until you can be sure you have been distinctly heard. A third person can be introduced to stand at your side and then you should speak again so that both your listeners can hear.*

Followed slowly and thoughtfully, this experiment will have shown how speech on stage involves concentrated attention, breath-control, projection, and choice of direction and that it requires both nervous and physical energy; one begins to discover that speaking to be heard clearly by an audience is a physical as well as an intellectual action. Besides these basic elements, attention must also be given to metre, rhythm, phrasing, intonation, modulation, and texture, together with motivation for speaking the particular words or for being silent when no more words follow. All this has to be taken into account before beginning to understand the complicated phenomenon of Shakespeare's text in performance: it involves more than speech and audibility.

Cicely Berry's *The Actor and his Text* (London: Harrop, 1987) explains how regular exercises improve 'relaxation, breathing and resonance, power and clarity' and yet:

> unless this work connects organically with an ever-fresh and developing response to language, it remains a technical accomplishment, which makes the voice stronger and more resonant, but does not necessarily make the speaking more interesting. ... We have to train ourselves to respond to words in a less obvious and stated way, so that their very movement contains our feeling. ... Exercises should make us ready for the intuitive response.
>
> (p. 24)

This is the advice of a voice teacher who has used Shakespeare's texts for the core of all her work:

> because it demands such a complete investment of ourselves in the words; because it is so rich and extraordinary we are forced to be bold and even extravagant and so perhaps discover more possibilities within our own voice than we are aware of; because, in a very practical sense, the connection between the physical and verbal life of the characters is totally apparent and palpable; and lastly because ... the structure of the thought demands both courage and discipline.
>
> (p. 9)

Elsewhere Cicely Berry calls for the very 'substance of words' – their shape, sound, and texture – to be taken into account; and so, too, must the sensations and emotions awakened by words and the speaking of them. All this should inform performance.

Actors are well aware of the many challenges the text presents. In their earliest training, they learn how to use words in different ways. A student will repeat a very simple sentence – such as, 'The man came into the room' or 'Now I understand' – and each time arbitrarily change pace, volume, pitch, phrasing, and emphasis so that a wide range of possible effects are identified. Then the same words are repeated while consciously changing the way of speaking to whatever seems appropriate for a number of specific and different situations. In answer to repetition of a simple question, single words, such as 'yes', 'no', 'never', 'perhaps', can be repeated in arbitrarily varied ways and each way of speaking will be found to communicate quite different answers. These exercises are taken from Michel Saint-Denis, *Training for the Theatre* (London: Heinemann, 1982), p. 117, the posthumous book which lays out his plans for the new Juilliard School at Lincoln Center in New York. So actors at the beginning of their training are shown that *how* to speak is as important as *what* to speak. Listening to 'Good morning' being spoken by people encountered by chance on a single morning is another simple way to discover, practically, how two words can carry very different messages.

A week before Peter Brook's *A Midsummer Night's Dream* opened at Stratford in 1970 – a production that would travel around the world and become a benchmark for later stagings – the director called John Kane, who was playing Puck, for a private session because he had said that he found repeating performances to be tedious. The actor reported how the two sat facing other on the floor of a quiet studio:

> Following his instructions, I closed my eyes and repeated the word 'Light' whilst simultaneously trying to analyse the process that led to the utterance of the word and the changes in its intonation. After a few minutes of this, he asked me to repeat the experiment this time using the word 'Dark'. After an equal amount of time had passed, he gently stopped me, told me to open my eyes and then to describe the sensations and responses that the exercise had aroused. ...
>
> Peter listened in silence and then asked me whether or not I thought it possible that such a precise examination of the word might take place during performance; and if it could, how much richer it would prove when applied to words in conjunction with one another as in a sentence or line of verse. Creation and exploration need not and, in fact, must not stop on the last day of rehearsal. The actor must always be open to change. 'You must act as a medium for the words. If you consciously colour them, you're wasting your time. The words must be able to colour you.'[1]

What is true of individual words is true of whole speeches and entire texts, in so far as time and skill will allow. Slowly, through rehearsal and performance, an actor aims at speaking every line in a part according to the changing situations encountered in the unfolding action of a play. Choices have to be made every moment, whether consciously or not: punctuation can be made lighter or heavier (that in printed editions having no authorial warrant), pauses can be introduced, some words stressed strongly and others passed over quickly and lightly. Some words need to be linked closely together in timing, pitch, volume, or quality of sound while others may be separated and treated individually. All this and more is dependent on each actor's discretion and inspiration; in our theatres, with a director's assistance.

Metre gives some guidance on how to phrase a speech. As Sir Philip Sydney explained in his *Apology for Poetry* (1580):

> The senate of poets hath chosen verse as their fittest raiment ... : not speaking (table-talk fashion or like men in a dream) words as they chanceably fall from the mouth, but peising [weighing] each syllable of each word by just proportion according to the dignity of the subject.[2]

Shakespeare, like almost all his contemporaries, used verse to control how words were weighted and sentences phrased but metre does not offer an unequivocal or complete guide for speaking the dialogue. Line-endings are usually significant and should be marked more or less lightly as sense and syntax dictate, but every other metrical feature is less definitive and less restrictive to an actor's delivery. A few pentameters may require five light and five stressed syllables to follow each other alternately, but such regularity is exceptional. Verse lines do not march ahead with both syllables of each iambic foot falling into their regular places. Most lines are variations of this norm: the first foot of a line often has its first syllable stressed; sometimes two strongly stressed syllables are placed together or three lightly stressed ones follow each other. With such a flexible metrical form, an actor will find that many variations are possible in delivery without loss of an underlying iambic beat and the on-going assurance that metre gives.

When Peter Brook started work on Shakespeare he believed 'to a limited extent in the possibility of a classical word music':

each verse had a sound that was correct, with only moderate variations; then through direct experience I found that this was absolutely and totally untrue. The more musical the approach you bring to Shakespeare, which means the more sensitive you are to music, the more you find that there is no way, except by sheer pedantry, that can fix a line's music ... While [an actor] has to keep certain consistencies in what he's doing or it's just a chaotic performance, as he speaks it, each single line can reopen itself to a new music, made round these radiating points.[3]

Syntax provides an actor with more certain guidance than metre. The varying length of sentences determines the duration of each line of thought and, by this means, it influences the phrasing of speech. Latin was taught in all Elizabethan grammar schools, such as King Edward's at Stratford-upon-Avon which Shakespeare almost certainly attended as a boy, and from this inflected language pupils learnt to respect a similar grammatical structure in English. In *The Merry Wives of Windsor*, Act IV, scene i, Shakespeare has the Welsh parson, Sir Hugh Evans, drill young William Page in the rudiments of Latin vocabulary and grammar. A common exercise was double translation, from Latin to English and then back again,[4] a practice which tested accuracy and also encouraged students to write English on the same grammatical foundations as Latin. Today, neither speakers nor writers have any form of syntax so firmly drilled into their subconscious minds and so actors in Elizabethan plays need to make a conscious effort to be aware of syntax and its shaping of the dialogue and controlling of emphasis. The main verbs indicate the impulse and activity of a speaker's thought; nouns are the objects on which this force works. The positions of both these elements in each complete sentence are like fixed stepping-stones in the changing current of speech. On these words, the main stresses should come and, once they have been set, the speaker will find that subsidiary clauses fall into place in support. A practical demonstration of this is easy:

Choose a continuous speech of some ten or fifteen lines that is not understood at first reading and mark its text so that its main verbs and the nouns that are their subjects and objects can be clearly seen. Then speak it aloud with emphasis only on these words.

To the reader, as well as a listener, the whole speech will be the better understood and a meaningful energy released. Usually syntax and sense will together direct an actor to three syllables in each line of verse that, when stressed, will give shape and clarity to speech. Beyond this, there can be considerable freedom in handling both verse and phrasing.

By responding sensitively to both metre and syntax, an actor will speak a series of varied sounds, linked together so that they hold attention and draw expectation forward. In skilled performances, the sound of a Shakespeare play creates an on-going and finely tuned music. The author of 'An excellent Actor' published in *New Characters* (1615) said as much, for 'what in the Poet is but ditty [i.e. is words to be spoken or sung], in him is both ditty and music'.[5] Audiences will be unaware that this spoken music is influencing their responses because it operates surreptitiously and subliminally alongside the conscious recognition of verbal meanings and physical performance. No two actors will create identical effects and, like much else in staging the plays, what happens is liable to vary each day of performance.

An Actor's Freedom of Response

Commentary on minutiae of vocal performance is bound to be clumsy because sound cannot be translated into words and can only with great difficulty be described. Yet an attempt to do this is necessary to show how Shakespeare's texts are continually open to alternative ways of delivery and how choice of these will affect the speaker's involvement in the action of a play and, in turn, affect an audience's experience of its drama.

A speech considered earlier on account of its imagery
exemplifies how the shape and sound of delivery become
part of its meaning and dramatic force, and how this
'music' can be created in various ways to different effect:

> A murd'rous guilt shows not itself more soon
> Than love that would seem hid: love's night is noon.
> Cesario, by the roses of the spring,
> By maidhood, honour, truth, and every thing,
> I love thee so that, maugre all thy pride,
> Nor wit nor reason can my passion hide.

> (*Twelfth Night*, III.i.144–9)

The opening unit of thought runs for almost two lines
and is followed by one of only four short words. In the
first, 'guilt' is syntactically juxtaposed to 'love' and then,
in the second, 'love' is repeated and linked with two contrasting nouns: 'Love's night is noon'. In the first, the
verbs 'shows' and 'would seem hid' are in opposition to
each other but the simple verb 'is' supplies the more
direct opposition in the second. With this sharper
antithesis, at the end of the second line, the rhythm will
almost certainly be strengthened and tightened, the
effect clinched by the rhyme. As we have noted earlier
(p. 48), this is also the point after which the speech
becomes verbally more sensuous in its appeal.

Olivia is bolder now, changing tack to address Cesario by
name. After this closer contact, however, she still holds back
her message until she has totally committed herself to what
she is about to say: phrasing lengthens within a regular pentameter – 'By maidhood, honour, truth, and every thing' –
until the direct avowal, 'I love thee so'. As the second syllable of a new verse-line and as a main and active verb, 'love'
will attract a strong stress and yet 'I' and 'thee' will also
have to be given some emphasis to clarify the syntax and
their opposed meanings. Because the fourth syllable of a
pentameter usually requires some stress in order to retain
the iambic measure, 'so' may also have to take some share
of emphasis. The balance achieved between these four
simple and monosyllabic words will strongly influence the

'music' of these lines, each variation of which will send differently weighted messages.

By the manner in which the last couplet is completed, rhyme bringing its own emphasis and a sense of necessity or compulsion, Olivia can seem most concerned with her 'wit' and 'reason', especially if the repetition of 'nor' is used to emphasize these nouns; an audible echo of the earlier 'hid' might also aid this impression. Alternatively, a strongly stressed 'passion' can so amplify and define 'love' of the previous line and offset 'wit' and 'reason', that it may seem the dominating force in Olivia's mind. But fear of Cesario's 'pride', or of his mere presence, could be a deeper reaction that she cannot speak about directly, an unwilled reaction that no amount of wit or reason can displace. This might have been sensed earlier in Olivia's physical bearing and in 'murd'rous', the only adjective in these lines and their first strong stress. Such a fear could develop on 'maugre', used only as a preposition but one that carries implications of fierce conflict;[6] the thought this represents might motivate the abrupt changes in rhythm and direction of thought that have already been noticed.

Whether Cesario is now facing Olivia or has turned away, he/she is given no time in which to reply; Olivia presses forward without interruption. While begging Cesario to be governed by reason and judgement, she uses metaphors of extortion and fettering. Phrases vary in length, natural word-order is reversed, and negatives are frequent; twice an imperative is sustained for a whole line; twice an antithesis is contained within a single line. Little of the poise the speaker possessed earlier is likely to remain as she concludes her speech:

> Do not extort thy reasons from this clause,
> For that I woo, thou therefore hast no cause;
> But rather reason thus with reason fetter:
> Love sought is good, but given unsought is better.

The last irregular pentameter starts energetically, with stress on both 'love' and 'sought' against the iambic norm. The second foot, 'is good', is regular but then the third and fourth feet are overloaded with 'but given unsought'. If 'but', 'given', and the negative 'unsought' are all sufficiently stressed to make the sense clear, a disturbed metre and rhythm will be the inevitable result. With three front vowels and an extra, unstressed final syllable, the sound of the last foot of the pentameter, 'is better', will be light and its force, perhaps, uncertain. How much confidence, insecurity, excitement, or fear is present – all very different sensations – will be influenced by the balance of sounds in the final couplet. In any performance, Olivia is now speechless, her continuing thoughts unspoken.

A huge contrast to the quick-changing moods of this encounter is King Lear's words on entry in the storm, having been rejected by his daughters and accompanied only by the fool. The dynamics of his opening speech are so strong that its sound and the physical effort of producing it would alone express his mind to an audience that did not know a word of English. Although weakened by his ordeal, Lear repeatedly calls out to the storm for assistance as his first active verbs crowd together and strain against the iambic mould. Very different thoughts follow each other without losing energy. With 'Singe my white head', the rhythm changes as he becomes aware of his age and suffering; then he turns away from such thoughts to call out again to the storm, anticipating that its irresistible power will destroy the entire, unfeeling world. The recurrent and varying mental energy that shapes the speech focuses finally on 'ingrateful man':

> Blow, winds, and crack your cheeks; rage, blow,
> You cataracts and hurricanoes, spout
> Till you have drench'd our steeples, drown'd the
>   cocks.
> You sulph'rous and thought-executing fires,
> Vaunt-couriers of oak-cleaving thunderbolts,
> Singe my white head. And thou, all shaking thunder,
> Strike flat the thick rotundity o' th' world;
> Crack nature's moulds, all germens spill at once,
> That makes ingrateful man.
>
> (*Lear*, III.ii.1–9)

The final and crucial choice for an actor, after negotiating the speech's technical and emotional demands, is how to bring everything to a close on the half-line. The Fool is the next to speak, begging Lear to take shelter and 'ask thy daughters' blessing'. Has Lear's fury supplied the main force of the whole speech, remaining unabated and now becoming stronger as it is directed against all conceivable enemies? Or does 'nature' and a strong final stress on 'man' indicate a shift of attention away from his own predicament as he calls for the destruction of all mankind? Or can the last one and a half lines draw all to a close in hatred of his own nature and the 'germens', or seed, that had engendered the daughters who have turned him out into the storm? Speech leaves Lear brooding in the silence that follows the half-line; for the moment, his spirit may be broken, or he may be using all his energy to struggle physically against the storm, or he may now identify with the storm's power and ruthlessness, showing this physically and emotionally. As much depends on how the speech is spoken as on its potent words.

Supplying another contrast, short phrases and simple words are sufficient to open up a wide range of options for both actors in the duologue during which Lear recognizes Cordelia. The king's attention shifts and his phrasing is broken, as if he fears to address the figure at his side:

LEAR   Do not laugh at me;
        For, as I am a man, I think this lady
        To be my child Cordelia.
CORDELIA   And so I am, I am.
                                (IV.vii.68–70)

Given either two or three stresses, 'as I am a man' can stand out from the flow of the short speech and emphasize Lear's self-awareness. But if the parenthesis is passed over easily, it will be a casual proviso that does not deflect his thoughts from Cordelia. The pause after the first half line, necessary for making sense and marked here with a semicolon, can be long or barely noticeable: a fearful hesitation that almost stops further speech, or a slight flicker disturbing the dawning of hope.

Tenderness and reassurance can be expressed in the phrasing and emphasis of the simple words of Cordelia's reply. Yet if the rhythm of its six monosyllables contrasts strongly with that of Lear's longer speech by being given three or, perhaps, four strong stresses, Cordelia's willpower, and not her sympathy, could dominate other impressions. If the second 'I am' is spoken less firmly than the first, it could be a sign that she still fears for his sanity or her own ability to reassure him; if spoken more strongly than the first, it would show growing confidence and joy. The delicacy of this simply worded encounter may have been recognized in early performances because Cordelia's final two monosyllables are found only in the Folio text, not in the earlier Quarto. They might have been added by an actor and subsequently recorded, to add more force to Cordelia's reply as originally written. Or the author might have been responsible when he found that the young male actor needed to repeat what he had said in order to gain sufficient attention for the simple speech.

Whichever version of Cordelia's reply is played, the balance between the two halves of the verse-line that Lear and Cordelia share will always be precarious because its metre is very irregular. Perhaps they should be spoken as two incomplete verse-lines with a pause separating them and, possibly, with another pause after Cordelia's reply as she fails to make contact with her father; his next speech does not answer hers, referring only to her tears. However this encounter is played, the two actors must be closely and continuously attuned to each other's performance if their words are to seem necessary and carry conviction.

Present-day Practices

Shakespeare's text lies continually open for the actors' imaginative engagement and quick invention as they create their own versions of its meanings, allusions, and music, and so develop their own interpretations of the roles they play. In rehearsal and performance many ways of bringing the words to life will be tried and tested. Speed can make a speaker seem less than fully engaged or eager to be finished. Drawing out each word can give an impression of speaking under duress, or in indecision, awe, or fear, or with uncommon deliberation. Actors can choose to emphasize any single element in a speech by highlighting particular words or introducing stage business. They find themselves so free in doing this that they are liable to recognize no boundary between what is suggested by the text and what arises from their own instincts and preoccupations.

In modern Shakespeare productions, with plenty of time for experiment and a director to develop whatever proves to be effective, idiosyncratic readings of the text are often so exaggerated that they play a major part in establishing distinctive interpretations of a role or an entire play. For instance, in a review of the Royal Shakespeare Company's production of *Macbeth*, the London *Times* reported (3 May 2000) that when Antony Sher's Macbeth enters saying, 'If it were done when 'tis done' (I.vii.1): 'the tone is conversational, reflective, aware – and he places a hand across his heart – that he will still have judgement *here*, in his conscience'. The interpolated gesture has attracted particular attention and defined a particular meaning. The egotism signalled by this diminishes the specific religious implications and antithetical emphasis of the words that follow:

> that but this blow
> Might be the be-all and the end-all here –
> But here upon this bank and shoal of time –
> We'd jump the life to come.
>
> (I.vii.4–7)

Later in the play, the same critic reported; '"O! full of scorpions is my mind!" he *snarls* at his vainly soothing wife' (italics added); in snarling these words, the actor disregarded the fact that this line is addressed to his 'dear wife' whom, a few lines later, he will call his 'dearest chuck' (1. 45), his most intimate and tender address in the entire play.

The text of a Shakespeare play is so written that it responds to the slightest impulse that the actors bring with them or discover in the text. Instructing actors in a series of television demonstrations, the Royal Shakespeare Company director, John Barton, told them:

> The words must be *found* or *coined* or *fresh-minted* at the moment you utter them. They are not to be thought of as something which pre-exists in a printed text. In the theatre they must seem to find their life for the first time at the moment the actor speaks them. Because he needs them.[7]

In so far as these instructions are followed – and actors find pleasure and growing confidence in doing so – a text is retuned and newly interpreted with every recasting and on every occasion it is performed, the actors making the parts their own. An audience is unlikely to be aware that this is happening but it may well sense that an unprecedented energy controls how the words are spoken. The meaning of the text, when part of a theatrical event, may be said to be immanent rather than fully expressed and determined, inseparable from the actors' performances and speaking to the senses as well as to conscious minds.

Elizabethan Practices

The special training and attention to minute details of performance that lie behind present-day productions are an entirely post-Shakespearean phenomenon. In his day, actors had no schools, studios, classes, directors, long rehearsal periods for a single play, or long seasons with only a few texts to remember. Instead, as members of a permanent and stable company, they had the advantage of years in which to learn from fellow actors and develop their own techniques and talents. With each new text that Shakespeare wrote, he made new demands on the actors to which they could continue to respond during the summers when only a few of the most popular and transportable plays were toured around the country until rejoining the company's repertoire in London. For much of this time these actors worked in close association with each other and with their principal author who had first been known as an actor and continued to perform until 1603, well into mid-career. These were enviable conditions for nurturing and maturing an actor's art and the skills necessary for subtle and ambitious texts. Working in this way, the company thrived, being called repeatedly to perform at court and winning a strong popular following.

Performances could, as always, go very wrong. Shakespeare's Hamlet tells us what might happen: that actors sometimes spoke their lines so that they made no sense, or they bellowed them like a 'towncrier' or said 'more than was set down' for them. Ulysses, in *Troilus and Cressida*, speaks of a player taking his mind off the play to listen to the sound that his own 'stretch'd footing' made on the scaffold stage (*Hamlet*, III.ii.7–12, 1–5, and 37–9; and *Troilus*, I.iii.153–6). On the other hand, audiences were capable of appreciating an actor's expert speech-technique: pedantic critics, like Polonius, could find fault, exclaiming that 'this is too long', and give praise when a speech was 'well spoken, with good accent and good discretion' (*Hamlet*, II.ii.491, 460–1). The author-poets who wrote for companies of boy actors were satirized in Joseph Hall's *Virgidemiarum* (1598), for sitting high in a gallery:

> ... watching every word, and gesturement,
> Like curious censors of some doughty gear [8]
> Whispering their verdict in their fellow's ear.
> Woe to the word whose margent in their scroll [i.e.
>   playscript]
> Is noted with a black condemning coal.

(I.iii.45–51)

Speech technique, at that time called 'pronunciation', was taught as a necessary part of rhetoric that was a basic subject in all advanced education; we do not know that any actor was especially well trained in this but it was said that 'whatsoever is commendable in the grave orator is most exquisitely perfect' in the excellent actor.[9]

The English language had comparatively recently become settled enough in usage for poets to 'peise' each syllable of their verses with confidence and take very conscious steps to develop its vocabulary. Writers of all kinds invented new words and new turns of phrase. When the old soldier Bardolph uses the word 'accommodated' in *Henry the Fourth, Part II,* Justice Shallow comments knowingly, 'It comes of *accommodo.* Very good; a good phrase' (III.ii.65–71). Sir Andrew Aguecheek, wishing to impress the Lady Olivia, listens avidly and competitively to Viola's courtly speech and vows to write down the rarest of her words so that he can use them himself:

> That youth's a rare courtier – 'Rain odours' well! ... 'Odours', 'pregnant', and 'vouchsafed' – I'll get 'em all three all ready.
>
> (*Twelfth Night,* III.i.81–8)

Although authors borrowed so freely from other languages and revived obsolescent usages to such an extent that they were sometimes hard to understand, their interest in language was sufficiently popular for many of their innovations to pass into common speech.

The most zealous attention that today's actors and their teachers give to Shakespearean verse-speaking and vocal delivery has warrant in the subtlety and variety of the plays themselves. As a composer can write with knowledge of the instruments to be played and the capabilities of those likely to be playing them, so a practised and popular dramatist would know how to use the resources of language and the most brilliant gifts of his actors. As a coach gives athletes or players the training that will stretch them beyond their current form, so a dramatist is likely to consider the development of his actors' skills. What was natural growth and refinement for Elizabethan actors working consistently in close contact with

Shakespeare has had to be carefully nurtured and kept under continuous watch by their modern counterparts.

Besides possessing a practised and well-honed vocal technique, all actors, Elizabethan and modern, need an active imagination and senses that are quick and sure in response if they are to speak the speeches that were written in 'the quick forge and working-house' of Shakespeare's mind (*Henry V*, V.Prol., 23). Words must be able to shine, strike, and surprise. Benedick, in *Much Ado About Nothing*, having talked with Beatrice, is lost in amazement: 'I stood like a man at a mark, with a whole army shooting at me. She speaks poniards, and every word stabs' (II.i.213–32). In the same comedy, speech is said to run 'like iron through [the] blood' so that listening to it is like drinking 'poison' (V.i.231–4). At another extreme, words should sound like the 'voice of all the gods' expressing great happiness and unexpected harmony, for 'when Love speaks' the sounds will 'ravish savage ears, / And plant in tyrants mild humility' (*Love's Labours Lost*, IV.iii. 340–5). Hamlet's utterance is, at times, 'grating' and 'harsh'; he also speaks of 'wild and whirling words' and 'cursing like a very drab' (III.i.2–3, 155–8; I.v.133; and II.ii.582). Speech must also sometimes seem to break down, the speaker unable to communicate, as at the end of *King Lear* when the old king 'knows not what he says; and vain is it / That we present us to him' (V.iii.293–4).

Great emotional range was also expected from the actors. As soon as the Players arrive at Elsinore, Hamlet calls for 'a passionate speech' and, later, he imagines the First Player would:

> ... drown the stage with tears
> And cleave the general ear with horrid speech;
> Make mad the guilty, and appal the free,
> Confound the ignorant, and amaze indeed
> The very faculties of eyes and ears.
>
> (II.ii.426 and 555–60)

Putting himself forward for the best roles of *The Tragedy of Pyramus and Thisbe*, Bottom offers to 'move storms' and also to 'condole', so that his audience will have to 'look to their eyes' (*Dream*, I.ii.20–2). In Shakespeare's plays, words alone are sometimes insufficient to express emotion and physical actions must take over: weeping, bodily shaking, or sinking to the ground are all specifically called for by the text. At other times, the actor's silent presence must express everything: moments like this have already been noticed for Ophelia, Juliet, Olivia, Lear and Cordelia; more will be discussed later. Shakespeare was well aware of the power that can be expressed in a silent presence: according to Claudio, 'Silence is the perfectest herald of joy: I were but little happy if I could say how much' and Viola can imagine a sister who 'never told her love' but 'pin'd in thought' (*Much Ado*, II.i.275–7; *Twelfth Night*, II.iv.109ff.). Words also cease when tension is heightened or concealment becomes necessary, as after Hamlet's 'But break my heart, for I must hold my tongue' or Volumnia's promise that 'I am hush'd until our city be afire, / And then I'll speak a little' (*Hamlet*, I.ii.159; *Coriolanus*, V.iii.181–2).

In Shakespeare's plays, speech and physical performance can seldom be disentangled. One of their most astonishing qualities is that 'in a very practical sense', as Cicely Berry puts it, 'the connection between the physical and verbal life of the characters is totally apparent and palpable' (quoted above, p. 67). Although words have altered in meaning and associations in the centuries since Shakespeare wrote and conditions for performance have greatly changed, in the simple setting of a rehearsal room, the more that actors work on speaking the words of a text, the more direction they find about what they should *do*. They are drawn towards a total involvement, physical, instinctive, and emotional, as well as mental and imaginative, an engagement that changes scene by scene and draws them onward in a journey through time. And a similar experience can be a reader's by asking similar questions of the text and, in imagination, committing to a full embodiment of what it suggests.

Notes

1. John Kane, 'Plotting with Peter', *Flourish*, 2, 7 (Stratford-upon-Avon: Royal Shakespeare Company, 1971).
2. Sir Philip Sidney, *Miscellaneous Prose*, ed. Katherine Duncan Jones (Oxford: Clarendon Press, 1973), p. 82.
3. Peter Brook, *The Shifting Point* (New York: Harper & Rowe, 1987), p. 94.
4. See, for example, Roger Ascham, *The Schoolmaster* (1579); *English Works*, ed. W. A. Wright (Cambridge: Cambridge University Press, 1904), pp.183–4 and 251.
5. *The Complete Works of John Webster*, ed. F. L. Lucas (London: Chatto & Windus, 1927), iv. 43.
6. It is not a word to be expected in a comedy: Shakespeare uses it only twice elsewhere, in *Titus Andronicus*, IV.ii.110, and *Lear*, V.iii.131.
7. John Barton, *Playing Shakespeare* (London and New York: Methuen, 1985), p. 50; italics included.
8. I.e., valiant talk or doings.
9. *New Characters (drawn to the life) of several persons, in several qualities* (London, 1615); see John Webster, *Complete Works*, iv 42.

5

Persons in a Play

The persons represented by actors in a Shakespeare play can seem startlingly real. Palpably present before an audience, they discover new resources during the course of a play and may appear differently from one performance to another. These are complicated phenomena for which Shakespeare has been praised down all the centuries. When a play becomes part of a theatrical event, the audience watches its leading characters as they seem to be driven by their own thoughts and feelings in a course of action that leads to a conclusion that is both fitting and revelatory. With each new performance this process will change, sometimes very slightly, sometimes surprisingly so, offering the actors a journey of discovery. By the end of the play, if all goes well, both spectators and actors will have shared in the unfolding of a seemingly complete world that had lain hidden within the text and now has a life of its own. It can seem so effortless and inevitable that both audience and actors wonder how it has all been done.

Shakespeare's Concept of 'Character'

Elizabethans did not speak of the individual characters in a play, as we do. The general use of *character* was for a letter of the alphabet, a distinctive mark or symbol, a style of handwriting, or a person's appearance: all signs of one sort or another. This is far from our sense of *character* as an individual person and still further from its use for the constituent mental qualities of any one individual. These meanings were introduced with regard to newly popular biographies and novels in the mid-seventeenth century and only later used with reference to dramatic texts and performances of plays. Until that time, characters in a play were referred to as *persons*. Prefatory notes to early printed editions use the word in various ways. The Latin *dramatis personae* is comparatively common and the phrase was varied in rough translations such as 'The Persons Represented' or 'The Persons Presented', that are found, for example, in the published texts of *A King and No King* (1626) and *The Roman Actor* (1629). The early editions of *The Duchess of Malfi* (1623) and *The Wedding* (1629) named the persons of the play alongside the members of the original casts who had played them and yet headed both lists with 'The Actors Names' as if performers had primary importance. In the 1616 collected edition of Jonson, only the 'principal' actors in each play were acknowledged, without listing the persons they represented. The implication is that a reader's knowledge of the actors who first performed the principal parts would increase appreciation of a play; they supplied a unique element to the original theatrical event and how they approached their task would have been a determining factor in that process – not unlike the filmstars whose appearance is advertised in preference to the roles they play.

The notion of *presenting* may have been current theatrical terminology. In Shakespeare's *Tempest* Ariel says he has 'presented' Ceres in the masque created at Prospero's command. In *A Midsummer Night's Dream* Quince calls for an actor 'to disfigure or to present the person of Moonshine' and, when *Pyramus and Thisbe* is about to be performed, the Prologue announces that 'This man, with lime and rough-cast, doth present/Wall, that vile Wall ...' and he is echoed later by the actor himself: 'I, one Snout by name, present a wall ... I am that same Wall; the truth is so' (III.i.54–5 and V.i.130, 155–61). When Hamlet greets the players on their arrival at Elsinore and asks for a taste of their 'quality' (II.ii.425), comments on the performance that follows are partly about the text and how it is spoken but, more extensively, about how the actor has presented the person of Æneas in his address to Dido. Polonius notes how he has 'turn'd his colour, and has tears in's eyes' (ll. 512–13) and, for Hamlet, it seems:

> monstrous that this player here,
> But in a fiction, in a dream of passion,
> Could force his soul so to his own conceit
> That from her working all his visage wann'd;
> Tears in his eyes, distraction in's aspect,
> A broken voice, and his whole function suiting
> With forms to his conceit.
>
> (ll. 544–50)

To this member of his audience, the player's physical enactment of imaginary emotion provided the dominating effect in performance, not the illusion of a certain kind of person, still less of a 'character' in our present-day usage.

The nearest Shakespeare's plays come to the modern concept of a dramatic character is after Menenius has described the appearance of Coriolanus at the head of a Volscian army surrounding Rome:

> The tartness of his face sours ripe grapes; when he walks, he moves like an engine and the ground shrinks before his treading. He is able to pierce a corslet with his eye, talks like a knell, and his hum is a battery. He sits in his state as a thing made for Alexander. What he bids be done is finish'd with his bidding. He wants nothing of a god but eternity, and a heaven to throne in.
>
> (*Coriolanus*, V.iv.18–23)

Menenius defends the truth of this description by saying 'I paint him in the character' (V.iv.26) but he has neither offered insights to the working of Coriolanus's mind nor supplied motives for his actions, as a critic would today when describing a dramatic character or a director when talking with an actor about the role he plays. Menenius is concerned with the effect of Coriolanus's presence, his actions and outward appearance, the sensations he felt and those he aroused: very much the same 'qualities' as those communicated when the First Player enacted Æneas' tale to Dido. The reasons why Coriolanus acted in this way, his interior and personal life, remain a mystery.

In non-dramatic literature of the years immediately following the end of Shakespeare's career, *character* came to be used of a particular form of writing. Prime examples are the '*many witty characters*' added to the second, 1614 edition of Sir Thomas Overbury's poem *A Wife, Now a Widow* and many times reprinted. Modelled on a series of 'Characters' written by Theophrastus, a Greek philosopher and pupil of Aristotle, these short essays included 'A Worthy Commander in the Wars', 'An Intruder into Favour', 'A Fair and Happy Milkmaid', 'A Roaring Boy', 'A Fantastic', 'An Excellent Actor'. While the title-page announces that the 'new characters of several persons' have been 'drawn to the life', they are not portraits of individuals but observations concerning various types of people and were meant to be generally true. They describe what persons 'in several qualities' do and what they feel, and how people react to them: for example, concerning the excellent actor:

> by a full and significant action of body, he charms our attention: sit in a full theatre, and you will think you see so many lines drawn from the circumference of so many ears, whiles the actor is the centre.

Often a general moral message underlies the description; for example, of the fair and happy milkmaid:

> She doth all things with so sweet a grace, it seems Ignorance will not suffer her to do ill, being her mind is to do well.

Occasionally *character*, in this sense, appears in Jacobean drama. So the Cardinal in John Webster's *The White Devil*

(1612) asks Vittoria: 'Shall I expound "whore" to you? Sure I shall;/I'll give their perfect character' (III.ii.78ff.). He then describes the typical actions of any whore, together with their consequences. Such a list is so similar to Menenius's description of Coriolanus that it might equally be called the 'perfect character' of 'A Ruthless Commander in the Wars'.

When evoking another person, a speaker in Shakespeare plays will sometimes adopt a method similar to that used in the literary 'characters', both noting specific actions and identifying emotions and sensations that are easily recognizable. In *The Tragedy of Coriolanus*, a comparatively late play, these twin aspects of the hero are clearly stated: for his actions, he 'fights dragon-like, and does achieve as soon/As draw his sword'; for his feelings and sensations, he is frequently reported to be a noble and courageous soldier who is proud, an inspiring leader of men who despises the 'common people' (for example, IV.vii.23–4 and II.ii.6). These judgements are repeated several times, as generally true of this man; and they are validated by what Coriolanus subsequently does. When his mother begs him to return to the market-place and speak mildly to the plebeians and their officers, he can only do so against these innate feelings:

> Would you have me
> False to my nature? ...
>   Must I
> With my base tongue give to my noble heart
> A lie that it must bear?

When he agrees to do as he is asked, he doubts if he can be such a person:

> You have put me now to such a part which never
> I shall discharge to th' life ...
> Away, my disposition, and possess me
> Some harlot's spirit.

> (III.ii.14–123)

When he does try to act like a 'mountebank' (III.ii.132), Coriolanus fails: he is defined by his 'disposition' that limits what he can truly speak or do; he has to be 'the man I am' (l. 16).

As the action of a play comes to its close, Shakespeare's text often draws attention to what Coriolanus calls his 'heart', a person's unchanging core of feeling and sensation. In the comedies, when journeys end in lovers' meetings, their 'true' feelings triumph: *As You Like It* concludes with 'rites' – and rights – of 'true delights' (V.iv.191–2). At the end of *Much Ado About Nothing*, letters betray the true 'hearts' of Beatrice and Benedick and they fall silent in a kiss which now speaks for them rather than their quick tongues (V.iv.91–2). *Twelfth Night* is not so confident but, even before he has seen through Viola's disguise as the page Cesario, Orsino experiences such a 'savage jealousy' that his 'heart' is ready to 'sacrifice the lamb that I do love'. Having experienced the strength of his true feelings, he and Viola must still wait until 'golden time convents' before a 'solemn combination' can be made of their 'dear souls' (V.i.111–25, 368–70). A tongue-tied 'truth', in some form, is common to the end of all the comedies; feelings and sensations overwhelm words and, in the ensuing silence, an audience can find itself drawn to the very being of the lovers so that it seems to share in their experience.

In the tragedies, the hero's 'heart' determines the final action. When Othello has committed suicide, Cassio acknowledges, 'This did I fear, but thought he had no weapon;/For he was great of heart' (V.ii.363–4). When Hamlet dies from the poison on Laertes's unbated rapier, Horatio says simply, 'Now cracks a noble heart' (V.ii.351). Caesar, seeing that Cleopatra is dead, knows at once that 'she ... being royal,/Took her own way' (V.ii.333–4); her inner nature would not allow her to live as a prisoner. No words describe the individual experience of deaths like these; at best, the text only points to a core of feeling and sensation that has driven the tragic hero and shapes the final actions. At the end of *King Lear*, the ebbing of the king's vital spirit holds attention while he says very little; comment is left to those on stage with him:

KENT   Vex not his ghost. O let him pass! He hates
    him
    That would upon the rack of this tough world
    Stretch him out longer.
EDGAR   He is gone indeed.
KENT   The wonder is he hath endur'd so long:
    He but usurp'd his life.

                                              (V.iii.313–16)

In *Macbeth*, a resurgence of courage takes the hero into a
final desperate fight:

                    Lay on, Macduff;
And damn'd be him that first cries 'Hold, enough!'
                                              (V.viii.33–4)

At the end of these tragedies, both these heroes are
defined by their actions and by the emotions and sensations that are expressed in and through them; their own
articulate speech adds nothing of comparable effect.

Elizabethan Practice in the Creation of 'Character'

The words of a text as they appear on paper are the one
fixed ingredient of Shakespeare's plays but when they
become part of a theatrical event and the actors speak
them, making sense as best they can, each word is sub-
sumed in a complete enactment and the effectiveness of
the words is determined in that process. For an audience
watching a performance, the 'heart' of a person, as mani-
fested in sensations and feelings, together with the actor's
presence, become inescapable and dominant elements in
its experience. The established processes of rehearsal and
performance in the theatres of his time were well suited
to this kind of drama.
    When an actor started work he had in his hands only
the words of his own part together with short cues that
showed him when to speak; the expense of copying an
entire play by hand for each member of a cast was not

considered necessary. An actor's first responsibilities would be to find how to speak the words clearly, to study metre, syntax and the structure of thought, and, not least, to memorize. For an actor already appearing in a repertoire of a dozen or more plays, this task was formidable but much could be done in private and in his own time. While focusing on his part from this detailed and independent point of view, he could also start to identify the basic feelings and sensations involved, the 'heart' of the person to be presented. With the first company rehearsals, physical activity would be added and, as the complete text began to be spoken and heard, the context for speech – the situations and interactions with other persons – could be more fully explored; appropriate emotions and sentiments could be found, tested, moulded, and strengthened. This complex process would have occupied more time than was available for on-stage rehearsal, since that was counted in hours rather than days;[1] it must have come from private study, an exploration that was continued on every occasion that the play was performed.

In theatres today, what the words mean and how to speak them are investigated in lengthy company rehearsals, commonly lasting a month or two. Improvisations are sometimes used to explore the context of a play's action so that the entire company can give credible life to the narrative and make it relevant to a contemporary audience. The words of the text are likely to be committed to memory slowly, along the way, while the whole production is beginning to come together and finding its preferred shape. Individual performances develop in interaction with each other and in the course of many experiments. As part of this long process, the characters, as we call them, are explored and gradually defined, so that their intentions are clarified and their effect on the play's action exposed for all to see. In contrast, when the plays were first performed there was time for none of this and, perhaps, there was no need because actors were, of necessity, more self-reliant. In those days, company rehearsals had little time for attention to individual performances; priority had to be given to the problems of large-scale entrances and exits, the more complicated and, sometimes, dangerous stage-business, and the choice and cueing of sound effects and music. There was no production in our sense of the word – another theatrical term that did not come into use until much later – and, without a director in charge, few meanings or interpretations could have been decided in advance of public performance, even if an actor had wished to work in that deliberate way. An audience would witness the play as its persons found their life and the text its current meanings in the course of each and every performance.

These working conditions were the more acceptable in Elizabethan theatres because many of the *dramatis personae* were easily recognizable and often-repeated types. Aristotle's *Rhetoric* had encouraged scholars to categorize men of different ages and fortune according to their emotions and habitual actions,[2] and these generalities, transmitted through Cicero and Quintillian, were often repeated. Thomas Wilson's *Art of Rhetoric* (1560) gave examples of the 'diversity of natures' as he saw them:

> a man of good years is counted sober, wise, and circumspect; a young man wild and careless; a woman babbling, inconstant, and ready to believe all that is told her … a soldier is counted a great bragger and a vaunter of himself; a scholar simple; a russet coat sad and sometimes crafty; a courtier flattering; a citizen gentle.[3]

In this tradition, the *dramatis personae* of Roman comedy were broadly conceived types: the deceitful pimp, eager lover, crafty servant, and so on. Some were given names to match, as *Simia* or monkey and *Peniculus* or sponge, or *Erotium* for a courtesan. Representatives of vices and virtues in early English plays and interludes had similarly descriptive names; for example, Mischief, Mercy, New Guise, Naught and Nowadays are found together with the titular hero in *Mankind* of the late fourteen-sixties.

Feelings and sensations that all men and women could recognize formed the basis for most *dramatis personae* in early modern playwriting. The Prologue to *Damon and Pythias* (1571) echoes Thomas Wilson:

> The old man is sober; the young man rash; the lover triumphing in joys;
> The matron grave; the harlot wild, and full of wanton toys.

Cast lists were often schematic in the same manner, proper names instructing actors what to feel and what to do: for example, besides its titular hero, the persons represented in *Ralph Roister Doister* (c. 1540) include Matthew Merrygreek, Tristram Trusty, Dobinet Doughty, and Tom Truepenny, together with Margery Mumblecrust and Tibet Talkpace. As late as 1605–6, the cast of *The Revenger's Tragedy* includes Lussurioso, Spurio, Ambitioso, Supervacuo, and Vindice, offset by Gratiana who is full of grace and Castiza who is chaste. The actors could scarcely expect any clearer instruction about the feelings and actions needed in performance; once the text had been memorized, rehearsals could be occupied with activity and action.

Shakespeare made occasional but significant use of this tradition in playwriting. In *Henry IV*, for example, Hotspur and Fal-staff are names that guide actors in performance, along with Shallow, Silence, Mouldy, Feeble, Wart, and Bullcalf. Proteus, in *The Two Gentlemen of Verona*, should clearly be changeable in affection, like the Greek god whose name he bears, and Valentine should emulate the patron saint of lovers after whom he is named; Speed's name is, however, partly ironic because, while he is quick-witted as might be expected, he is slow in action, on his first entry failing to meet with his master and, on arrival in Milan, arriving so late that his running is unlikely to make amends (I.i.72–3 and III.i.361–70). Names sometimes work indirectly: in *The Tempest*, Prospero is eventually fortunate, as his name implies in Italian, but that cannot always be evident; Miranda's name is relevant to sensations she arouses in others, not those she herself feels – 'Admir'd Miranda!' exclaims

Ferdinand, 'Indeed the top of admiration; worth/What's dearest in the world!' (*Tempest*, III.i.37–9). Gonzalo, from *gonzo*, Italian for simpleton or thick-head, indicates what Antonio and Sebastian think of him, not the sentiments and courtesy shown in many of his words and actions. Other names in this play are allusive: Ariel being suitable for an 'airy spirit' and Caliban echoing *cannibal*, a race described as 'wild' and 'savage' by Montaigne in an essay which was one of Shakespeare's sources for this play.

In *Measure for Measure*, the name Angelo indicates only one impression an actor should give in the part, this person being no more than 'outward-sainted' (III.i.90); other descriptions of his feelings must, in the end, be given emphasis: 'his stricture and firm abstinence' and his 'sensual race' and 'sharp appetite' (I.iii.12; II.iv.160–1). This discrepancy is the more noticeable because so many other names in this play are directly appropriate: the simple-minded Froth; Escalus who holds the scales of Justice; Lucio whose name in Italian means 'light' and, hence, both fantastic and wanton; Mistress Overdone, an old whore who has had nine husbands and is now a brothel-keeper. Pompey, a tapster and bawd, is named ironically after a Roman hero while his surname, Bum, draws attention to what he says is 'the greatest thing' about him (II.i.206–7).

Creating typical *dramatis personae* in this way was supported by the medieval belief that human bodies were composed of four chief fluids or 'humours' – blood, phlegm, choler, and melancholy – and that differing proportions of these determined physical and mental qualities. As Ben Jonson explained, a humour implied that:

> ... some one peculiar quality
> Doth so possess a man, that it doth draw
> All his affects, his spirits, and his powers,
> In their confluxions, all to run one way.[4]

Many plays were given characters of this kind, Jonson's own 'humour' plays among them: for example, in *Every Man in His Humour* of 1598 George Downright is a plain squire, Thomas Cash a cashier, Justice Clement an 'old merry magistrate', and Roger Formal his clerk, all true in manner to their names. But Jonson himself was quick to see that this way of playwriting could become a mere trick, defining a person by the wearing of 'a pied feather' or 'three-piled ruff', trivial affectations that were 'more than most ridiculous'.[5]

With the needless repetitions of the humour-conscious Corporal Nym, Shakespeare also made a mockery of the device that was enjoying a vogue at the end of the century: 'My humour shall not cool', he says: 'I will incense Page to deal with poison' and immediately makes much the same point again: 'I will possess him with yellowness; for the revolt of mine is dangerous. That is my true humour' (*Merry Wives*, I.iii.96–8). Nym's addiction to humours trivializes even a matter of life and death and this narrow theory about life and art is ridiculed in some way almost every time he opens his mouth. Although Shakespeare sometimes used names that indicated a certain constant quality, the persons who have a major part in the action of his plays are based on a core of feeling and sensation that cannot be defined as either a 'type' or a 'humour': his word for it was the 'heart' or 'truth' of a person.

Creating an Inner Consciousness

Shakespeare's writing was influenced both by traditional dramaturgy and by accepted conditions of rehearsal and performance. The stock characters of ancient and early modern plays have often been derided by later criticism but, by founding the persons in his plays on easily identifiable emotions, sensations and professions as earlier writers had done, Shakespeare reaped some advantages not likely to be possessed by the 'characters' of much later plays that are based on psychological idiosyncrasies and individual histories. When persons are identified by single-track feelings in his plays, they are immediately recognizable by an entire audience and, when given appropriate acting and staging, offer open access for an empathy that will encourage reactions ranging from affirmation to opposition. Shakespeare did not, however, rely solely upon the common stock of dramatic characters; the principal figures in his plays also have individualities that are the result of observation and a wide reading. Fiction in prose and verse that supplied the narrative source for some plays also furnished details for creating the persons involved. The kings, queens, nobles and common people as depicted in the *Chronicles* and Plutarch's *Lives of the Greeks and Romans* were modified by Shakespeare but often retain both small details of behaviour and basic motivations. Inspiration also came from more general reading that ranged from Erasmus's *Praise of Folly* to Montaigne's *Essays*, and more specialized accounts of travel, duties of constables, and practice of witchcraft. Shakespeare's *dramatis personae* have many sources and their words and actions make immediate impact; their 'true' natures, or 'hearts', however, are more mysterious and are revealed more slowly, over the course of a whole play.

On first seeing Olivia, Viola tells her, 'I see you what you are: you are too proud' (I.v.234), and, for the time being, an audience is likely to recognize common signs of this feeling and agree with the judgement. Later, when Olivia has said more and done more, the simple label will no longer serve. As we have already seen in discussion of the text (see above, pp. 48 and 72–4), Olivia can also be fearful, flirtatious, anxious, dependent: the actor can choose which of many aspects to emphasize and her 'true' nature will not be disclosed at once. Soon she acknowledges both perplexity and fear:

> I do I know not what, and fear to find
> Mine eye too great a flatterer for my mind.
>
> (I.v.292–3)

Sebastian finds her bearing to be 'smooth, discreet, and stable' and yet senses that 'There's something in't/That is deceivable' (*Twelfth Night*, IV.iii.17–21). Often she acts on the impulse of easily recognizable feelings and yet, especially when she hesitates, she seems to withhold further secrets. In this play, the same is true of Viola, Orsino, Sebastian, Malvolio, Sir Toby, Sir Andrew, Maria, and even the relatively minor part of Fabian: all are strongly grounded in their basic feelings and yet varied in their impulses and capable of being acted in significantly different ways. In the course of the play, they change and develop, holding attention by what they may become, as well as what they are.

While feeling and sensation were fundamental in all the persons he created, rather than intellectual attitude or personal idiosyncrasy, Shakespeare seldom allowed them, in Jonson's phrase, 'to run one way'. His method was to imagine several emotions and sensations in one person and set them over against each other. At the time this was an almost revolutionary dramatic device and he was sometimes careful to draw attention to what was happening: for example, by having both enemies and supporters draw attention to the same divergent qualities in Coriolanus (see pp. 88–9, above). In a scene that was subsequently cut from the later Folio version of *King Lear*, an anonymous Gentleman describes Cordelia's feelings before she returns to the stage after a long absence, explaining that 'patience and sorrow strove ... [to] express her goodliest' (*Lear*, IV.iii.16–19): perhaps Shakespeare thought he had asked too much from a young male actor but found, subsequently, that the scene worked well enough without this preparation. Elsewhere he varied emotions with extraordinary boldness, for example in the sudden and shocking eruptions that reveal the strength of Othello's jealousy: his behaviour 'would not be believ'd in Venice', especially since, earlier in the play, he had appeared to be 'the noble Moor' whose nature 'Passion could not shake' (*Othello*, IV.i. 238, 261–5). Macbeth, planning regicide, swiftly changes so that he imagines 'Pity, like a naked new-born babe,/Striding the blast' in opposition to the 'horrid deed' that moments before he had been ready to commit (I.vii.21–5). Later, when obviously motivated by 'slaughterous thoughts', he also thinks of 'honour, love, obedience, troops of friends' and experiences what it means to have lost them (*Macbeth*, V.iii.25; V.v.14). From the start of *Antony and Cleopatra*, its hero is both an 'amorous surfeiter' and the commander whose 'soldiership/Is twice' that of other generals; when he is 'dispos'd to mirth, ... on the sudden/A Roman thought' takes possession of him. Just before her suicide, Cleopatra claims 'I have nothing/Of woman in me' and then, in the moment of death, she imagines 'my baby at my breast/That sucks the nurse asleep' (see II.i.32–5; I.ii.79–80; V.ii.237–8, 307–8). Contradictions that are suggested early in a play will later begin to pile up in stronger form. In his opening scene, Hamlet shows many of the obvious 'forms, moods, [and] shapes of grief' for the death of his father but speaks more vaguely of 'that within which passes show' (*Hamlet*, I.ii.76–86). His uncle-king acknowledges what is 'sweet and commendable' in his nature but also rebukes his 'impious stubbornness' (I.ii.87, 94). Oppositions soon multiply: Hamlet tells Ophelia 'I did love you once' and, almost immediately afterwards, 'I loved you not'; Ophelia speaks of him as having been 'Th' expectancy and rose of the fair state' and yet he has just condemned himself as 'very proud, revengeful, ambitious; with more offences at my beck than I have thoughts to put them in, imagination to give them shape, or time to act them in' (III.i.115–19, 152, 122–9). In the play's last scene, he is prepared to accept providence and 'let be', as if 'readiness' were all, and yet, minutes later, he fights Laertes, becomes 'incensed', and kills the king in three different ways, by rapier and two kinds of poison (V.ii.211–16, 293).

Such contradictions draw attention to emotions and actions that are more varied than those of an older tradition of playwriting and yet, like those, they shape an audience's experience and often dominate it. The leading persons of a Shakespeare play are drawn forward by what they feel, at least as much as by any conscious intention or intellectual idea. Arguments, ambiguities, and uncertainties, together with wit, humour, 'paper bullets of the brain'[6] and every product of fancy and imagination, are all activated by a great undertow of feeling and sensation, a slower and stronger drama that is only partly suggested by what is spoken. The effect of words, deriving from the 'quick forge and working-house of thought',[7] is sometimes to direct attention to feelings that cannot be expressed in words and exist only in the senses. In his last three speeches Hamlet insists that he cannot speak his mind fully; before he gathers strength to die, Othello's passion suffuses his whole body and obliterates thought; Macbeth's last defiance is a wordless fight that needs all his remaining energy and passion; Cleopatra's suicide brings an unprecedented calm and assurance. At these climactic moments, words direct attention to what is happening and then scarcely register while the heroes of the drama are absorbed in their feelings and in what they have to do; in consequence, the actor's performance changes and an audience, left to sense what is happening, may be drawn closer to the inner consciousness at the centre of the play.

Our attempts to understand what one of Shakespeare's plays achieves when it takes its place in a theatrical event must be prepared to look beyond words and their expression of thoughts to seek the heart of the matter in feeling and sensation. Sometimes overpowering in a theatre, this part of a play scarcely registers on the page and yet, if it is not taken into account, a distinctive aspect of Shakespeare's writing will be neglected and our judgement of a play skewed away from a central feature and its culminating moments.

Notes

1. See above, pp. 12 and 26, and, below, 161.
2. Aristotle, *Rhetoric*, II. xii–xvii.
3. Thomas Wilson, *Art of Rhetoric* (1560), p. 179.
4. Ben Jonson, *Every Man Out of His Humour* (1599), Induction.
5. Ibid.
6. *Much Ado About Nothing*, II.iii.217.
7. *Henry V*, V. Prol., 23.

6

Parts to Perform

The relation of speech to performance can be closely observed in soliloquies, for which dramatic focus centres on one person alone on the stage. The changing style of these sustained speeches throughout a play marks a changing relationship of text to performance and of performer to audience that affects the nature of the entire theatrical event. In the course of his career, Shakespeare came to use soliloquies differently, seeming to develop a greater trust in an actor's ability to draw upon the instinctive depths of his being. Increasingly, he called into play physical sensations and feelings that cannot be put into words because they are beyond the scope of conscious thought.

A Text's Changing Demands

A soliloquy will often begin with a comparatively simple explanation or questioning of the speaker's situation; this is then interrupted or counter-stated so that an audience has to look and listen more intently to follow what is happening. An early example is Richard the Third's opening soliloquy. As verbal exposition, it starts simply enough and yet its full effect is complicated by his physical malformation that he does not mention but an audience is liable to notice as soon as he walks onto the stage. It may seem as if Richard is well able to deal with the misfortune even though the opposition of fair and foul informs every thing he says:

Now is the winter of our discontent
Made glorious summer by this sun of York; ...
Grim-visag'd war hath smooth'd his wrinkled front,
And now, instead of mounting barbed steeds
To fright the souls of fearful adversaries,
He capers nimbly in a lady's chamber.

Individual words, puns, and obvious ironies, mock ordinary persons and the actor will have to choose whether
Richard is taking pleasure in his own superior intelligence or being driven towards hatred by his misfortune:
some unspoken source of energy and confidence is
needed to load these opening lines with so much detail;
they can tingle with submerged feeling long before
Richard speaks directly of himself:

But I – that am not shap'd for sportive tricks,
Nor made to court an amorous looking glass –
I – that am rudely stamp'd, and want love's majesty
To strut before a wanton ambling nymph –
I – that am curtail'd of this fair proportion,
Cheated of feature by dissembling nature,
Deform'd, unfinish'd, sent before my time
Into this breathing world scarce half made up,
And that so lamely and unfashionable
That dogs bark at me as I halt by them –
Why, I, in this weak piping time of peace,
Have no delight to pass away the time,
Unless to spy my shadow in the sun
And descant on mine own deformity.
And therefore, since I cannot prove a lover
To entertain these fair well-spoken days,
I am determined to prove a villain
And hate the idle pleasures of these days.

With verbal brilliance together with variations of phrasing and rhythm Richard holds attention while he
explains his origins and intentions in a way that raises
unanswered questions. His cool, verbally straightforward,
decision to 'prove a villain' takes only a moment to speak

and establish, indelibly, Richard's egotism and lack of compassion; yet, simultaneously, syntax and repetitions may be betraying a deep-seated pain or dangerous will to self-destruction.

A lot has been left to the actor: how 'unshapely' and awkward is Richard's body, how assured his manner? Is he satisfied with his own explanations; does he take pleasure in his own humour; does he feel thwarted by his 'deformity' or take pride in knowing how to cope with it? With those and other questions unanswered, not caring if they have been formed in anyone's mind, he then breaks off:

> Plots have I laid, inductions dangerous,
> By drunken prophecies, libels, and dreams,
> To set my brother Clarence and the King
> In deadly hate the one against the other;
> And if King Edward be as true and just
> As I am subtle, false, and treacherous,
> This day should Clarence closely be mew'd up –
> About a prophecy which says that G
> Of Edward's heirs the murderer shall be.
> (*Richard III*, I.i.1–40)

After defining his immediate purpose so clearly, he again changes tack because his first victim has entered: 'Dive thoughts, down to my soul. Here Clarence comes.' His brother is already under guard on his way to prison and, finding fate on his side, Richard immediately pretends to be sympathetic and concerned, transforming his appearance. Although he has made all this clear to an audience, other thoughts remain his own, in what he calls his 'soul'.

For almost all the play an audience will be fascinated by Richard's performances. As he plays with one victim after another, so he plays with spectators in the theatre, telling them what he intends to do but disclosing little about his own thoughts until he has entered '*in pomp*', asking for Buckingham's hand while he '*ascendeth the throne*' (IV.ii.0, S.D., 3, S.D.). Now the dramatic focus alters: thanking his chief accomplice for 'assistance', Richard puts him to 'the touch' to see if he is 'current gold indeed' by openly wishing that the two young princes imprisoned in the Tower were not alive. When Buckingham does not respond positively, he is more outright, 'Shall I be plain? I wish the bastards dead' (l. 18): the mask of kingly behaviour and political finesse has slipped or, perhaps, he is still confident enough to make a joke of being 'plain'. When Buckingham leaves, asking for time before responding, Richard becomes still more unguarded and transparent, sending for someone 'whom corrupting gold / Will tempt unto a close exploit of death' (ll. 34–5) and giving orders to eliminate others who stand between him and the throne. Alone once more, a short soliloquy follows in which fluent explanations of what is happening are soon broken by an exclamation and, then, by four very simple monosyllables at the end of a verse-line, 'But I am in'. Introducing a new rhythm and new mood, they are followed by a complete line of monosyllables – a metrical device requiring a slow delivery if its sense is to register, its sense clinched with a rhyme:

> I must be married to my brother's daughter,
> Or else my kingdom stands on brittle glass.
> Murder her brothers, and then marry her!
> Uncertain way of gain! But I am in
> So far in blood that sin will pluck on sin.
> Tear-falling pity dwells not in this eye.
>
> (ll. 62–7)

Within the tight confines of these lines ideas are packed that have not been expressed before and, in so far as the actor gives credibility to them, a shift in tension and attention will occur. The word 'sin', twice-repeated, has not been used before by Richard, only by those opposing him; 'Pity', of the following line, is also new for him. He does not speak of *fear* but his insecurity and pain is present in the nightmarish fantasy of immersion in blood and sin that will 'pluck' on sin; the phrasing of speech suggests a physical tugging or dispirited loss of impetus. Richard is, now, aware of his sin, knows the demands of pity, and finds that he is liable to weep. Words, now, say so much in little space that outward, physical signs of inward struggle may be necessary to ensure that his transformation is credible to an audience. Alternatively, the actor could decide to conceal how deeply Richard feels and speak of sin only to mock at such thoughts; so Richard would seem the stronger for his admission and, therefore, likely to be watched more closely in future. Either way, attention will now be focused more intently on the play's hero than it was at first and on the changes that are likely to come.

When the Earl of Richmond arrives to claim Richard's throne and restore England to prosperity, the two commanders have contrasting dreams the night before battle. Richard wakes from his for a soliloquy that breaks free from the syntactical control which has characterized almost all his previous speeches. Consecutive sense yields to exclamation, question, assertion, and command. While no incomplete verse-line insists on a silence, the changes of intention and feeling are so extreme that speech must draw from the actor a strikingly varied physical performance and sudden disruptions of feeling as he responds to experiences that strain his comprehension:

> Give me another horse. Bind up my wounds.
> Have mercy, Jesu! Soft! I did but dream.
> O coward conscience, how dost thou afflict me!
> The lights burn blue. It is now dead midnight.
> Cold fearful drops stand on my trembling flesh.
> What do I fear? Myself? There's none else by.
> Richard loves Richard; that is, I am I.
> Is there a murderer here? No – yes, I am.
> Then fly. What, from myself? Great reason why –
> Lest I revenge. What, myself upon myself!
> Alack, I love myself. Wherefore? For any good
> That I myself have done unto myself?
> O, no! Alas, I rather hate myself
> For hateful deeds committed by myself!
> I am a villain; yet I lie, I am not.
> Fool, of thyself speak well. Fool, do not flatter.

Although he starts boldly, Richard's words soon require him to be almost prostrate: alone, afraid, guilty, fearful, sweating, trembling. He speaks what he does not want to speak and is unable, as he later admits, to escape from a 'fearful dream' (l. 212). Very little scope is here for the buoyant energy of mind that was able to convert almost every other circumstance to his own advantage. Words now act as knives that cut him open to the 'soul' – to what Shakespeare elsewhere calls the 'heart' – exposing before the theatre audience his tortured feelings, the 'I' that is within his shaking body.

A build-up of parallel phrases and emphatic repetitions achieves the only sustained climax in the soliloquy and that is followed by the short and simple, 'I shall despair':

> My conscience hath a thousand several tongues,
> And every tongue brings in a several tale,
> And every tale condemns me for a villain.
> Perjury, perjury, in the high'st degree;
> Murder, stern murder, in the dir'st degree;
> All several sins, all us'd in each degree,
> Throng to the bar, crying all 'Guilty! guilty!'
> I shall despair.

With this unique soliloquy, Richard voices new and irrepressible feelings: despair, the loneliness of isolation, and an appetite for love and pity;

> I shall despair. There is no creature loves me;
> And if I die no soul will pity me: ...

> (V.iii.176–206)

An actor, who had studied and rehearsed in private, with only his own part written out, could find, in these few words, emotions and sensations that would be able to supply the unspoken drive behind the confident opening soliloquy and the successful villainy of the narrative.[1] If action and speech are founded on these enduring and basic feelings, rather than on passing thoughts or expressed intentions, the part of Richard will be a journey towards a deeper and truer exposure. For an audience, the play becomes a progressive experience that deepens and widens perceptions – in effect, a journey towards understanding and, perhaps, empathy or compassion. On some occasions, audience and actor may come to share with the protagonist a triumph in the presentation of self, a daring affirmation of all the consequences of being different from other people and more intelligent than everyone else on stage.

For some in most audiences, however, Richard's progress will only heighten their condemnation of his sins against the God whom he momentarily evokes in his cry 'Have mercy, Jesu!' and to whom others in the play have turned repeatedly for help or consolation. But the final scenes direct the focus of attention elsewhere: Richard foretells a 'black day', orders his army, denigrates his enemies, calls his soldiers to fight, deals harshly with a deserter, and leaves for battle calling on Saint George. Then, after a general '*alarum [and] excursions*' and a report that he is 'seeking for Richmond in the throat of death' (V.iv.5), Richard enters alone crying 'A horse! a horse! my kingdom for a horse!' As his words again express need and emotion, courage and determination probably register most strongly; certainly, any need for pity and love has vanished. The actor's voice and body are likely to be wearied after the long and strenuous performance so that Richard's cry may sometimes sound like bravado, a pretended courage that is taken on because he fears defeat and capture:

> A horse! a horse! my kingdom for a horse!
> *Withdraw, my lord; I'll help you to a horse.*
> Slave, I have set my life upon a cast
> And I will stand the hazard of the die.
> I think there be six Richmonds in the field;
> Five have I slain to-day instead of him.
> A horse! a horse! my kingdom for a horse!
>
> (ll. 9–13)

Catesby assumes the horse is needed to make an escape, as in Shakespeare's source for the play it was intended. But Richard scornfully denies the charge of cowardice, puns about risk and dying, strives to be ahead of his enemies' plans, and commits himself to fight; while his courage is likely to be obvious, he may be desperate too. As he leaves the stage, the actor's bearing, his very presence in the role, and how the cry is repeated, will engage an audience's attention at least as much as the words he utters.

After a futher '*alarum*', the audience has another view of Richard that is entirely without words. He and Richmond re-enter and fight, man to man, until Richard is slain. Courage is probably obvious, or recklessness; also, perhaps, a sense of doom. Choices that the actor makes here, and has made earlier with regard to the 'heart' of Richard's feelings, will largely determine the way an audience views the play's conclusion. Its force and quality does not depend on political issues or verbal declarations but on whatever mental, emotional, and physical resources each individual actor can bring to the part and is able to sustain to the end.

Change in an Audience's Focus of Attention

To follow any major part through a Shakespeare play is a continual challenge to a reader's understanding and sympathies; for an audience it can be an engrossing adventure into a largely unmapped territory that usually culminates in a sense of discovery. Over the long sequence of his plays, physical involvement and unspoken feelings were given increasing importance. The sensations involved may eventually be identified in words but they are made present – given outward form – only in the performance of an actor.

How quickly Shakespeare developed this dramatic strategy is shown by the soliloquies of *Richard the Second*, written in 1595–6, one or two years after *Richard the Third*. The hero here speaks repeatedly about his own thoughts, feelings, and actions and is hypersensitive to their effect on himself and, sometimes, on others, and yet a mystery remains because Richard changes his mind frequently and often surprisingly, without verbal explanation. For example, he orders a trial by combat and then cancels it; he ignores the

Duke of York's advice and, the next moment, makes him Regent of England. When he cannot resist the military power of his cousin Henry Bolingbroke, whom he had earlier banished from the land, Richard withdraws, leaving his rival in charge:

> Go to Flint Castle; there I'll pine away;
> A king, woe's slave, shall kingly woe obey.
> 　　　　　　　　　　　　　　　　(III.ii.209–10)

When he does confront Bolingbroke, he knows that his feelings of grief, inadequacy, and shame are in conflict with his pride and former greatness:

> 　　　　　O that I were as great
> As is my grief, or lesser than my name!
> Or that I could forget what I have been!
> Or not remember what I must be now!
> Swell'st thou, proud heart? I'll give thee scope to beat,
> Since foes have scope to beat both thee and me.
> 　　　　　　　　　　　　　　　　(III.iii.136–41)

Although his words remain dignified and coherent, his opponents can see that 'Sorrow and grief of heart / Makes him speak fondly, like a frantic man' (III.iii.185), as if Shakespeare had relied on the actor maximizing the contrast of grief and pride that are explicit in his speech. Later, in the crucial scene when he relinquishes the crown, Richard acknowledges that words cannot represent what he feels:

> 　　　　my grief lies all within;
> And these external manner of laments
> Are merely shadows to the unseen grief
> That swells with silence in the tortur'd soul.
> There lies the substance. ...
> 　　　　　　　　　　　　　　　　(IV.i.295–8)

Richard's one sustained soliloquy comes in his very last scene when he is in prison and Bolingbroke has been crowned Henry the Fourth:

> I have been studying how I may compare
> This prison where I live unto the world; ...

He makes a determined attempt to express what he feels
himself to be and what he suffers:

> Sometimes am I king;
> Then treasons make me wish myself a beggar,
> And so I am. Then crushing penury
> Persuades me I was better when a king;
> Then am I king'd again; and by and by
> Think that I am unking'd by Bolingbroke,
> And straight am nothing. But whate'er I be,
> Nor I, nor any man that but man is,
> With nothing shall be pleas'd till he be eas'd
> With being nothing.
>
> (V.v.1–41)

As he contemplates death, two interventions occur that
are both Shakespeare's invention, not being found in any
of the play's sources and not necessary for its story-line.
With them, suddenly, words direct attention to feelings
that have been concealed, or not recognized, and soon
very different words and actions follow.

Shakespeare's first addition was to have music played
off-stage, prompting Richard to reflect on his own inabil-
ity to find a timely response to discord in the land and in
himself: 'I wasted time, and now doth time waste me.'
Eventually, his feelings get the better of him and he
orders the playing to stop: 'This music mads me. Let it
sound no more.' The burst of anger and fear are not his
only reactions; soon a gentler impulse appears:

> Yet blessing on his heart that gives it me!
> For 'tis a sign of love; and love to Richard
> Is a strange brooch in this all-hating world.
>
> (ll. 42–66)

This soliloquy is interrupted by the second of
Shakespeare's interventions when, unheralded and

unnamed, a 'poor groom' from the royal stables is let into the prison. Almost certainly he will bow as he greets the prisoner with 'Hail, royal Prince!' to which Richard replies ironically with equal courtesy, 'Thanks, noble peer!' This unknown man reports that, 'with much ado at length', he had sought leave to see his 'sometimes royal master's face' and that it had 'ern'd my heart' to see Bolingbroke riding on Barbary, King Richard's mount. With this, the encounter changes and other feelings take over:

> Rode he on Barbary? Tell me, gentle friend,
> How went he under him?
>
> (ll. 81–2)

The Groom hesitates, since the half-line is left uncompleted, and then answers: 'So proudly as if he disdain'd the ground.' In an instant, Richard angrily rails against the horse that did not 'break the neck / Of that proud man', and then, at the very next instant, asks forgiveness of the horse that 'was born to bear' (l. 92). These contrary feelings lead Richard back in the direction of soliloquy, aware of his own weakness in bearing 'a burden like an ass, / Spurr'd, gall'd, and tir'd, by jauncing Bolingbroke' (ll. 93–4). Here, the actor's task is to represent the feelings indicated by his words: they well up instinctively within the king and take possession of him, sensations of anger, pain, frustration, guilt, compassion, weakness, ass-like stupidity.

At this point, as if alarmed by a violence in Richard's voice, the Keeper of the prison enters and orders the Groom away. The sudden disruption leads to two lines of dialogue that suggest, by the simplest of verbal means, a mutual understanding between these two men, although still strangers to each other:

> If thou love me, 'tis time thou wert away.
> *What my tongue dares not, that my heart shall say.*

If time is taken to express these feelings of 'the heart', an audience will focus attention on the two silent figures and may, in imagination, be united with them for the moment. Even the 'sad dog' who brings Richard's food (ll. 70–1) is affected by the tongue-tied exchange, for his tone changes: 'My lord, will't please you to fall to!'

Hearing that Bolingbroke has sent Sir Pierce of Exton as emissary, Richard changes yet again, momentarily wary and then angry:

> The devil take Henry of Lancaster and thee!
> Patience is stale, and I am weary of it.
>
> (ll. 102–3)

As the Keeper cries out for help, the stage fills with assassins and, in the turmoil, Richard kills two of them, only to be struck down by Exton.[2] Threat of death has, once again, transformed Richard. His Queen, seeing him led away to prison, had accused him of passivity:

> Hath Bolingbroke depos'd
> Thine intellect? Hath he been in thy heart?
> The lion dying thrusteth forth his paw
> And wounds the earth, if nothing else, with rage
> To be o'erpow'r'd, and wilt thou, pupil-like,
> Take the correction mildly, kiss the rod,
> And fawn on rage with base humility,
> Which art a lion and the king of beasts?
>
> (V.i.27–34)

Thrusting forth his power in sudden action and denouncing his murderers, Richard is king-like now and then, in two rhymed lines, aspires to heaven:

> Mount, mount, my soul! thy seat is up on high;
> Whilst my gross flesh sinks downward, here to die.
>
> (V.v.111–12)

This last change to pious aspiration may resolve the 'unseen' swellings in Richard's 'tortur'd soul': Exton replies with homage and an admission of his own guilt: 'As full of valour as of royal blood. / Both have I spill'd.'

Again, Shakespeare has left a great deal to the actor and, this time, to the other actors on stage with him. In killing two assailants, Richard's physical strength is bound to be impressive, but how weakened is it in death and how painful are his last moments? How confident is the call to his mounting soul, how hurried the whole episode or how deliberate? Will the audience believe that Richard's 'soul' is able to mount to its throne in heaven like an eagle, the king of birds?[3] In *Richard the Second* words have established many themes that remain unresolved at its conclusion: the nature of a ruler's political authority, the roles of expediency, finance, and religion in government, the worth of family lineage, the influence of history and destiny, and more. But the journey taken by its central figure frequently awakens emotions and sensations at which words can only hint and it is these that are likely to hold an audience's attention as his story ends in violence and may be made somewhat clearer in his final actions and consequent silence.

Varied Strategies for Disclosure

Shakespeare did not usually wait until so late in a play to introduce a soliloquy that significantly alters an audience's perception of a central figure. For example, in *Henry the Fifth* two are placed at the start of Act IV, immediately before the king and his army meet the French in the crucial battle of Agincourt. The first is long and ruminative, Henry's mind reaching back over his whole reign and outwards towards his lowly subjects. There is, perhaps, a studied self-consciousness in these thoughts – certainly they lack the abrupt changes of subject and mood found in Richard the Third's last long soliloquy – but soon, as the testing time of battle draws closer, a second soliloquy is compact and urgent. It starts as a prayer for his soldiers:

> O God of battles, steel my soldiers' hearts,
> Possess them not with fear! Take from them now
> The sense of reck'ning, if th' opposed numbers
> Pluck their hearts from them.

But soon Henry speaks of his own guilt in holding on to the throne his father had won by rebellion and confirmed by the murder of his predecessor; his 'fear' and 'sense of reck'ning' become very evident as he repeats a crucial phrase and enumerates multiple acts of contrition:

> Not to-day, O Lord,
> O, not to-day, think not upon the fault
> My father made in compassing the crown!
> I Richard's body have interred new,
> And on it have bestowed more contrite tears
> Than from it issued forced drops of blood;
> Five hundred poor I have in yearly pay,
> Who twice a day their wither'd hands hold up
> Toward heaven, to pardon blood; and I have built
> Two chantries, where the sad and solemn priests
> Sing still for Richard's soul.

Before he finishes, a sense of hopelessness also emerges:

> More will I do;
> Though all that I can do is nothing worth,
> Since that my penitence comes after all,
> Imploring pardon.
>
> (IV.i.285–301)

Had Henry expressed these feelings earlier, he would have undermined the appearance of authority and recti-tude with which he rules his people, administers justice, and fights the war with France. He will not be viewed in the same way again.

An actor will have to decide how much of Henry's long-standing guilt shows through in performance, both before this verbal acknowledgement and afterwards. An audience could be encouraged to sense it when he insists that the church should justify his war against France, or warns that 'Treason and murder ever kept together' and treats traitors as if their fault were 'another fall of man' (II.ii.105–81). Later, when he woos the French princess, Henry's pledge of his 'good heart' that 'keeps his course truly' may sound hypocritical or forgetful (V.ii.159ff.). The imaginative experience of praying on his knees before battle can feed into the entire play, not least towards the end when Henry listens in silence to Burgundy's description of war-ravaged France and the French Queen's warning of divorce and fell jealousy in marriage. Much will depend on the audience: did it come to the theatre determined to acclaim 'this star of England' (Epilogue, 6) and take pleasure in an English victory over French enemies? Will it be appalled at the bloodshed and Henry's manipulation of less powerful people?

The conflict between Henry's guilt and assurance can become a major element throughout the playing of the part, even though he only speaks directly of it once. In later plays, however, similar conflicts are repeatedly debated, especially as the narrative draws to its close. In *Julius Caesar*, the extensive 'quarrel scene' between Brutus and Cassius (IV.iii) turns repeatedly on suspicion and trust, pride and courage, motivation and instinct. Earlier, Brutus had debated these issues with himself in a series of soliloquies that ensure the audience knows how his innermost feelings threaten to tear him apart:

> Since Cassius first did whet me against Caesar,
> I have not slept.
> Between the acting of a dreadful thing
> And the first motion, all the interim is
> Like a phantasma or a hideous dream.
> The Genius and the mortal instruments
> Are then in council; and the state of man,
> Like to a little kingdom, suffers then
> The nature of an insurrection.
>
> (II.i.61–9)

The Tragedy of Hamlet, following only a year or two later in 1600–1, develops this awareness throughout the entire leading part. Hamlet asks questions of himself continually and responds to very different impulses within moments of each other. By these means Shakespeare ensured that an audience recognizes Hamlet's hideous dreams and phantasmas and follows the councils and insurrections of his divided being.

With *The Tragedy of Hamlet,* Shakespeare had developed many ways to make inner experiences present to an audience: besides soliloquy and disturbed dialogue, Hamlet has been given wild and whirring words, satiric bitterness, seeming inconsequence, both real and feigned madness, deliberate debate about instinctive responses, strangely studied speech, private thoughts in public places, minor figures with contrasting behaviour. These devices, that distinguish sensation and feeling from conscious thought and speech, are used throughout this entire play, not only in presenting its central figure. Claudius knows that his 'words fly up [while] thoughts remain below', Gertrude that 'words like daggers' can reach to the 'very soul', Laertes that 'nature her custom holds, / Let shame say what it will' (*Hamlet,* III.iii.97, III.iv.89–96, IV.vii.188–9). Behind the words of Shakespeare's texts and largely beyond their reach, lies a more pervasive and, ultimately, stronger presentation of a life that is based in sensation and feeling. It becomes a hidden and yet palpable presence, sometimes frightening or daunting, sometimes fragile or tender, that gives to the plays an appeal that speaks directly to an audience's instincts and common experience. More familiar and less intellectually demanding than the concerns of subtle and complicated speech, actors nourish this inner life and feed upon it. When audience members come to recognize it, they can discover multiple images for what might otherwise elude them in their own lives.

By giving an audience the opportunity to see more of the play than many of the persons on stage, perhaps more than all of them, and by making its response to that view awaken their own senses, feelings, and imaginations, theatre performances of *Hamlet* can command a lasting popularity among persons from a wide range of cultural, social, and personal circumstances.

Notes

1. The three long soliloquies (see, also, I.ii.227–63) will stand out in the actor's written-out part, offering constant and easily located points for reference while preparing his performance.

2. Shakespeare's dialogue follows Holinshed's *Chronicles* closely here. Stage directions and speeches, as variously printed in the Quarto and Folio editions, call in rather vague terms for hurried and fierce activity in which Richard takes the initiative. If Shakespeare asked the actors to follow his source in their actions as they do in speech, the assassins would number 'eight tall men … every of them having a bill in his hand'. Seeing this, Richard:

   > stepping to the foremost man, wrung the bill out of his hands, and so valiantly defended himself, that he slew four of those that thus came to assail him. Sir Piers being half dismayed herewith, lept into the chair where King Richard was wont to sit, while the other four persons fought with him, and chased him about the chamber. And in conclusion, as King Richard traversed his ground, from one side of the chamber to another, & coming by the chair where Sir Piers stood, he was felled with a stroke of a poleaxe which Sir Piers gave him upon the head, and therewith rid him out of life, without giving him respite once to call to God for mercy of his passed offences. It is said, that Sir Piers of Exton, after he had thus slain him, wept right bitterly, as one stricken with the prick of a guilty conscience, for murdering him whom he had so long time obeyed as king.

3. The image of the royal eagle may well be implicit in Richard's words: early in the play, he had condemned Bolingbroke's 'eagle-winged pride / Of sky-aspiring and ambitious thoughts' (I.iii.129–30).

7

Actions and Reactions

Because so much attention has been paid to individual parts in the tragedies, Shakespeare's reliance on the interaction between the persons of a play has almost escaped attention. They speak to each other, obviously enough, but they interact across a much wider spectrum of responses than their words indicate. As these people move on stage, they react physically and instinctively to each other's presence. Coming together, they can be in agreement or fierce opposition. They can enter on stage together and then leave separately, or the other way about. A vast range of actions and interactions are set in motion by the texts and arise almost without premeditation during performance. Just as naturally, an audience responds to this ever-changing show. If the actors' parts in the comedies had been considered, these processes could not have been missed, for in these plays location and mood shift frequently and the grouping of figures is constantly changing to reveal further possibilities inherent in their basic relationships and individual resources and qualities.

Actors in action on stage can provide a spectacle that is endlessly interesting in detail and also capable of large-scale effects as the narrative of a play unfolds. Gordon Craig used to tell theatre directors:

> it is the large and sweeping impression produced by means of scene and the movement of the figures which is undoubtedly the most valuable means at your disposal. I

say this only after very many doubts and after much experience.[1]

Shakespeare knew the power of such choreography. By
its means a play is experienced in the minds of audiences
without passing through their verbalizing intelligences,
without raising resistance or needing explanation.
Responding to actions on stage, we can be affected
unconsciously and arrive where we had no intention of
journeying.

A Play's Visual Language

The word *Choreography* was introduced into English
during the second half of the nineteenth century for
dance notation, the description of dancers' movements
in space and time. Over the years, it came to refer more
generally to the sequence of steps and movements in a
dance. Although not usually considered essential to
drama, a term such as this is necessary if we are to understand how physical actions and movements are implied
in the words of Shakespeare's texts and their effect inven-
tively exploited by the dramatist. The extent to which this
original choreography has been ignored in study of the
texts and downgraded in production is a result of study
based on literary principles and a theatre dominated by
the spoken word. We are often told that Shakespeare's
pre-eminence is due to his use of words, his poetry, or
psychological insights, without acknowledgement that
inherent in the texts is a mastery of choreographic detail
that calls for a varied deployment of actors on stage
throughout the course of a play.

The bias that ignores a play's choreography is not new.
In the nineteen-thirties, Antonin Artaud declared that
the 'psychological and spoken depiction of the individual' had obsessed European theatres for over a hundred
years to the exclusion of almost everything else. He
wanted to see an immediate return to 'the oldest theatrical tradition' that would entail the rediscovery of an

earlier 'theatre of action' using 'dynamic and plastic' movement, physical language, and compelling visual images.[2] This argument is in tune with Gordon Craig's view that, in performance, 'the large and sweeping impression produced by means of scene and the movement of the figures' can exert the strongest hold over an audience. While present-day theatre directors handle action so that it makes a strong visual impression along with the words, few of them work as if Shakespeare had considered these matters; they tend to invent their own choreography and their own stage-business with little regard to those implicit in the texts.

The physical actions and interactions of individual figures that can be deduced from details of the text represent only one part of Shakespeare's choreography. The whole stage and the whole play have to be taken into account, with larger groups of figures, recurrent patterns, and variations in timing and rhythm. All this is easier to say than to do, because the only records of how plays were staged in Shakespeare's day are the practical instructions in surviving promptbooks and the stage-directions, seldom complete and not always authorial, that are found in early printed texts. What Shakespeare intended to be done must also be sought in small details of the dialogue, calls for stage-business and activity, and the handling of narrative. Enough is there to show that he paid careful attention to movement and visual effects throughout a play – so did other dramatists of his time, no doubt because action could be 'large and sweeping' in effect, as well as variable, on the broad space of an Elizabethan stage.

Manuals used today in the training of actors can help us to identify the actions implicit in the texts. One of the earliest but still in use is Rudolph von Laban's *Mastery of Movement for the Stage*, first published in 1950 and revised for a posthumous edition by Lisa Ullmann (London: Macdonald & Evans, 1971). Laban had developed his own system of dance notation and so his book is able to teach how to analyse movement as well as identify what the text requires. Not all the evidence is in the words that are spoken because physical movement is able to express the more instinctive feelings that originate in the body rather than the head. Chapter headings in Litz Pisk's *The Actor and His Body* (London: Harrap, 1975) indicate the range of non-verbal consciousness that can be expressed in body language: Awareness; Non-resistance; Tuning and Resilience; Confluence; Empathy. The exercises described in both these books, intended to develop an ability to perform, can also be used as a practical introduction to the variety and strength of physical action in stage plays.

An objective view of our own behaviour is sufficient to give some sense of how non-verbal expression operates and the ways in which movement and action will, almost inevitably, bring about changes in consciousness.

Choose almost any speech of two or three lines from a play by Shakespeare and speak them as you walk slowly towards another person; then repeat the same words in the same manner as you walk quickly, and then as you back away or remain seated.

Vary the experiment along these lines and the words will register differently on each occasion and your awareness of the other person will also change. Repetition itself will change the value of both movement and consciousness because the passage of time, as well as the use of space, modifies the effect of action. These are the twin factors in choreography that are to be taken into account when analysing movement on stage. Scale has further effects: a large number of persons can make a broad and often overwhelming impact if they move with co-ordination to the strong beat of footsteps or music. With less regular placement, movement, and rhythm, a crowd will have more subtle effects and critical assessment become more difficult.

A play's visual statement at any one moment is more easily considered. By holding the figures on stage still in the mind's eye, as if arrested in mid-action, they can be examined in much the same way as a painting or a group sculpture. Rudolf Arnheim's *Visual Thinking* (Berkeley: University of California Press, 1969) will assist in this by showing that we cannot actually see every detail that is in front of us at any one time. Visual perception actively discriminates, depends on memory, and notices gaps and discrepancies; certain details are likely to be missed while others register strongly. Our vision is naturally influenced by pairing and grouping together, by distortion or disproportion, and by what has recently been seen; what we see at any one moment will depend on contrasts, innovations, and repetitive elements within our view. His later book, *The Power of the Center: a Study of Composition in the Visual Arts*, issued in a revised edition by the same publisher in 1988, deals more extensively with the organization of objects in space and the effects of imbalance, stability, tension through deviation, polarities, perspective, and centricity: all these are terms that can be used to describe the changing shapes and organizations that occur on stage in a theatre and help us to understand an audience's reaction to them. We will never be certain about all the physical and visual implications of a text, but some crucial ones can be identified and many possibilities of reaction recognized. In the course of time, we are able to develop a sense of what a text implies should happen on stage and begin to judge its effect on an audience. Arnheim warns us that what is seen often takes precedence over verbal recognition.

To deal at first in simple terms, we may say that, on an open stage like those in Elizabethan theatres, 30 or more actors can be called upon to fill the space with formally ordered groups or in free-flowing movement; the difference in effect will be large and inescapable. Many deployments are possible, and they may change with the narrative. Two armies can confront each other in ordered ranks before battle and then join in conflict; or a single body of soldiers can be variously engaged in small groups in preparation for battle, or in reaction to one that has already been fought. Members of a crowd can stand close together or be dispersed in several directions. Two or more actors can follow each other through a crowd or stand in opposition to everyone else. By remaining quite still or pursuing an independent purpose, one actor can stand out in a restless crowd.

After many actors have left the stage together, a single remaining figure will be given very close attention, as at the end of *Twelfth Night* when the solitary Feste draws an audience's attention and leads it, as if through the eye of a needle, to consider another much wider and timeless view of what has just been represented on stage. When a particular configuration of actors is repeated after some time has passed, it can lose its effectiveness or, by small alterations or additions, gain new values; for example, the Prince in *Romeo and Juliet* stands in a commanding position on a crowded stage on three occasions and, on the last, seems almost powerless as attention is drawn to new and very different elements of the stage picture. When Othello stands half hidden at a distance from Iago and Cassio who are engaged in talk about Bianca, an audience may be uncertain where to look and yet, if physical alertness shows that Iago is fully in charge of both aspects of the situation, he will hold most attention; if Othello's anguish at his wife's supposed infidelity is expressed as strongly physically as it is verbally, he is likely to dominate everything else that is seen on stage even though he may be off-centre.

Shakespeare's Choreography

Action, movement, spectacle and narrative are all intimately connected. A good story can set the persons of a play in pursuit of contrasted objectives and on journeys towards confrontation and eventual failure or satisfaction. In *Twelfth Night*, for example, two contrasting households are brought on stage. At Count Orsino's court, fanciful whims are satisfied by obsequious and almost indistinguishable attendants. Having stood around him during the first scene, they are sent off in a small procession and then he follows on his own:

Away before me to sweet beds of flow'rs;
Love-thoughts lie rich when canopied with bow'rs.

(I.i)

Orsino is the centre but not always the prime focus in this stable composition; on at least one occasion, Viola, dressed as Cesario, draws all eyes away from him. The other main spectacle is Olivia's household; she is a young widow, with neither parents, brother, nor sister to console her, but attended by servants and a fool who all, in different ways, have minds of their own. This visual composition is less settled than the first since Olivia, its centre of power, is not always in view and not for long constant in what she does. Sir Toby, a needy relation, lodges here and has introduced the simple-minded Sir Andrew to the household as a suitor to his niece and a supplier of cash for himself. Action moves from the lady's private rooms to the buttery bar where the mistress does not go, then to a garden and, just before the end, to a 'dark room' that acts as a prison. The location for a third strand of the narrative is not fixed at all: early in the play, events happen on a sea coast immediately after a frightening storm and then the action moves to the streets of a port where, later, fighting will break out in 'private brabble' (V.i.59).

Within the illusory worlds on show during a performance of a Shakespeare play, individual persons make a sequence of contrasted appearances that mark the steps in their progress in the narrative. Each new entry makes a physical statement that would register strongly on the broad stages of Elizabethan public theatres where six or seven metres might have to be traversed before making contact with persons already present or before reaching a position from which the whole audience could be addressed. A great variety of entries was possible and their effect would be heightened by contrast with what was already happening on stage. An actor could enter eagerly at speed or slowly in fear; he could walk deliberately, hesitantly, respectfully, irreverently, or complacently; or he could run. For a new play in Elizabethan theatres, the one major expense was on the wardrobe which suggests that the distinctive nature of many entries would have been emphasized by changes in clothing: sometimes introducing signs of rank or service, sometimes wearing voluminous outer garments for travelling on horseback along uneven roads, often marking the huge differences between court finery and everyday wear. So an entry would both alert an audience's attention and demonstrate changes in fortune, feelings, or intentions without the aid of words.

In *Twelfth Night*, Viola will behave differently on each entry and often wear different clothes. She is first seen reaching the seashore after being shipwrecked, her dress and hair dishevelled, her behaviour apprehensive on finding herself the only woman among unknown sailors. The next time she enters it is along with others in Orsino's entourage; now she is disguised as the boy Cesario and probably dressed in a uniform livery; some signs of uncertainty are bound to be evident in her presence, especially when called and addressed by her new master. Her next appearance is as Orsino's messenger arriving at Olivia's house and dressed for an official embassy; she probably wears a sword, as she certainly does on a similar visit later in the play. On this occasion, the text insists that she appears confident at first and, even, 'saucy' (I.v.185–7) but this is likely to be a mere pretence, a performance like the speech she has prepared for delivery (see ll. 179–83). For Act II, scene iv, as the most favoured attendant in Orsino's private quarters, she will be less formal than before, speech less guarded and behaviour more intimate. A sequence of silences, indicated by incomplete verse-lines, establish a mutual sympathy between master and servant.

With each succeeding scene, Viola's entries call for new physical language and provide further demonstrations of instinctive feelings and silent sensations. At the start of Act III, scene i, competing in verbal wit with Feste, the wise fool, she probably avoids too close a scrutiny; later, when Olivia enters, she becomes carefully, perhaps overly, polite. When her message is disregarded, she breaks decorum by showing both 'contempt and

anger' (l. 143). When Olivia answers with protestation of
love, Viola leaves precipitously and almost rudely,
perhaps alarmed under a thinner veneer of politeness.
On visiting Olivia again, which is her next entry on stage,
the two walk side by side with Viola subdued in spirit and
reserved in speech. This time, Olivia leaves first and Viola
is immediately faced with Sir Toby delivering a challenge
to fight with Sir Andrew. Her physical actions now
become awkward and very obviously terrified; she does
not know how to use a sword and has heard that she is to
fight a knight who is 'a devil in private brawl' and has
already killed three adversaries. When Sir Andrew,
equally alarmed, is brought on stage to fight with her,
everything becomes broadly farcical: Viola 'pants and
looks pale, as if a bear were at [her] heels' and Sir
Andrew turns to bribery and prayer (III.iv.279–80, 294).
Sir Toby says that 'oxen and wainropes cannot hale them
together' to engage in the duel (III.ii.56–8). Antonio's
surprise entry saves the day for both contestants and by
the next scene, when she enters at the side of Orsino,
Viola has regained every appearance of ease.

In the play's last scene, Viola is rapidly drawn into a
succession of very different physical actions by the turn
of events. She is faced with unexpected news, accused of
lying, and threatened with death by Orsino who is now
driven by 'savage jealousy'. Immediately afterwards she is
called 'husband' by Olivia and reproved for being afraid.
Having been reported to be 'the very devil' in a fight, she
is then struck dumb by the arrival of her brother whom
she had thought drowned at sea (V.i.113, 174). After
these sudden and rapid transformations, mutual recognition is slowly and delicately established; whereas
Sebastian is ready 'to let fall upon [her] cheek' his tears
of joy, she delays any embrace until more is known
(ll. 231–45). Her gender having been revealed, she now
swears true and everlasting love for Orsino and then falls
silent until the very end of the play, even when he
promises a 'solemn combination ... of our dear souls'
and vows to be her servant (ll. 369–74). As if no words
can express what is in her heart, it is left to the actor to

realize Viola's feelings and sensations in her physical bearing. Now, after very many different appearances and actions, only Viola's silent presence on stage tells members of an audience what is happening in her body and in her 'heart': both actor and spectators will respond at this moment as the entire performance has led them.

So much happens physically in a performance of *Twelfth Night* that choreography is a constant element in performance. Around Viola and in interaction with her, the contrasting behaviour of other figures sets up their varied and distinct rhythms and patterns of movement. At the start of the play, Olivia is a young widow dressed in black and occupied in daily rituals of mourning but, after she has unveiled so that Cesario/Viola can see her face, her behaviour changes. Soon alone, for the first time in the play, she realizes that everything is happening 'too fast' and then decides, only moments later, to 'let it be' and send a ring as gift to Orsino's young messenger. 'I do I know not what', she says; her excitement shows as she surrenders her self-possession:

> Fate, show thy force: ourselves we do not owe;
> What is decreed must be; and be this so!
>
> (I.v.292–6)

For subsequent scenes, mourning clothes and behaviour are discarded. On her next entrance, finding Cesario /Viola already on stage, she is silent, holding in her feelings while others talk, and then, sending everyone else away, becoming progressively more unguarded and passionate. This time, Viola breaks off the meeting, leaving Olivia speechless and having to make her exit alone. After many variations in the dance of behaviour, Olivia enters to find Sebastian fighting with Sir Toby. Because Viola's brother is dressed exactly like his sister and is her identical twin, Olivia thinks he is Cesario and orders the fight to stop, begging Sebastian not to be 'offended'. After a longish silence, in which he must try to take in what has happened, Sebastian expresses his astonishment and agrees to be 'rul'd' by this unknown lady and leave in her company. It is now her turn to be almost tongue-tied: 'O, say so, and so be' is all she can reply while her bearing and movement will express much more (IV.i.63–4). Sebastian soon reappears alone, both enraptured and fearing some madness has taken hold of them both. When Olivia arrives accompanied by a Priest and excusing 'this haste of mine' (IV.iii.22), Sebastian vows that he 'ever will be true' and she calls the heavens to witness her act of engagement. They leave, with the silent priest, in scarcely believable and shared solemnity (IV.iii.32–5).

Each strand of the play's narrative has its own pattern of behaviour and action. In contrast with persons engaged in pursuit or avoidance, Sir Toby and Maria, Olivia's 'waiting gentlewoman', are at ease with each other from the start, even though she tells him to respect the 'modest limits of order' (I.iii.7–8). When Sir Andrew enters, Toby creates a diversion by setting him to 'accost' Maria and, when she leaves, having made a fool of her new gallant, he calls for a demonstration of Andrew's dancing abilities, urging him on, with 'Ha, higher! Ha, ha, excellent!'; they leave the stage in high spirits with Toby very much in charge. When the location shifts to the buttery bar at night, these two are together again and more at peace. They are joined by Feste from whom they request a love song that causes a wistful lyricism to take hold of all three, dispelled only when they agree to join together in a 'catch' or part-song. Maria enters to quieten their 'caterwauling' but not in time to forestall Malvolio, Olivia's steward, who enters to reprove them all, including Maria, for turning his lady's house into an alehouse. The fun deriving from their contrasted behaviour proves irrepressible and, once Malvolio has left accompanied by their jeers, Maria proposes a practical joke that will make a fool of the spoilsport. In their next scene, the conspirators set the trap and hide, like children, to enjoy what happens. Malvolio enters alone as expected and in soliloquy reveals himself to be what the others call an 'overweening rogue' and 'rare turkey-cock'. Eventually he sees the letter that has been dropped for him to find; he swells in self-importance as he reads it aloud and is totally deceived by its coded declaration of love in what appears to be Olivia's handwriting. The eavesdroppers struggle to suppress their incredulity and laughter, and later their fury as well.

The overall visual composition and balance change as Malvolio becomes the central figure in the comedy. Believing himself beloved by his mistress, he discards puritanical composure for extravagant postures and broad smiles: 'I do not now fool myself to let imagination jade me', he triumphantly declares (ll. 146–7), as everything he has dreamed about in secret can now be played out in public. When he next appears, having put on yellow, cross-gartered stockings as the letter instructed, he greets Olivia with 'ridiculous boldness', calling out sweet nothings, smiling, and repeatedly kissing his hand; he interprets her expression of concern as an invitation to 'go to bed' with her (III.iv.29–31). After this total exposure, he is next seen locked in a dark room as a cure for his 'madness'. He is taunted in this 'prison' by Feste disguised as Sir Topas the Curate while Toby and Maria watch the humiliation that they have brought about; eventually, aware that their joke has gone too far, they leave, telling Feste to revert to his own voice. Malvolio cannot see the 'beard and gown' of Feste's disguise (IV.ii.61–3) so that only his own face and hands are likely to be visible through the bars of his prison as the bewildered victim cries out in frustration, his words stumbling and repetitive. Before he leaves, Feste breaks into song and the scene ends with Malvolio having nothing more to say and Feste transformed into a figure from an older kind of moral drama:

> *I'll be with you again,*
> *In a trice,*
> *Like to the old Vice, ...*
> *Who with dagger of lath,*
> *In his rage and his wrath,*
> *Cries, Ah, ha! to the devil; ...*
> (IV.ii.116–27)

Feste may dance as he sings, for that was an important part of a fool's repertoire, and he probably beats out an emphatic rhythm on his 'tabor' (see III.i.1–2). The comedy has turned into a nightmare, either absurd or frightening, according to how performances have developed, physically and emotionally. Malvolio's last appearance is in huge contrast to his first. Then he had been precise and authoritative; now he is bedraggled and baffled, isolated in front of both assembled households and in the midst of other people's happiness. Hearing that the letter had been a forgery, he is silent during further explanations and Olivia's promise of a fair hearing. Then, as if from the depths of his being in a violent tragedy or, alternatively, in still more frenzied frustration at ultimate humiliation, he cries out, 'I'll be reveng'd on the whole pack of you' and leaves the stage alone, all eyes on him. The choreography of his role will have led an audience to pay increasing attention to Malvolio and, at the same time, have left the actor to define by his physical and emotional performance the terminus of one, increasingly dominant, strand of the play's narrative.

Feste is the only other isolated person in this last scene although, with a fool's licence to mock and find fault, he had earlier spoken individually to everyone who is now present. At first he has business to do: he asserts ownership of Malvolio's letter and announces the Count's arrival but, after this, he is progressively sidelined. When he reappears supporting Sir Toby who, together with Sir Andrew, is limping towards his bed, his fooling has little scope beyond reporting that the surgeon who should dress Toby's wound is blind drunk. He enters again with Malvolio's letter and, taking a prominent position, starts to read it, demonstrating again that he 'is for all waters' (IV.ii.61) by using an appropriately mad voice. But his fooling is now out of key with the situation and Olivia orders Fabian to take over the reading; when asked to confirm that Malvolio had indeed written the letter, all Feste contributes is 'Ay, madam'. He then falls silent and no one in the play or the audience is prompted to think of him again until, when everyone else has left, he remains on stage to sing a song about the entire course of his life:

> *When that I was and a little tiny boy,*
> *With hey, ho, the wind and the rain,*
> *A foolish thing was but a toy,*
> *For the rain it raineth every day.*

The song continues with *But when I came to man's estate, ... But when I came, alas! to wive, ... But when I came unto my beds, ...* As the visual focus of attention centres on the play's most enigmatic figure, Feste sets a riddle for the audience to solve that ignores the play's fictional narrative and gives prominence to very ordinary and real-life events. His singing concludes the play with an address to the theatre audience:

> *A great while ago the world begun,*
> *With hey, ho, the wind and the rain,*
> *But that's all one, our play is done,*
> *And we'll strive to please you every day.*

With this reminder that everything on stage has been a pretence and an effort to give pleasure, the lonely Feste awakens a sense of the life to which everyone will shortly and variously return.

Stage-business, Activities, and Ceremonies

Shakespeare's handling of stage action that was appropriate to the theatres of his time can still be effective in present-day productions if the scenery, lighting, and sound effects of our technically advanced theatres are used in support of what happens between the actors. The stage setting has always contributed to the choreographic effect of these plays, even though the background to the actors in Elizabethan theatres was other members of the audience sitting opposite and the unchanging and formal arrangement of entrances and other features on the two levels of the tiring-house facade. The entrance through which an actor came onto the stage and how close he then stood to a section of the audience would have had immediate visual impact. In addition to varying use of these background effects, the setting for performance changed whenever large properties were brought on stage, altering the focus of attention and identifying the location or occasion for on-stage action. Thrones, gateways, graves, and funeral monuments had particular symbolic implications and other properties called for practical business, for example seats of varying importance, tables, arbours, beds, mounds of grass, rocks, carts, cannon, and so forth.

The stage picture viewed by an audience was also changed by the activity and behaviour associated with many smaller properties. For example, wearing a sword altered posture, carrying a pistol could make others more wary. Military equipment such as banners and pikes could be paraded and handled; trumpets and drums carried at the ready as well as played. Cooking utensils and plates of food, casks and flagons of drink, purses, books, papers, letters, baggage of various sorts, torches, lanterns, and so on: all these and more, used in a wide assortment of ways, introduced expressive and eye-catching visual effects. Much variety was possible: preparations for eating and drinking in *Romeo and Juliet*, *Much Ado about Nothing*, *As You Like It*, and *Macbeth* all need special management, no two having the same occasion or ingredients. Mourning in *Romeo and Juliet*, as Juliet lies as if dead on her bed, is expressed individually and in unison, with inarticulate, repetitive cries and with elaborate speeches, music, and procession. In contrast, mourning for Hero in *Much Ado About Nothing* is formal, restrained, and accompanied with torchlight and a 'solemn hymn' (V.iii.11). Fighting with various weapons and in various modes occurs in almost every play and can be spontaneous, rough, skilful, organized, enraged, dangerous or, in single contest, decorous and formal. The duel at the end of *Hamlet* occupies very little of a reader's time but, for the actors, it is a lengthy business in several distinct stages that grow increasingly strenuous and tense; they are especially taxing for the actor of Hamlet, who has been active on stage for a large proportion of the preceding two and a half or three hours. This fight holds an audience's close attention, even though not every thrust and parry can register; at times, Hamlet's deeply and uniquely involved presence may obliterate everything else from notice.

Sometimes the use of stage properties prolongs or foregrounds a particular action. An elaborate example is in *Othello* Act IV, scene iii, when Desdemona prepares for bed by removing her jewellery and, probably, loosening and brushing her hair. Her actions will, necessarily, be delicate and precise, setting slow rhythms for the scene. Emilia will be close and attentive to her mistress as she helps and this physical relationship encourages a shared intimacy in which both women are able to speak with exceptional candour. A list of properties needed to stage any play is a useful indication of the experience it will give in performance. In *Othello* further very personal and domestic articles are required, notably the embroidered handkerchief which Desdemona has always about her during the first three Acts and which is subsequently handed around by Emilia, Iago, Cassio, and Bianca; the last scene is dominated by a bed and its furnishings. All these are in strong contrast to other recurring properties: swords and a variety of weapons, seafarers' gear, lanterns, cups and flagons of wine for celebration, letters and official papers, purses, and once, exceptionally, coins. Musical instruments are brought on stage to be played very briefly or not at all; a chair for carrying the wounded Cassio is called for and duly appears. From off-stage, a loud bell is heard, capable of frightening the entire garrison and population of Cyprus. Desdemona's stage-properties and accompanying actions are so different from those of the numerous males in the play that she always stands out, seeming to occupy a very different space. Yet, when she has been murdered with a pillow on a bed,

Othello falls down beside her and roars out in pain (see V.ii.201). Later, at the very end, he leaves the assembled witnesses and goes to kiss his wife as she lies dead on the marriage sheets. The soldier-hero now occupies his wife's space and his going there speaks for him as eloquently as any words he utters.

Manners and ceremonies in regular use during Shakespeare's lifetime ensured that entrances and exits, or the handling of certain properties and changing of costume, held greater significance than they would today on stage or in life. Personal relations were expressed in a variety of ways. Removing a hat, clasping hands, saluting with or without a sword, and standing up when one had been seated were among the simplest and are still readily understood today. Other greetings, such as bowing very low, kneeling, taking backward steps, or exchanging a formal embrace could hold up the on-going narrative. Whatever the greeting, the entry of someone of greater social status would bring about a significant regrouping of every one else on stage. Exits, as well as entrances, would normally be strictly in order of social precedence, in domestic situations as well as public places. When this protocol was forgotten or wilfully altered, an audience would be almost sure to notice and probably want to know the cause. The history plays, that are much to do with authority, allegiance, and power, have numerous situations in which words draw attention to a missing ceremony. For example, when Northumberland delays kneeling before his king, Richard the Second demands 'how dare thy joints forget / To pay their awful duty to our presence?'; this show of respect should have been an instinctive or deliberate action. Audiences familiar with the appropriate ceremonies, as many Elizabethans had to be, would view encounters on stage with certain expectations and mark any modifications rapidly.

In *Richard the Third*, the Duke of Gloucester is very aware of protocol on his way towards the throne but, once crowned, acts in some unexpected ways. Having hesitated about the murder of the young king Edward V, Buckingham leaves the royal presence neither asking for nor being granted permission. To this provocative action, Richard says nothing but is seen to be angry as he 'gnaws his lip'. He then ignores protocol himself by calling a nameless 'boy' to his side for a secret conference, enquiring if he knows 'any whom corrupting gold / Will tempt unto a close exploit of death?' (IV.ii.24–35). Later, in the early morning before battle, Richard says he will engage in still less kingly activity:

> Under our tents I'll play the eaves-dropper,
> To see if any mean to shrink from me.
>
> (V.iii.221–2)

Even when no one in the play comments on these lapses in decorum, an Elizabethan audience would be unlikely to miss them. The sight of Richard leaving the stage preparing to act as a common spy would be seen as an expression of craven thoughts and feelings that no one in the play dares to mention.

The procession, bell, and signs of mourning that set the scene and appropriate behaviour for Act V, scene i of *Hamlet* are totally counterstated when Laertes leaps into Ophelia's grave and Hamlet follows him. This shocking breakdown of decorum is followed by others. Hamlet leaves ahead of the king and his mother, and with a threat, not a farewell:

> Let Hercules himself do what he may,
> The cat will mew, and dog will have his day.
>
> (ll. 285–6)

This unexpected behaviour heightens a growing sense of crisis that will affect everyone on stage and, probably, in the audience as well: Claudius speaks separately and tersely to Horatio, Laertes, and Gertrude, without regard for precedence or the public occasion. No one makes a reply but everyone leaves the stage saying nothing. The next scene starts with Hamlet talking volubly to Horatio in what must be strictest privacy. The contrast with the preceding scene is great and, in many physical ways, unusual and puzzling so that it adds a sense of uncertainty or danger. Why should 'young Osric' enter when he does? Does he play with his hat to cover his own anxiety or to direct Hamlet's attention away from a surveillance that has been ordered by Claudius? He cannot act so affectedly because he is stupid, since he is clever enough to be trusted with crucial distribution of weapons for the murder that has been planned to follow. Is the Lord who enters to ask Hamlet to confirm what Osric has just reported a sign of insecurity in Claudius or one of a team of surveillants? Or was he a simple way of forwarding the narrative added by Shakespeare in case Osric's manner of speech had obscured what is about to happen? His entry is missing from the later Folio text, suggesting second thoughts about its necessity. The organization of on-stage action at such a juncture is a matter for very fine judgement because every detail could affect an audience's experience of the play's conclusion.

While Shakespeare's choreography, the visual and physical aspects of his plays, contributes continuously and, often, silently to performance and to the effect the plays have on audiences, much of it is disclosed only after careful study or in exploratory rehearsals. We adapt comparatively quickly to unfamiliar words and ways of thought but the visual statements of a play are not so easily understood or translated into recognizable behaviour. To visualize what the text tells us should or could happen on stage is only part of the job because the formal manners, heraldry, and colour symbolism of Shakespeare's times mean little today. Almost everywhere ceremony is reduced and we have grown suspicious of its validity; we are more at ease in approaching other people, especially our parents, teachers, and employers. We show our bodies more openly and few people wear body-restricting clothes. So the passage of time has introduced many unavoidable changes in our view of a play and these, in turn, have affected our understanding and enjoyment.

Today it is unlikely that more can be done to bring performances into line with the original choreography since theatre practice is by nature conservative and audiences have changed in expectation. Directors and designers prefer to add their own visual statements of meaning that tend to obscure what the text holds in store. Present-day scenography and stage management are seldom employed to enhance what is implicit in the text. It is not surprising that Shakespeare's choreography has fallen into neglect. For readers, however, these circumstances are not an inevitable disability; with a text in hand and working slowly, it is possible to retrieve more of what Shakespeare created and so enhance our readings of the plays.

Notes

1. Gordon Craig, *On the Art of the Theatre* (London: Heinemann, 1911; ed. 1957), p. 21.
2. Antonin Artaud, *Collected Works*, vol. ii, trans. Alastair Hamilton (London: Calder and Boyars, 1972), pp. 160, 165–6; these ideas recur repeatedly in his writings.

8

Visual Interplay

Small details of physical performance and staging are closely related to the words of a text and are therefore more readily understood than actions larger in scope. But actions that involve many persons and evolve over a long period of time affect the whole of a theatrical event and the value of any single moment will depend on its relation to these larger movements. This is partly due to a scale effect, the more substantial and slower actions drawing lighter and quicker ones along with them, as if in their wake. It is also a consequence of the progressive nature of a theatrical event which enables an audience to accumulate impressions, retaining the least transitory and becoming increasingly, if subconsciously, aware of contrasts, similarities, and interconnections. The interplay between different visual elements in a play should to be considered in the widest and most sustained terms possible; it contributes significantly to the overall effect of a play.

Contrasts in Physical Presentation

In Shakespeare's plays, action is both complicated and clarified by his practice of following several lines of narrative, each one establishing visual patterns of action and behaviour that interplay with those of others. The first Act of *King Lear*, which follows the fortunes of two separate families, provides notable examples of recurring and developing actions and their cumulative effect. The very first scene makes three distinctly different visual impressions. Its main episode sets out a formal and public assembly in which the old king announces his retirement as active ruler, transfers power so that it is shared among his daughters and their husbands, and deals with two suitors for the hand of his youngest daughter, Cordelia. At first everyone on stage takes up a position in relation to the central figure of the king and their speeches are pronouncements rather than contributions to talk or debate. Cordelia, however, will not join with her two sisters in answering their father's demand that they should each say how much they love him. Rather than competing for their father's gift of territory, she breaks the regular pattern to speak brief asides and then returns towards the centre to give the disturbing, riddle-like answer, 'Nothing, my lord' (I.i.86). This immediately provokes an incredulous and, then, a passionate reaction from Lear that disrupts the ordered proceedings at their very centre. Next, the Earl of Kent steps out from the symmetrical grouping and attempts to dissuade Lear from disinheriting his child. Face to face, he calls the king 'mad' and, raising a 'clamour', dares to invoke Apollo, as Lear has already done. Answering Kent with a great oath, Lear banishes the 'recreant' from the land (I.i.159–79). The broad focus and regular tempo of corporate ceremony have been replaced by passionate and individual intensity. A new order is briefly established when Kent stops before leaving the stage and, in turn, addresses the king, his daughters and the assembled lords.

In addition to this main business of the first scene, that calls upon the entire strength of an acting company, Shakespeare introduced private talk between a few individuals and so alerted an audience to an alternative view of the action that will follow. Kent and the Earl of Gloucester begin the play by speculating about the king's intentions and then Gloucester introduces his younger and illegitimate son, Edmund, who has entered silently along with his father. Although he says very little beyond offering his 'service' to Kent, Edmund's presence will attract an audience's keen attention: he is said to 'promise well' but what he does subsequently in the play implies more than that. He is a person who draws all eyes; rather than serving others, he has the potential to lead an army and his sexual attractions are so strong that both Lear's older daughters will be desperate to enjoy them. However shrewdly Kent and Gloucester discuss the political situation, providing the focus of attention, an audience may well sense – perhaps without consciously recognizing this – that Edmund, standing apart, represents another force that lies in wait to take over the play. He may also alert spectators to look for outward signs of Cordelia's inner strength when she stands apart from everyone in the subsequent action.

After the main public business has ended, on a comparatively empty stage and with eyes 'wash'd' by weeping, Cordelia bids farewell to Goneril and Regan, her older sisters (ll. 267–9). An audience's attention in this third section of the first scene will focus on the three women in turn because, while committing her father to their care, Cordelia does not hide her knowledge that 'plighted cunning' has hidden their true feelings under protestations of undying love (ll. 280–1). When she has left with her betrothed husband, the King of France, Goneril and Regan, by common, unspoken consent, remain on stage and, in sharply phrased prose that contrasts with the sustained verse of their public speeches, speak of their father as a mentally disabled old man; instead of making him welcome in retirement, they agree to curtail his freedom. While the dramatic focus is now shared between the two sisters, they are physically and emotionally contrasted: Regan's last words are direct yet reserved while Goneril's imply purposeful and physical effort:

> – We shall further think of it.
> – We must do something, and i' th' heat.
>
> (ll. 305–7)

They probably leave separately or in different directions, contrasted in the way they walk.

Edmund starts the second scene by taking sole possession of the stage and introducing new action in fluent and energetic soliloquy: 'Thou, Nature, art my goddess; to thy law / My services are bound ...' As he declares his independence and asserts the right to do whatever suits himself, an audience's attention will be focused on him more consistently than on any single person earlier in the play. Contrary to the established ordering of society and the strictures of ordinary morality, he intends to displace Edgar, his older and 'legitimate' brother:

> ... if this letter speed
> And my invention thrive, Edmund the base
> Shall top th' legitimate. I grow; I prosper.
> Now, gods, stand up for bastards!
>
> (I.ii.19–22)

At this moment, Gloucester enters questioning what had happened in the previous scene and at once Edmund starts to play a trick on him by very obviously concealing the letter that he wants his father to read. Were it not for his opening soliloquy and were the letter not concerned with politics, social order, and an intended murder, he could be performing in a stage comedy for an audience's relaxed amusement. Gloucester, blind to his son's deception, quickly becomes convinced that his other son, Edgar, is trying to kill him and, before leaving, instructs Edmund to 'find out the villain'. Any pity that might be felt for the old man's plight is likely to be forgotten when Edmund has another soliloquy, this time in high-spirited prose, and Edgar enters, coming 'pat', his brother says, 'like the catastrophe of the old comedy' (I.ii.127–8). As if Shakespeare wanted to taunt his audience, Edgar discloses little about himself, his few words being gentle and bookish; he is so concerned with what others are thinking that he seems to lack a mind of his own. With surprising speed, Edmund is able to convince him that his life is in danger because their father is enraged against him for some unspecified misdeed. He hurries Edgar off-stage to seek safety and then, once more, holds the stage alone and, in a soliloquy, gives an audience opportunity to enjoy his spirit even if it is appalled by what he intends to do:

Let me, if not by birth, have lands by wit:
All with me's meet that I can fashion fit.

(ll. 74–5)

In these two opening scenes, Shakespeare has drawn
the audience's attention in different ways to actions of
several distinct kinds, each with its own basic tempo,
rhythm, and pitch. Visually, the scenes vary in pattern
and by this interplay gain in clarity and impact. Starting
with two figures close together in confidential discussion
and a third who stands apart saying nothing, the silent
one is then drawn into the talk and plans are made for
his future. The stage now becoming fully occupied, everyone knows where to stand and what to say until a succession of individual figures draw attention away from the
centre and what had seemed firmly established suddenly
becomes so fractured and unpredictable that an audience may momentarily fail to grasp all that is happening.
Eventually, two sisters stand alone, revealing hitherto
hidden intentions. The following scene is dominated
throughout by one individual with his own clearly
expressed intentions as, one at a time, he deceives his
father and brother. A number of timely entries and a
series of visual and verbal echoes combine to give a
further impression of inevitability, implying that what is
being done could not be other than it is: although not
verbalized, this will gradually become a pervasive element
in an audience's experience of the play.

In the remaining scenes of the first Act, the narrative
proceeds along a single line but markedly different kinds of
physical action repeatedly modify an audience's experience
of the drama. The location shifts at once to Goneril's castle
where she is now the centre of attention as she instructs
her obsequious steward, Oswald: her father's gross crimes,
she says, are setting us 'all at odds' and the knights attend-
ing him 'grow riotous'. As horns signal Lear's approach,
she tells Oswald what she thinks of him – an 'Idle old man,
/ That still would manage those authorities / That he hath
given away' (I.iii.17–19) – and that she wants matters drawn
to a head. As they both leave, a new scene begins with the

solitary entry of another member of the servant class. An audience is likely to be puzzled until a brief soliloquy reveals this unknown man to be the Earl of Kent in disguise. When horns are heard again, Lear enters from a hunt and attended by his knights: it is likely to be a busy and noisy entrance, filling the stage and quickly dispelling other impressions.

The vigorous sport of killing wild animals is a surprising pastime for an old man who had said he was about to unburden himself and 'crawl toward death' (I.i.40). He may well enter 'bloody as a hunter'[1] so that, during the dialogue that follows, he is helped to wash and change his clothes; at least boots and outer garments will have to be removed. Meanwhile, he interrogates Kent, who now calls himself Caius and, bluntly and humorously, asks to be accepted as a servant. Although an audience will laugh at Kent, it may also be apprehensive because, for security reasons, a king would not accept an unknown person as his personal servant without at least one authenticating recommendation; a visual contrast with Edmund being formally received into Kent's 'service' may be perceived here. From now on, physical action becomes progressively more riotous and absurd, an audience being both surprised and entertained.

Although Lear calls repeatedly for his supper, nothing in the text suggests that it comes. Instead, Oswald enters and, giving Lear a surly answer, leaves abruptly; he re-enters shortly afterwards and is still more disrespectful. For this the king strikes at him and, as he starts to leave, Caius/Kent trips him up so that he falls full-length on the floor. As Lear commends him, with 'I thank thee, fellow: thou serv'st me, and I'll love thee' (I.iv.86–7), Caius forces Oswald onto his feet and off-stage; this brings a gift of money as a promise of further service and reward. At this point, the fool enters and, seeing what is happening, offers his coxcomb to Caius/Kent to signify that he is now the king's fool. Although Lear had several times called for 'my fool' and greets him now as 'my pretty knave' (ll. 94–5), Fool ignores his master, continuing to address Caius who is now silent.

To the view of a Jacobean audience, the entire opening of this scene is packed with activity that transgresses civilized behaviour and courteous service. One of Lear's knights does speak with proper respect, asking pardon for plain speaking when he reports the 'great abatement of kindness' shown by their hosts and their servants (ll. 56–65). He is, in effect, the one sober man who shows up the behaviour of a gang of drunks. Fool's performance – his wit, pranks, questions, denunciations, songs – leads the drama into even less restricted and more fantastic territory, where he, and not the king, takes charge. At one point, he makes Lear stand in his place as a fool (ll. 139–47); at another, he so castigates his master that he is threatened with 'the whip' – perhaps one that Lear had held and was cracking when he came in from the hunt, having used it on his horse or dogs (l. 109 and ll. 162–3, 178–85). As many of Lear's 100 knights as the acting company can muster are likely to join in the games initiated by the fool, perhaps clapping or stamping in time with his doggerel, or following him as he dances and sings around the king:

> *Have more than thou showest,*
> *Speak less than thou knowest, …*
>
> (ll. 117–26)

They are unlikely to stand around passively: Hamlet says that Yorick, the king's jester, was 'wont to set the table on a roar' (*Hamlet*, V.i.184–5) and Feste's companions in *Twelfth Night* are said to 'caterwaul' together and 'gabble like tinkers' (II.iii.70–1, 83–8). Lear stands like a man at a mark with the whole company on stage and in the audience ready to laugh at whatever the fool dares to say about him. Sometimes the knights may be shocked by Fool's temerity and a joke may fall flat in dead silence – for instance, at 'I would not be thee, nuncle: thou hast pared thy wit o'both sides and left nothing i'th' middle.' Eventually, laughter and noise bring Goneril on stage where her silent, frowning presence at once draws Fool's attention and, momentarily, silences even him.

As Lear and the fool had been previously, Goneril is now the centre of attention, able to take time before denouncing the 'rank and not to be endured riots' and her father's encouragement of them (l. 202). At first Lear is incredulous, the fool responding before he does. When he does bring himself to address Goneril, she stands her ground and replies by laying the blame squarely on him, threatening to discipline or dismiss the knights herself if he will not do so. Having listened in silence, Lear can bear it no longer:

> Darkness and devils!
> Saddle my horses; call my train together.
> Degenerate bastard! I'll not trouble thee;
> Yet have I left a daughter.
>
> (ll. 251–4)

All eyes will focus on Lear as that last incomplete verse-line shows him to be stunned, unable to move or to say more. Goneril continues to upbraid him, more specifically now, while he prepares to go to his other daughter, Regan. His anger and misery are whetted by a contrasting realization of his own mistakes: 'Woe [to him] that too late repents!' (l. 257). The focus is divided now between father and daughter, others on stage remaining quiet and, probably, quite still – there is an echo here of the confrontations in the play's opening scene.

Goneril's husband, the Duke of Albany, enters at this point but stands watching silently, even when Lear addresses him; only later does he speak briefly and ineffectively: 'Pray, sir, be patient' (l. 261). Nothing deflects Lear until he suddenly remembers the 'most small fault' in Cordelia that had:

> ... like an engine wrench'd my frame of nature
> From the fix'd place; drew from my heart all love
> And added to the gall.
>
> (ll. 266–70)

Recoiling from that memory, the flow of words stops and, as if convulsed and helpless, he repeatedly calls out his own name and beats upon his head. Then, having ordered his followers to leave the stage, he regains his strength for a sustained and very precise curse:

> Hear, Nature, hear; dear goddess, hear.
> Suspend thy purpose, if thou didst intend
> To make this creature fruitful.

The incomplete verse-line indicates that everyone else is silent and implies that overwhelming emotion takes possession of him before he continues:

> Into her womb convey sterility;
> Dry up in her the organs of increase ...
>
> (ll. 275–89)

Finishing the curse, he remembers the biting pain Goneril has inflicted, 'sharper than a serpent's tooth', and then, impetuously, he calls out, 'Away, away!', as if fleeing from the loss of love and respect.

Physically Lear has become alarmingly unpredictable and deeply disturbed. At this point both the original texts are unclear about what should happen. The Folio has two stage-directions, one for 'Exit' and another, only three and a half lines later, for '*Enter Lear*': these imply that the king should leave and almost immediately return. Most editors adopt this reading and direct the fool to go with him. On his return Lear says that within a fortnight 50 of his followers have been dismissed 'at a clap' and one editor[2] has suggested that an audience would be expected to imagine that two weeks have passed before his re-entry, during which time Goneril and Albany remain on stage. The Quarto text, however, avoids placing this burden on both audience and players by giving no stage-direction at all at this juncture. This may well be the better reading, implying that Lear would remain on stage weeping, only able to speak after a painful physical and emotional struggle (see ll. 296–8).

Goneril has already threatened to reduce the number of knights so Lear's heightened and turbulent imagination might have raced ahead to specific consequences. When Lear does speak again, he is still concerned with his wrongs but says nothing to imply that he has been pondering them for a fortnight: instead he speaks of his 'hot tears' and Goneril's 'power to shake [his] manhood' (ll. 294–9) as though these had been his most recent experience; he threatens to 'pluck' out his 'old fond eyes' should they weep again (ll. 301–4).[3] Lear leaves the stage finally, either for the first or second time, to go to Regan and resume the power that he had intended to 'cast off for ever'. Frightened by what he has witnessed, Fool has said nothing for more than 80 lines and now he does not move until Goneril orders him to follow his master. In a context that draws all eyes to him, the way he leaves the stage will be the physical expression of a new and frightened relationship to his master.

The actor playing Lear must transform himself during the course of this scene. He changes from a king, who has 'authority' (I.iv.30) and is the centre of attention, to a passionate and affronted father whose suffering is as plain to see as his anger and frustration is to hear; finally, he becomes an isolated man who leaves the stage racked by memories and with all emotional resources spent: 'Ha!', he exclaims, 'Is't come to this?', before adding, 'Let it be so' (ll. 304–5). With Lear's physical changes, an audience's reaction to him will have changed too: whatever judgement it makes about his mental instability and arrogance or about Goneril's justification for taking command, it will know, as Lear does not, that Regan will disappoint his hopes. It will also have witnessed the pain that he feels and its instinctive sense-reactions to this may be the strongest response of all: suffering has been sustained through much of the scene and made visually manifest in repeated actions, without need for words and regardless of rights and wrongs.

So far, the only other person who so dominates a scene has been Edmund. He is very different from Lear in being young and without rights or possessions; besides, he is in control both of himself and of the events he has set in motion. He also speaks in soliloquy, as Lear does not, and so can share his thoughts directly with an audience. Nevertheless, the attention they both receive by being continuously centre-stage will encourage an audience to view them in relation to each other as they pursue their own purposes and not the customary demands of society or patterns of family life. Nothing that is spoken draws these connections to an audience's attention but the way Shakespeare has handled the play's action will do so inevitably. Because any perceptions that arise from this will seem to be their own discovery, an audience will be drawn into a close involvement with both persons before further events unfold.

For the next short scene, Shakespeare arranged a contrast to the pomp and authority of Lear's first entry in the play and to the commotion and conflicts of the preceding scene. The king, dressed now for travelling, is alone with Caius/Kent, the fool and, probably, one gentleman; they are on the move, Kent being sent off at once to Gloucester and Regan, and Fool and the Gentleman asked if horses are ready. During this business, Fool tries to serve and engage with his master as he had done before; but as he quizzes him and warns that Regan will be as hostile as Goneril, Lear follows what he is saying with only half his mind. No longer goaded by Goneril, no longer weeping or racked by passion, hardly paying attention to anything but his own predicament, he speaks out of experience in a series of short, disconnected utterances that together function like a painful and unwilled soliloquy: 'I did her wrong ... I will forget my nature. So kind a father! ... To take't again perforce! Monster ingratitude!' (I.v.24, 31-2, 38-9). When Fool chides him for being old before he is wise, something snaps within Lear. In the first verse-lines of this scene, he forgets his daughters and prays to the gods for his own sanity:

> O, let me not be mad, not mad, sweet heaven!
> Keep me in temper; I would not be mad!
>
> (ll. 43–4)

The repeated *mad* could hardly be more effectively introduced. Lear's isolation from his retinue and family, his
inner concentration, the simplicity of the entire sequence
of his short speeches, and the posture he takes for prayer
to a 'sweet heaven' all mark this scene apart from everything that has come before. Visual contrast with the violence of earlier scenes accentuates the new isolation and
the depth from which his fear of madness springs. With
'How now! are the horses ready?', Lear leaves without
ceremony but calling 'Come, boy' to his fool, as if he
needs to know that he is not entirely alone. Fool has an
almost irrelevant bawdy couplet to complete the scene,
suggesting that he needs to assert his professionalism in
an effort to maintain sanity or find courage. Whether
Lear waits for him or Fool has to run to catch up with his
master, these two lone figures, as they draw physically
together, will make a further, non-verbal comment on
what has happened within Lear and in relation to his
family and realm. The text offers no guidance on how
they leave and so whatever they do is almost bound to be
improvised and will depend upon how they have sever-
ally acted until this moment. This means that an audience will focus on them as they come silently to terms
with all that has happened; it could be an intimate
moment shared between actors and spectators.

Physical contrasts and visual interplay are vital elements
in the choreography of Shakespeare's plays, changing
from scene to scene and within each scene. Like Lear's
daughters, Edgar and Edmund are presented in contrasting ways. While Edmund's dominance relates him to Lear
in the early Acts, Edgar's more private nature and subsequent service to his father awaken echoes of Cordelia.
Both Gloucester's sons are misunderstood by their father,
as Goneril, Regan, and Cordelia are by theirs. Disguising
himself as poor Tom, the mad beggar, and meeting with
Lear and the fool on the heath, Edgar's pretended
madness and baffling speeches will echo the professional
folly of the fool and help to identify the beginning of real

madness in the king. Almost as soon as they meet, Lear will later direct attention to Edgar's near nakedness as an image of his own dispossession and defencelessness. The long 'pilgrimage' of Edgar with Gloucester (V.iii.196) has parallels with the journey of Lear, Fool, and Kent. All these parallels and more, some involving other persons in the play, are marked in speech as well as action and so their significance in the structure of the play will be noted by any thoughtful reader. But when the text becomes part of a theatrical event, the nature of this interplay changes: embodied in performances, these contrasts and correspondences draw on the actors' instincts, as well as intelligence, and bring about major changes in physical behaviour and expressiveness. Thoroughly realized, they command an audience's attention visually and so awaken an additional response that is sensuous and bodily – and one that operates, as Arnheim has demonstrated, in advance of verbal communication. The effect of this is to create an impression of actuality without recourse to words: spectators are encouraged to seek out what is happening for themselves in whatever way imagination and individual life-experience suggest.

Notes

1. *Twelfth Night*, III.iv.213–14.
2. G. K. Hunter, New Penguin edition (London: 1972).
3. Another explanation of why Lear speaks of the dismissal of 50 knights might be that Shakespeare wanted to draw the narrative forward strongly and knew that a varied and passionate performance would allow an audience little opportunity to notice an inconsistent exposition.

9

Improvisation

Between Shakespeare's time and our own, theatre has changed in many ways, in the composition and behaviour of audiences and in the setting and staging of plays. Among these changes, although not always obvious, the degree of improvisation used by actors and stage technicians has been a major influence on the staging and reception of Shakespeare's plays. Today, productions are carefully prepared to ensure that one chosen interpretation of the text is expressed throughout the actors' performances and in the play's setting and technical support. The aim is to give the strongest possible effect to each distinctive production. The public benefits from this in that, having a good idea of what they will see from pre-publicity and journalistic reviews, they can choose what they pay for. Successful producers are able to offer the same production, essentially unchanged, over a period of many months and sometimes several years.

Yet comparison with what can be deduced about the plays' original performances is not entirely in favour of the new; we pay dearly for theatrical assurance and its promotional advantages. An audience no longer shares the excitement of fresh discovery and productions have little scope for responding to topical and local events. Worst of all, actors' performances run against the grain of Shakespeare's playscripts by trying to fix what was written to be flexible and, occasionally, mysterious. Actors are tempted to play safe instead of putting themselves at risk each time they take on a person of

Shakespeare's invention. They find themselves pretend-
ing to be spontaneous in response to the energy of the
writing, its rapid changes of mood, fresh sensations, and
questing intelligence. Their performances seldom come
into first life before the eyes of their audiences or seem to
take unexpected flight, as the early improvised ones
might have done.

The Potential of Improvisation

The notion of improvised performances of Shakespeare
is open to ridicule because theatre production has
become a serious business and its artifice intricate and
studied. Almost all the theatres that perform his plays
today neglect the skills needed for improvisation and, in
consequence, no longer believe that they should be
developed. In professional circles, this kind of acting is
associated with creative drama classes in schools, stand-
up comedians, and theatre companies that perform in
streets and public places, for whom bold words and clear
action are necessary staples rather than the subtlety of
Hamlet or *Twelfth Night*. Or improvisation is, more simply,
what happens when something goes wrong and anything
is better than nothing.

Improvisation has a far wider range than this. The *commedia dell'arte* companies of Italy were conspicuous among theatres of the past that knew its power and depended on it.
Following the outline provided by a *scenario*, not written dialogue, assuming standardized characters, and using the
stage-business of well-practised *lazzi*, their actors improvised
whole plays that reflected topical and local life. They could
give lively impressions of immediately recognizable people
and speak directly to their audiences. Dramatists learned
from this Italian success and soon were writing plays in
which dialogue and much of the stage-business allowed
plenty of scope for improvisation. Among these, Molière
was pre-eminent. The time he spent touring the provinces
in makeshift conditions, before audiences unschooled in
polite and quiet appreciation, would have taught him the

basic skills of improvisation. When he settled in Paris, his company was in competition with a highly successful Italian *commedia* company. Even his mature plays call for improvisation.[1] In *Dom Juan*, for instance, the actor of Sganarelle, alone on stage at the very start of the play, must hold his audience's attention with a long and complicated speech about the benefits of tobacco. In the play's last moments, having watched his master descend into the flames of hell, this servant has two words with which to express his own feelings. The actor – in the first performances he was the play's author – must discover how to call out 'My wages! My wages! My wages!' so that the play is brought to a satisfactory conclusion.[2] On the page, this may seem a weak ending for a strong narrative, but with skilled improvisation the two words can be varied each time they are spoken so that they express Sganarelle's growing realization of his new predicament. They can provide a dark and heartless ending or an eminently clear-sighted one. The simple, everyday words are able to suggest panic, ineptitude, fatalism, determination to seek compensation, or, possibly, satisfaction at Juan's death, the flames being Sganarelle's wages given in recompense for mistreatment. Throughout the play, the actor of Dom Juan also needs to be a skilful improviser if he is to make all his seductions credible, especially when he woos two peasant girls at the same time and must keep each competitive and suspicious victim from realizing what he is doing with the other. Actors in Molière's plays need to have cool heads and instantaneously inventive performances.

In ancient Greece, where many months were taken to prepare a play, it might seem that actors had little call to be able to improvise, but these festival offerings were performed only once a year, on one special day. With neither previews nor out-of-town try-out, an actor would have only that single opportunity to appear in an entirely new role, making whatever adjustments were necessary as he responded to the inevitable accidents of a first performance and the unforeseeable reactions of a huge audience. Few actors today have to handle the stress of such a competitive occasion and adjust their performances to its last-minute demands. Much the same problems were faced in medieval mystery plays and the civic and princely celebrations of the renaissance. Actors experienced in these conditions must have accepted them as opportunities to shine and show their improvisational skills. In some cases their audiences would have known the narratives that were to be enacted so that, consequently, *how* the actors performed and *how* the plays reflected topical and local concerns would have been keenly observed, enjoyed, and encouraged; it is probable that here lay a large part of their appeal. Ability to cope with these ephemeral performances would have been found in any company that, like the King's Men, appeared regularly in plays for only one night at a time, toured for weeks to many ad hoc theatre-spaces, and were hired for occasional appearances in court masques and civic triumphs.

Popular forms of theatre, such as vaudeville, burlesque, and melodrama, in which performers are in close contact with their audiences, kept improvisation alive and well regarded until comparatively recent times. But nowadays only a few clowns and fools are expected to improvise 'more than is set down for them' (*Hamlet*, III.ii.37–9) and play each moment freely in response to an audience. As the physical staging of a play became more complicated and more impressive, the task of actors was bound to change. The unstoppable progress of technology, starting with gas and then electric lighting, has meant that they have lost contact with their audiences sitting 'out front' in the dark and are no longer so free to address them directly or respond to their reactions. Stage-managers and the specialist operators of light, sound, and remote-controlled scenic effects, keep strict charge of a production but find difficulty in accommodating any changes that actors might make during a performance. Some scholars and critics who study the texts with exceptional application have tended to encourage these practices by arguing that the words, that at one time were freely spoken, should be given certain exact and inflexible meanings.

In general, only simply equipped and simply run theatres have much use for improvisation today, and then only in comedy. Kathakali and Kuttiyattam performances, in Kerala of southern India, are among the exceptions. They present highly sophisticated and carefully prepared dramas for which actors start training in childhood and spend many years in developing the necessary physical and vocal skills to improvise both words and elaborate physical gestures on stages that are small, bare, and without changeable scenery. These actors need to possess detailed knowledge of dramatic form, great concentration, and vivid imaginations so that they can awaken their audiences' imaginations and draw them into a world where passions are strong and dramatic conflict, both metaphysical and dynastic, of crucial importance.

While twentieth-century theatres belittle or downgrade improvisation, the public still has an appetite for witnessing highly skilled performers operating at full stretch and reacting to momentary opportunities. These are among the qualities that attract enthusiastic crowds to football stadiums and intent spectators at top-line tennis tournaments. In a game of cricket, two or three players can hold attention as they respond to unforeseeable challenges over a long period of time. Almost any team-sport mirrors improvised theatre in requiring a close and mutual understanding between players and in offering spectators a shared sense of a unique occasion. It is tempting to believe that, if our actors deployed similar skills while giving challenging and unique performances, our theatres would be as crowded with enthusiastic spectators as the stands of sports grounds. The excitement to be gained by not knowing which way a game will go or who will play a major role in victory would seem to be entirely missing at a performance of a set text and yet, to some extent, that too can be found at an improvised production. While the audience knows that Macbeth or Hamlet will die and many of them remember the circumstances in which this will happen, no one can know *how* these heroes will die, what will be the effect of death and what emotions and sensations will be involved at that moment. Shakespeare's plays offer plenty of scope for improvisation and are open to unexpected development and conclusion.

The Scope for Improvisation in Shakespeare's Texts

Theatre practices of Shakespeare's day encouraged improvisation. The open stage of the Globe and the simpler stages encountered on tour, together with a circled audience many of whom would be standing, were conducive to performances that evolved freely on each occasion according to the moment-by-moment life of the play and the response of its audience. The ever-changing repertoire of Elizabethan theatres, with one out of many plays chosen for performance each day, meant that actors could not repeat how all their hundreds of words in a particular text were spoken from one performance to another, days and perhaps weeks later. Appearing in ten or more plays within weeks of each other, remembering a single role, how and where essential movements were to be made, and how stage-business was to be shared with other actors would have been burden enough for the most retentive memories. The rest of the performances must have depended on improvisation and fresh invention as the cast came together to re-create the persons of the play and carry its narrative forward. Fortunately and co-incidentally, the long-lasting, close-knit company of the King's Men would have been more able to respond to the corporate challenge than the short-lived or continually changing theatre companies of today. To stage Shakespeare well in present-day theatres, instead of downgrading improvisation to being a comic device of limited usefulness, we should recognize it as a highly skilled aspect of an actor's art. Actors should develop this facility if the plays are to be staged in a style that respects the way in which they were written.

The need for improvisation has been argued several times in the course of this book. If the persons of a play are to come convincingly to life on stage their words must seem to spring from thoughts and feelings that are experienced, unexpectedly, moment by moment. Assurance must seem to be founded on inner necessity, hesitation on present uncertainty. Seldom should Shakespeare's speeches be spoken with a settled and one-directional energy, most of them being articulated and varied by the writer's darting, far-reaching intelligence. The variety of metaphor and rhythm will only be credible in speech if quick sensations as well as active minds shape and empower performance. When two or more actors engage in dialogue, their words should be able to give the impression of quite separate and unprepared minds engaged in pursuit of their independent objectives; at other times, they should reach out to express more than either person could conceive on his or her own account. When played with spontaneity and imagination the texts light up with fresh invention and inspire actors to give astonishing and unique performances.

To improvise in this way, actors must have mastered the techniques of verse-speaking, phrasing, syntax, multiple and far-fetched meanings, and all the other refinements of Shakespeare's writings, so that response can be instinctive and quick, as if second nature. Constant practice and natural aptitude are both required, so that the technique, once acquired, can be forgotten in performance without loss of its benefits. In much the same way, when we are at the wheel of a car, we do not consciously think about what we were taught in driving lessons long ago. As well as this individual preparation, the cast of a play need to be practised at acting together so that they can develop rapport or antagonism with equal facility and draw on the extra energy and concision that arise out of mutual engagement. A company of actors brought together to perform only one play, as sometimes happens today, will always lack an adequate synergy for presenting the inner forces that drive a play's narrative. Small touring companies that spend long periods together on the road, in this respect are more likely to serve the plays well, their communal off-stage life giving them unusual freedom in acting Shakespeare because experienced group-knowledge has been added to self-knowledge.

Perhaps the closest a present-day audience can come to improvised Shakespeare will be found in a public workshop which 'explores' a text to show students the demands it makes on actors and the range of meanings it

can communicate. Here nothing is fixed and the actors
are ready to experiment, knowing that variety is expected
and not 'finished' performances. For example, actors
from a National Theatre production of *As You Like It*
showed in workshop how the scene at the beginning of
Act IV might go between Rosalind, Celia, Jaques and
Orlando, roles they were not playing in the evenings. The
Orlando played at first as if he was always talking to a
shepherd called Ganymede and not to 'his Rosalind', and
then, as if he had forgotten the deception, he began
instinctively to think of Ganymede as a girl. Between
these two ways of playing the text no decision was made
about which should be preferred and so the relationship
between Rosalind and Orlando changed continuously, in
humour, intelligence, physical contact, and sexual suggestion. When the actor played as if he had an inkling or
was sure that he was speaking to Rosalind, he would
sometimes come closer to her and sometimes be reluc-
tant to do so. Faced with these changing performances,
Rosalind spoke her confident lines either because she
was sure of her love for Orlando or because she was
trying to hide her doubts of his love for herself. Celia's
presence was not noticed and she was forgotten until the
actress began to come forward to be an on-stage audience for the charade and became increasingly active in
laughter and applause. Her single verbal intervention –
'he hath a Rosalind of a better leer than you' (ll. 59–60) –
was tried at first as a warning to her cousin not to take
the pretence too seriously and then, since it follows talk
of horns and horn-making, as a warning not to go too far
in sexual innuendo. She then used it as a similar warning
to Orlando, then as a means of testing how far both were
deceiving themselves, and then as a way to heighten her
own enjoyment of the comedy of courtship. As these different ways of playing were attempted, with greater or
lesser degrees of intimacy, the actors found that the text
nowhere provided clear instructions either for or against
any of the interpretations.

    The scene starts with talk between Rosalind and Jaques
about 'acquaintance' and 'melancholy', topics of concern

to both persons. When Orlando enters, late for his appointment, this Rosalind instinctively turned the talk into a veiled reproach for her declared lover. Orlando's first words seemed simple in contrast but Jaques' response raised a whole clutch of possibilities:

> ROSALIND ... I had rather have a fool to make me merry than experience to make me sad – and to travel [or travail, i.e., work] for it too.
> ORLANDO   Good day, and happiness, dear Rosalind!
> JAQUES   Nay, then, God buy you, an you talk in blank verse.
> ROSALIND   Farewell, Monsieur Traveller; ...
>
> (ll. 24 ff.)

How could Jaques, with the most senior actor in the company normally cast in this role, make an effective exit with such a seeming irrelevance or cheap jibe? Should he puncture an overly theatrical flourish that Orlando has assumed to divert attention from his late arrival? Or, since Jaques has been talking to Rosalind, does he continue to address her as she is obviously on the point of answering Orlando in a similar fashion ? Or are Jaques's words a response to the absurdity of Orlando addressing the boy Ganymede as if she were a woman, so that he puns on 'blank' in its other current meanings of 'void, empty, meaningless'? These alternatives may not seem of much significance either to the progress of the scene or the presentation of Jaques but then the actor tried leaving the stage on the last word of his short speech and not half-a-dozen lines later during Rosalind's response, which is where most modern editions insert an unauthorized *Exit*. With this physical emphasis, Jaques's short speech became much more decisive and drew laughter and applause from its audience in the theatre: he was fireproof while the lovers were left momentarily speechless. Rosalind was the first to recover and followed Jaques's exit across the broad spaces of the Olivier stage speaking words to which he did not bother to reply and which seemed intended to strengthen her position in relation to Orlando, making him wait before his presence is acknowledged as a punishment for his lateness; they also gave herself time to prepare a sharp reproof. The timing of an exit and the way one line was delivered had changed the progress of the scene and the relationship between all three persons involved. None of this is inscribed in Shakespeare's text but actors will always have to respond to each of the many issues that the speeches present to them. So loose is the text's control here, as it is on countless other occasions, that the players either have to spend long rehearsals in deciding what they should do or they must respond spontaneously as each performance develops before an audience. Speaking lines and being the person who speaks them comprise only part of an actor's task: Shakespeare's words presuppose a fuller performance than that, one that is infinitely variable and, in many significant respects, impossible to fix.

When speaking the words of one of Shakespeare's texts, innumerable possibilities open up in small details of physical performance. As Antonin Artaud wrote:

A movement, a gesture in the nick of time sometimes does more to elucidate a complicated thought than all the treasures of the spoken language.[3]

Such fine details are even more difficult than speech to repeat in exactly the same form from one performance to another. Although actors and their director become aware in rehearsals of how movement, gesture, timing, and phrasing can change performances, a common practice today is to make a number of choices for the actors to hold on to in order to keep the play running along consistent lines and strengthen a particular interpretation of the whole play. The alternative of improvised performance is far riskier and can lead to unmanageable confusion.

Even without an audience, too great a freedom can be thought dangerous today. In a rehearsal of the last scene of *The Tempest*, the Miranda was frightened as well as amazed when she looked around at the assembled company and so, having said 'O brave new world / That has such people in't!' (ll. 183–4), she ran, instinctively, across the stage to cling to the one person she had known all her life. Prospero's very brief reply, "Tis new to thee', then spoke of his concern for his daughter, not only of his bitter knowledge of the world as it had done in previous rehearsals: he felt with her and comforted her, as well as warning her of disappointment. This way of playing was not retained in the production; her movement was judged too great a surprise and the feelings expressed too disturbing for Prospero because they were contrary to the resignation and weariness he felt and would cause his 'every third thought' to be of his grave (l. 401). In performance of the production, Prospero spoke across the stage, at a distance from his daughter, and seemed self-absorbed as he did so. Another director and another leading actor might have judged otherwise: at the beginning of the play, taking place on the same day, Prospero had spoken of Miranda as 'a cherubin' who had preserved him (I.ii.152–3) so there is precedent for being instrumental in preserving his compassion now.

Although actors have fixed words to speak, the rest of their performances will always exist on a sea of opportunity that is largely uncharted. Shakespeare's plays are a very special case because, whatever course the actors take, they find the texts continually suggestive and supportive; their writer must have visualized free performances as he set down the words.

If the plays are kept open to the contributions of actors, they will be forever updated to reflect the interests of persons living in the time and place of each performance. However distant or exotic the events presented in the play, its performance draws imaginatively on familiar reality and everyday concerns.[4] No one on stage or in the audience will have 'supp'd full with horrors' or thought of plucking her nipple 'from the boneless gums' of her own baby and 'dashing' its brains out (*Macbeth*, V.v.13 and I.vii.54–8), but the present-day experience and imagination of actors can give to *supping full, plucking, boneless gums,* or *dashing out* an immediacy that will carry all amazing action of the play into performances that allow an audience to share in the sensation of being the persons involved. With skilful improvisation, developed in long practice, the effect is both recognizable and startling: the play takes on such vivid and imaginative life that actors and audience share in a moment of discovery and triumph. This kind of theatrical event has an attraction that can make theatre truly popular, as Shakespeare's plays were in his own day.

Notes

1. See Gerry McCarthy's *Molière's Theatres* (London and New York: Routledge, 2002), pp. 36–40, for an account of how the Italians were received in Paris and their influence on Molière.
2. '*Mes gages!*' was first found in an edition published at Amsterdam in 1683 in which lines that had been cut by the censor had been restored. Earlier French editions had provided a moral reflection with clearer meaning in the place of the two words, perhaps as an acceptable or prudent alternative.
3. Antonin Artaud, *Collected Works*, trans. Alastair Hamilton, vol. 3 (London: Calder & Boyars, 1972), p. 211.
4. See examples on pp. 48–9, above, and pp. 199–200 below.

PART III: CONTEXTS

10

Stage Space

Anyone with a grammar school education in Shakespeare's day would have known that the word *theatre* derived from Latin, with the meaning of a place for viewing or a public arena. *Playhouse* was a more specific word, a document of 8 January 1600 referring to 'the late erected playhouse on the Bank ... called the Globe'. This word seems to have been a new coinage, the first literary citation in the Oxford *New English Dictionary* being Shakespeare's *Henry V* of 1599 (II. Chorus, 36). But earlier, John Norden's map of London in his *Speculum Britanniae* of 1593 shows two circular buildings just south of the river which he identified as 'The Bear house' and 'The Play house', the latter representing the Rose theatre that had been built in 1587. These inscriptions defined purpose: actors were to be seen performing in the playhouse and in the bearhouse animals were watched being baited. The older *theatre* came to be used with much the same intention, as in 'An Excellent Actor' in the collection of *Characters* of 1615:[1]

> sit in a full theatre, and you will think you see so many lines drawn from the circumference of so many ears, whiles the actor is the centre.

Playhouse, plays, actors, and audience were all that was needed to create a theatrical event, a stage set up within the auditorium providing space for performance with little other physical support. Shakespeare's plays could be performed almost anywhere that could accommodate an audience: they toured to the various palaces of the court, to great houses, town halls, schools, and colleges, to inn yards and, sometimes, to suitable spaces out of doors. Unlike its well-equipped successors in later centuries, the stage was little more than a space – an 'unworthy scaffold' (*Henry V*, Prol. 10) – with small, even negligible, resources. Within this constant context, however, what today would be called the setting for a play could be varied continuously by the deployment of actors. Elizabethans sometimes spoke of plays as *shows*,[2] so eye-catching were the changing images created.

Changeable Settings in Performance

Costume-changes and stage-properties, that have already been noticed for their effect on the actors' performances,[3] were among Shakespeare's means for creating a varied sequence of visual settings for dramatic action. In *Hamlet*, for instance, after a first scene set at night and in bitter cold, with armed sentries and a questing Ghost, the action moves to a wedding celebration at the royal court, full of rich clothes, pomp, and political confrontations. A little later, two students arrive from a distant university and they are followed by a band of players who will perform before the reassembled court. Mother and son meet in a private room. A foreign army marches across the stage as Hamlet leaves for England; Ophelia enters in crazed distress; a rabble of insurgents try to break onto the stage and Ophelia returns to sing and distribute flowers; 'seafaring men' briefly appear delivering letters. The action moves to a graveyard where the gravedigger talks with his assistant and sings; then the prince returns disguised in a 'sea-gown' and, briefly, attention is held by a skull and dead men's bones, a funeral procession, and hand-to-hand fighting. Back indoors, for a third time the court assembles, a duel is fought, the prince and others die, and the foreign army returns in victory, accompanied with English Ambassadors, drum, colours, and attendants; four of its captains carry the dead prince off-stage while cannon fire in salute. Even this brief and selective summary indicates how the coming and going of actors, with what they wear and what they do, combine to give the tragedy a changing visual context; the play is a 'show' as well as a story told in words and action.

Shakespeare would sometimes create a world with two different faces by varying the deployment of actors on the open stage. The action of *The Merchant of Venice* moves repeatedly from Venice to Belmont and back again, each place given a distinct visual setting by different concerns, manners, ways of speaking, costumes, and properties. For *Othello*, the action shifts from the palaces and streets of Venice to a military outpost on the island of Cyprus; for *The Winter's Tale*, from a sophisticated court in Sicily to a pastoral retreat in Bohemia, and back again. In some plays, the movement and grouping of actors radically alter the visual show without involving any change of location. For example, in *Much Ado About Nothing*, the scene in Leonato's chapel is established by processional entries, formal words and restrained behaviour; Hero is in her bridal dress and, as the custom was, her hair is loose. This solemn order is then shattered when Claudio denounces his bride as 'an approved wanton' (IV.i.43); soon Benedick and Beatrice are alone on stage and the chapel no longer registers: they are free from its restraints.

While scenic flexibility is a mark of almost all plays of the period, Shakespeare was especially adroit at effecting unexpected and swift changes of mood by the introduction of strikingly new elements. In *As You Like It*, for example, the entrance of the god Hymen, either in supposed reality or in a masque-like or simpler folk celebration, stops everyone in their tracks and bars all 'confusion' (V.iv.119). In later plays, gods appear even more impressively and are greeted with silent awe: in *Pericles* Diana appears to a silenced king, in *Cymbeline* the roof, or 'heavens', over the stage opens so that Jupiter can descend on his eagle to address the ghosts of Posthumus's family. In *The Winter's Tale*, Apollo's oracle is neither heard nor seen, but two messengers enter still affected by a ceremonious sacrifice at the temple and a voice that had 'so surpris'd my sense, / That I was nothing' (III.i.1–11). In *The Tempest*, three goddesses appear in the masque that Prospero offers his daughter and her betrothed; their performances make Ferdinand full of wonder, as if he were in 'paradise' (IV.i.118–24).

The actors' physical actions are sufficient to change the mood of a setting. Midway through *Henry IV, Part One*, Lady Mortimer asks her husband to lie down on 'wanton rushes' and rest his 'gentle head upon her lap' and, when the scene has been reordered in this way, she sings to him tenderly in Welsh (III.i.207 ff.). Just before battle in Act IV of *Julius Caesar*, Brutus sits reading a book with a lit taper beside him and the boy Lucius, who plays music and sings to him, falls asleep during the stillness (IV.iii.254 ff.). Music often contributes to a change of setting and mood, for example when a boy sings about the loss of love as the action of *Measure for Measure* moves to Mariana's 'moated grange' (IV.i.1–6). In *Troilus and Cressida*, music is heard from off-stage when the location shifts to the house of Paris and Helen (see III.i.16–32). Act IV, scene iii of *Othello*, in which Desdemona prepares for bed and talks intimately with Emilia, seems to move into another time and place when she sings the 'Willow Song' that mad Barbara, forsaken in love, had sung in her mother's house years before. Nowhere else in this tragedy is action so static or the setting so delicately realized; the scene prepares for the final change of location that follows alarms and action at night, reminiscent of those at the play's opening. Dressed only in her night clothes, Desdemona then lies on the bed that will provide the constant point of visual focus throughout the violence and terror that follows.

At the opposite extreme from changes of setting by means of small physical movements or music are those achieved by filling the stage with many actors; in Shakespeare's day their numbers could be swelled by doorkeepers, musicians and casual hirings. These crowds that could convert intimate scenes into theatrical shows of visual variety and strong physical impact were introduced by Shakespeare even when the story had no absolute call for them. At the start of *Much Ado*, when Leonato's household greets the return of Don Pedro and his soldiers from military action, 12 actors in named roles are needed on stage but they are supported by another dozen in the anonymous roles of musicians and the servants to heighten the celebrations. Later in the play '*Attendants*' are specifically required for Hero's wedding to Count Claudio and the 'great coil' involved in its preparation (IV.i.0, S.D. and III.iii.86–8). In the midst of this on-stage business, a band of watchmen has to be assembled who will require very different costumes and must be numerous enough to take command of Conrade and Borachio, two drunken and belligerent soldiers. The dialogue names only two watchmen as well as the Constable and Headborough but the more that are present the more credible will be the change of setting and the more effective its contrast with scenes of aristocratic and witty leisure.

History plays and tragedies in which rival factions and armies confront each other have the most spectacular crowd scenes and make the largest demands upon the acting companies. *Titus Andronicus, Richard the Third, Julius Caesar,* and *Coriolanus* call for numerous citizens to contrast with the princes, politicians and soldiers. *Titus, King John, Henry the Fifth, Troilus and Cressida,* and *Coriolanus* call additionally for racial differentiation, realized visually with contrasting costumes and insignia and with traces, at least, of different speech and behaviour. Theatres that are short of funds, as many are today, can stage these plays with minimal casts and much doubling of the parts – *Timon of Athens* has been produced with just three actors[4] – but then recorded speech and sound, computerized lighting effects and projections, mechanical devices, puppets and changeable scenery are likely to be introduced to compensate for lack of actors and retain, as far as possible, the variety of showmanship that is called for by the playscripts. An alternative economy is to cut or change a text radically and not pretend to stage the play as Shakespeare wrote it; in the present financial situation, this is often the only practicable possibility although it limits the play's spectacle and so shrinks its appeal. Experience has shown that productions of Shakespeare that do not fill the stage with actors are unlikely to fill theatres with audiences: not only is less left for the eye to see but the narrative goes forward without showing the repercussions of individual decisions and actions.

A few plays, notably *Twelfth Night* and *Othello*, can be produced with a cast of 10 or so actors without extensive doubling or cutting and yet, to stage the action in an appropriate context, 20 or more are desirable. In *Twelfth Night*, to set the scene in Orsino's court, he should have numerous attendants whenever he is on stage, even though they may be sent away almost immediately. When Viola makes her entrance to the play as a survivor from shipwreck accompanied by a Captain and an unspecified number of '*Sailors*', the more men who are present on stage to set the scene the more exposed will be the heroine's predicament. Maria is Olivia's one 'waiting gentlewoman' but the countess also has '*Attendants*' who establish her more feminine environment although only one of them speaks when delivering a message (V.i.90, S.D. and III.iv.55–8). Additionally, at least two Officers are called for at the end of Act III and again later: their presence establishes Orsino's power and peace-keeping responsibilities. Besides augmenting the spectacle and marking changes of location, a cast of at least 16 will mark the contrasting expectations of the two households.

Othello illustrates how Shakespeare was intent on placing a play's central action within a wider social context and, in doing so, would write with little or no thought of economizing in cast numbers. Although its action can be made sufficiently clear with 10 actors, the playscript calls for 20 or more and they would serve the tragedy far better. When Desdemona first professes love for her husband, the scene starts with 'the *Duke and senators, set at a table with lights; and Attendants*'; two messengers, one after another, bring news from the galleys at sea and then Brabantio, Othello, Iago and Roderigo enter accompanied by two sets of '*Officers*': Desdemona enters with yet more '*Attendants*'. Seventeen actors is the smallest possible number to do all that the playscript requires here and yet, in the preceding scene when Othello, Cassio, and Brabantio have entered separately, each of them was supported by '*Attendants*' or '*Officers*' carrying torches and weapons who proceed to fight against each other in two factions: more than a dozen actors are needed to stage this encounter adequately and none of them will have time to change into the robes of a duke or senator for the council of war that follows. After the two ships carrying Iago and Othello have arrived in Cyprus and after the riot that Iago engineers in Act II, scene iii, most of the following action requires no more than ten actors, the majority of scenes only two or three. Throughout most of the last three Acts, the task of establishing the setting depends on only three or four persons; it seems as if a noose is being pulled tighter by an inevitable and unwilled process.

When scenes that are crowded with actors are followed rapidly with ones in which only one or two persons are present, the focus is immediately narrowed and more personal issues dominate. All the plays use this alternation of scenes by which those with only a few figures are viewed with a closer focus that can increase the narrative's grip on an audience's attention. In the tragedies, especially *Romeo and Juliet, Hamlet, Macbeth* and *Lear*, the focus narrows frequently and produces scenes of exceptional intensity. Occasional use in *Richard the Second*, the Henry the Fourth plays, and *Henry the Fifth* brings a sense that, in isolation, the hero has reached a deeper and truer realization of what is at risk in the play's action.[5]

Imaginary Settings and Present-day Scenography

A context wider than any seen upon the stage is established when words create an imaginary setting in the minds of actors and audiences that is both evocative and limitless. This overreaching of the bounds of the stage is very characteristic of Shakespeare and gave rise to some of his most famously poetic passages. For example, after the Ghost has 'faded on the crowing of the cock' towards the end of the first scene of *Hamlet*, Horatio's speech directs attention to the distance:

> But look, the morn, in russet mantle clad,
> Walks o'er the dew of yon high eastward hill, ...
>
> (ll. 166-7)

The theatre did not, of course, contain a hill and, in Shakespeare's day, the light was what chance provided during an afternoon performance on a stage that was open to the sky or, alternatively, whatever was provided throughout the play in a candle-lit hall. Yet Horatio speaks as if the hill were actually present and evokes that landscape by images of a rising dawn and the slow passage of time, an illusion that is touched with transitory 'dew' and coloured by autumnal 'russet'. The suggestion of a physical figure that has clad itself in a mantle gives a further evocation of activity that contrasts with the slow dawning of the eastern light. While all this is unlikely to register at the moment of performance in the consciousness of either the actor or a member of his audience, it lurks within Horatio's words and can stir in a mind subconsciously.

Sometimes an imaginary context tends to obliterate every other impression. A prime example is in *Macbeth* when the newly crowned king has experienced the affliction of 'terrible dreams / That shake us nightly' and recognizes that 'we have scotch'd the snake, not kill'd it' (III.ii.13–22). Already he has set about the murder of Banquo but does not tell his wife of this; instead, having counselled her to be 'jocund', he speaks of an awesome and minutely imagined world that he inhabits in his mind:

> Ere the bat hath flown
> His cloister'd flight; ere to black Hecate's summons
> The shard-borne beetle with his drowsy hums
> Hath rung night's yawning peal, there shall be done
> A deed of dreadful note.

Lady Macbeth, having sought this meeting, now senses
her exclusion and asks 'What's to be done?' Macbeth
brushes the practical question aside almost tenderly – 'Be
innocent of the knowledge, dearest chuck, / Till thou
applaud the deed' – and then becomes still more
obsessed with darkness and violence, sensuously and particularly imagined:

> Light thickens, and the crow
> Makes wing to th' rooky wood;
> Good things of day begin to droop and drowse,
> Whiles night's black agents to their preys do rouse.
> (III.ii.40–53)

This context for action, that could never be physically
presented on any stage, is created in the imagination by
words that are sustained by slow but assertive rhythms
and driven home by rhyme. Lady Macbeth says nothing
and, if more were needed to establish the vast space that
Macbeth inhabits in his mind, her new passivity marks
their distance apart; she is now the one who seems to be
'lost so poorly' in her thoughts (II.ii.71–2):

> Thou marvell'st at my words; but hold thee still:
> Things bad begun make strong themselves by ill.
> So, prithee go with me.   [*Exeunt*]
> (ll. 54–6)

Imaginary contexts like these have rendered Shakespeare's plays highly susceptible to late twentieth-century
scene design or, more properly, scenography, an art that
can use recently developed technology and encompass the
structure of the theatre as well as everything visible on
stage. Each new production of a play is given a distinctive
look by changeable scenery, lighting, and sound effects, all
painstakingly developed in studios and workshops during
long weeks of preparation and rehearsal. The cost can be
high and the design so striking that it affects an audience's
response even before an actor steps onto the stage.
Contrast with original conditions of performance could

scarcely be greater. In those days, as we have seen, actors were the centre of attention and their physical and vocal performances largely responsible for establishing the context for a play's action. By present-day standards, these means were very simple and incapable of the broad vistas and carefully constructed interiors that are now common-place in well-financed productions. Today, seemingly without effort, large stage settings can disappear or open out to new perspectives or more subtle mysteries. Special lighting and sound effects can make any speech or small movement more impressive than the actors could ensure by their own efforts. A stage set can ensure that a certain mood is unmistakably established or draw attention to whatever aspect of a play's argument the director has chosen to emphasize. Even in our poorer theatres, especially designed and constructed costumes mark historical or topical references almost regardless of the performers' qualities. Visually, a Shakespeare production is likely to be more striking than formerly, the setting making its own independent contribution to the theatrical event.

Modern scenographic inventions can be intrusive, reducing the impact and freedom of individual performances and sometimes running counter to the demands of the text. On the other hand, they can also serve the plays by creating a visual context to which audiences will readily respond. The stage-space can be made to represent a contemporary or otherwise familiar world to offset obsolete word-usages and arcane references in the dialogue and avoid the sword fights, ancient pieties, and royal ceremonies, and other features required by the action and which, on their own, are likely to give a half-achieved and faked historicity to a production. Scenography is also able to represent the context of dramatic action by giving visual form to verbal images that are otherwise only passingly glimpsed along with many other effects of the spoken words. Hamlet or Macbeth can be seen to inhabit the world of his own nightmares, a politician to be in a hostile or unsettled environment, a lover seem to step on air. The blood of battle, mystery of witchcraft, sweetness of spring, or unrelenting cold of winter can seem to envelop the stage. The setting of a performance is now a major element in many theatrical events, mingling with what the author envisaged and the actors achieve.

Although uniquely of the present time in its ways of representing the context for dramatic action, contemporary stage spectacle can be subtly sensitive to Shakespeare's text and supportive of the actors. Pamela Howard, who is a teacher as well as scenographer, has explained how:

> I especially listen out for the sound of the words, the 'musicality' of the text, the timbre and texture of speech, trying to decide for myself what makes this play different from any other ...

Because 'the sense of sound is very near to the sense of colour', the music of a play can lead 'to a choice of colour keys in the major or the minor that visually mirror the music of the words'.[6] Such consonance between the stage-setting and what is seen and heard in the actors' performances can heighten an audience's response to both so that, in their experience, the play becomes more apparently and more completely alive. At its best, scenography is both tactful and ambitious, sensitive and variable, in its reponse to Shakespeare's plays.

Many theatre directors and producers argue that, in an age when potent visual images have become commonplace in film, television, advertising, and mass culture, all Shakespeare's plays need the help of skilled and well-resourced scenographers. Others wish to keep the principal focus on the actors and what they say and do, confident that this regime will not lessen the impact of the plays but will direct attention away from reproducible images and generalized sentiments, back towards theatre as a site for individual experience and communal awareness.

A Mythological Context

One aspect of the setting for Shakespeare's plays cannot possibly be presented physically on stage and calls for a digression here.[7] In the youthful days of modern Europe, a mythology inherited from the Greek and Roman empires offered a sportive freedom to the imagination in the company of pagan gods and goddesses, fabulous creatures, and unnatural marvels. By resorting to myth, writers and other artists were able to escape from the practical necessities of everyday life and the strict patterns of thought imposed by religious and political authorities. The early Europeans wrote about the world which they inhabited in ways that were expected and proscribed and, in another vein, indulged themselves in a very different existence, seeking a more personal and private satisfaction. In their imagination and fantasies, they could align themselves with mythical persons and so inhabit a lost civilization, the ruins of which could still be seen throughout southern Europe.

At the end of the fifteenth century, the painters of the frescoes that adorn the Salone dei Mesi in the Palazzo di Schifanoia in Ferrara created a series of tableaux, one for each month of the year, and arranged them anti-clockwise, starting at the west end of the southern wall. Each is divided into three levels on the lowest of which, at eye level with any viewer, are depicted members of the d'Este family and the daily life of the city and neighbouring farmsteads of the Po basin: here the rich and powerful sit on their thrones or astride great horses and are surrounded by labouring peasants and attentive lackeys. On the second level of each month the comparatively simple and demonstrative signs of the zodiac are depicted while on the topmost and most extensive level are displayed the triumphs of pagan gods. Here fantastic creatures are depicted, together with bridled swans and nibbling rabbits, the delights of Venus, and, in the background, vistas of pellucid seas and unscalable mountains. Music is playing and there is dancing. Elsewhere, in a stillness that seems to have escaped the effects of time, young lovers touch and arouse each other, sharing half-dazed and tender looks; Mars is in bed with Venus, their discarded clothes on the floor beside them: the Graces pose unselfconsciously naked for all to see. By depicting the gods of pagan myth, the artists of that time were able to create an intimate and sensual world that was beyond reality.

Shakespeare and his fellow poets in England also used myth to give freedom to the mind and freshness to sensation. Using words and not paint, they did not have to segregate the real from the mythological on separate levels; tangible experience could co-exist with flights of fancy, dangerous ideas with acceptable dogma. So Shakespeare's King Richard the Second is keenly aware of the political reasons why he must descend from the top of the castle walls and yet, even in that moment, as he is about to make his way down a spiral of stone steps in some dark turret, he also sees himself as Phaethon, the sun-god, and feels the horses pulling his chariot as if they were so many restless cart horses:

> Down, down I come, like glist'ring Phaethon,
> Wanting the manage of unruly jades.
> (*Richard II*, III.iii.178–9)

The god's 'unruly jades' are Richard's political opponents and also his turbulent, irresistible, and frightened thoughts. They come to his mind, and so to his spoken words, together with the 'glistering' sun-god, who is heaven-born and dazzling. As Richard conjures up these images, an audience can share the moment's sensuously realized context, an unmanageably dangerous situation in an imaginary space far more extensive than that of the stage.

When Portia, in *The Merchant of Venice*, waits to see if the good-looking Bassanio has the intelligence or luck to choose the dull-looking casket and so win her hand in marriage, she thinks instinctively of the sacrificed virgin, Hesione, not naming the victim but identifying her suitor as 'young Aclides' and her attendants as married women with tears and harrowed faces:

> I stand for sacrifice;
> The rest aloof are the Dardanian wives,
> With bleared visages come forth to view
> The issue of th'exploit.
> (*Merchant*, III.ii.57–60)

In her mind, Portia is chained to a rock and a 'sea-monster' threatens to devour her as the heartless sea reaches into the distance like her own uncertain future at which she is daring to look. She may also remember that Alcides did not rescue Hesione for love, but merely to win some horses that her father had offered as reward. It might be argued that classical allusions such as these are the product of a little learning and were used to decorate a moment's dialogue with small pedantic flourishes. In Shakespeare's earliest plays this will sometimes be the case, but in more mature works the effect is poised, the words simpler and the effect more passionate and sensuous.

Modern scholarship is able to fill out the details of each individual myth, defining them all, tracing their ancestries, and comparing one usage with another, but this was not the way of Shakespeare or the poets of his time. For them, the myths were malleable: occasionally precise for a special purpose or passing moment and yet as complex and vivid as the most intimate of personal experiences and fantasies. When Ben Jonson wanted to explain how a poet's imagination could soar to great heights and yet remain in touch with lived experience, he used a trio of myths: a poet, he wrote, has a divine instinct or rapture which:

> contemns common and known conceptions. It utters somewhat above a mortal mouth ... it gets aloft, and flies away with his rider, whither before it was doubtful to ascend. This the poets understood by their Helicon, Pegasus, or Parnassus.[8]

This spacious and amazing world was conjured into imaginary existence as actors performed upon a bare and open stage.

Shakespeare's handling of space was not confined to entries and exits, the specification of certain groupings, or the introduction of properties and stage business. The use of stage space, both actual and imaginary, must have been a continual concern as he wrote the plays because, at every turn, the dialogue holds clues to what he saw in his imagination and to what he wished his actors to perform in physical and sensuous terms. Scenographers, directors, and actors will benefit by searching out and using these clues. Readers, too, should keep the persons of a play in their mind's eye and allow Shakespeare use of stage space to work in their imaginations.

Notes

1. See above, p. 87.
2. See, for example, *Love's Labours Lost*, V.i.95, 104; *Midsummer Night's Dream*, V.i.126; *II, Henry IV*, III.ii.273; *Sonnet XV*, l. 3.
3. See pp. 123–4 above.
4. By the Bremer Shakespeare Company at Bremen, Germany, in 2000–1.
5. See pp. 112–14, above.
6. Pamela Howard, *What is Scenography?* (London and New York: Routledge, 2002), p. 20.
7. This section was developed from a paper given at a symposium of the Connotations Society at Cologne in July 1995; it was published in *Connotations*, 5 (1995/96), 2–3, 339–54 as 'The Woods, the West, and Icarus's Mother: Myth in the Contemporary American Theatre'.
8. *Discoveries*, ed. Ian Donaldson (Oxford: Oxford University Press, 1985), p. 584.

11
Off-stage Space

In performance, Shakespeare's plays appear to occupy a space far wider and deeper than any stage. The persons of a drama arrive as if from other places, sometimes from long distances, sometimes from within earshot, and the course of a story will often depend on off-stage action that is independent of any event shown on-stage. Since it is never visible, neither text nor actors can do more than suggest the presence of this off-stage space; it needs to draw upon the imaginations of spectators if it is to become effective. Doing so will involve them closely with the play's action by making it seem to take place within the space of their own minds.

Verbal References to Off-stage Happenings

When Romeo and Juliet lie dead together in the Capulet's monument, cries and activity surround the stage as if a whole city has been awakened in alarm:

CAPULET What should it be that is so shriek'd
    abroad?
LADY CAPULET The people in the street cry 'Romeo'.
  Some 'Juliet' and some 'Paris'; and all run,
  With open outcry, toward our monument.
PRINCE What fear is this which startles in our ears?
                  (V.iii.189–93)

Here the entire force of the acting company, doorkeepers and everyone else, can join in giving an impression
of off-stage space. Often, however, a verbal reference or
a more extensive report must do this work. Early in the
same play, Benvolio sets an off-stage scene for Romeo:

> ... an hour before the worshipp'd sun
> Peer'd forth the golden window of the east,
> A troubled mind drew me to walk abroad;
> Where, underneath the grove of sycamore
> That westward rooteth from this city side,
> So early walking did I see your son.
> Towards him I made; but he was ware of me
> And stole into the covert of the wood.
>
> (I.i.116–23)

In this imaginary off-stage space, timing and mood are at
the dramatist's command and have few bounds.

Benvolio reports what he has seen but other persons in a
Shakespeare play travel only in their imaginations when
they speak of times and places not represented on stage.
On first meeting, both Romeo and Juliet envisage a holy
shrine and devoted pilgrims in some space far from Juliet's
home where the on-stage action takes place. After being
banished for killing Juliet's kinsman Tybalt, Romeo enters
alone on a stage that represents the streets of Mantua
emptied for a holiday but, when he hears that Juliet is dead,
his mind moves rapidly to different locations. Before
knocking on the door of an apothecary's shop, his mind is
already inside:

> ... and about its shelves:
> A beggarly account of empty boxes,
> Green earthen pots, bladders, and musty seeds,
> Remnants of packthread, and old cakes of roses,
> Were thinly scattered, to make up a show.
>
> (V.i.37–48)

When the owner comes on stage, Romeo recognizes in
his face the signs of a world that is not represented in the
rest of the play:

> Famine is in thy cheeks,
> Need and oppression starveth in thy eyes,
> Contempt and beggary hangs upon thy back,
> The world is not thy friend, nor the world's law.
>
> (V.i.69–72)

Here the appearance of the actor playing the Apothecary will join with Romeo's words to give the impression of a world of hunger and vagrancy beyond the reach of the law and outside the bounds of the stage. Alone once more, Romeo's thoughts travel back to Juliet's grave, needing only a couplet with which to effect the imaginary journey.

Some of the most crucial incidents in this story are enacted off-stage. In the penultimate scene, when the action is once more located in Friar's Lawrence's cell outside Verona, Friar John enters unannounced and explains that he comes from a distant part of Verona that is stricken by the plague:

> Going to find a barefoot brother out,
> One of our order, to associate me,
> Here in this city visiting the sick,
> And finding him, the searchers of the town,
> Suspecting that we both were in a house
> Where the infectious pestilence did reign,
> Seal'd up the doors, and would not let us forth,
> So that my speed to Mantua there was stay'd.
>
> (V.ii.5–12)

While an audience will forget Friar John very quickly, his account of selfless charity and strictly enforced laws in a place off-stage evokes scenes and raises issues that are not represented elsewhere in the tragedy. Yet, as Friar Lawrence will remind an audience in his own defence (see V.iii.249–51), the result of this visit to a house suspected of the plague leads, directly, to the final catastrophe. Because Romeo did not receive the vital letter, he commits suicide with the Apothecary's poison, believing that Juliet is dead and not drugged by Friar Lawrence's helpful potion.

Both the perspectives to other places that these two minor characters introduce are carefully detailed and so placed that they make an immediate impression. The off-stage environment that Shakespeare has constructed for this play is an arena for other dramas that affect the main action and, with their own passions and intentions, awaken questions of cause and effect that remain provokingly unanswered except in Friar Lawrence's deference to 'a greater power than we can contradict' that has manipulated events (V.iii.153). If all is 'the work of heaven', as he will later affirm (V.iii.260), then happenings off-stage are the chief instruments of judgement rather than the Prince who concludes the play, promising pardon and punishment. An audience is left to make its own assessment of where responsibility rests.

Verbal Evocations of Other Places and Times

Off-stage space can be far-reaching in extent and exist in several epochs. The ultimate source for *The Tragedy of Hamlet, Prince of Denmark* is a history of pre-Christian Denmark by Saxo Grammaticus but the scope of its setting is European and Christian, both Protestant and Catholic, with occasional references to classical and barbaric worlds. Early in the first scene on the battlements of Elsinore, talk is of a star's pathway in the heavens and then the Ghost of Hamlet's father enters from his 'prison house' of purgatorial fires (I.v.10ff.) and silently stalks the stage. Horatio, the prince's fellow student, now speaks of events in Norway during a past conflict and of ghosts gibbering in the streets of ancient Rome at the death of Julius Caesar. On its second appearance, the Ghost starts 'like a guilty thing / Upon a fearful summons' and departs as soon as a cock crows off-stage (ll. 148–9) which leads Marcellus, one of the soldiers, to speak of the time and place of Christ's nativity. Before Hamlet has made an entry, a complex and varying off-stage space has been sketched in that will become the environment for the play's action.

The second scene further establishes the court of Elsinore in Europe, as Claudius the king despatches ambassadors to Norway, gives leave for Laertes to go to Paris, and urges Hamlet not to return 'to school in Wittenberg'. By Shakespeare's time, Wittenberg had become renowned as the home of Martin Luther, spokesman for the many restless Protestants in the Christian church. The arrival of touring players, the despatch of Hamlet to England, and the march of Fortinbras's Norwegian army on its way to Poland, are among other indications of the Europe-wide context. Its Christian practices are present in Hamlet's reference to churchyards, Claudius's prayer speaking of Old Testament guilt and heavenly angels, and the 'churlish priest' who officiates at Ophelia's funeral. Yet the Player's speech about the Trojan war and Polonius's account of his performance as Julius Caesar, together with Hamlet's recollection of weeping Niobe and fiery Vulcan, Jephthah, Judge of Israel, and Nero, the Roman tyrant, are notable references to pre-Christian thought and times. With no hint arising from historical accounts or Denmark's geography, Shakespeare also evoked an off-stage countryside that is very like his native Warwickshire. This rural world is fleetingly present in Hamlet's talk of the country game of 'hobbyhorse' (III.ii.128–30) and more consistently in Ophelia's crazed talk and songs in Act IV, scene v, with their references to folk customs of wooing and burial, a 'grass-green turf', 'sweet flowers', and the 'cold ground'. The herbs she distributes are such that might be found in a country garden and the lore she associates with them in an aural folk wisdom. A still more sustained displacement to this green world is Gertrude's account of Ophelia's death: here is space for the 'hoar leaves' of a willow, countryside flowers and 'liberal shepherds', simple old-fashioned songs, a flowing brook, and a 'muddy death' (ll. 166–84). On-stage action stands still during this speech and an audience is given enough detail for its imaginations to feed upon: sense-memories of other times and inbred prejudices are capable of creating a very specific world in attentive minds. Laertes begins to weep and precipitately leaves the stage, with everyone else following straightaway. An evocation of

Warwickshire has opened the play to sentiments that, from now onward, will be an incipient element in the drama that infrequently surfaces into speech, mostly in the graveyard.

In their opening words, the Witches in *Macbeth* speak of an off-stage space that is vast, rather than local, in scope and will continue to surround the play's action with thunder, lightning, rain, a setting sun, and darkest night. Further off-stage space and closer to home is in their talk of the hurlyburly of a battle taking place on 'the heath'. Then, at the very start of the next scene, the result of that battle is actualized on stage with the arrival of '*a bleeding* Sergeant' (I.ii.0,S.D.) whose account of 'reeking wounds' extends the off-stage space with a recollection of 'Golgotha', the 'place of a skull' to which Christ was taken to be crucified. The play's imaginary setting is extended still further in the Witches' second scene with their claim to be 'Posters of the sea and land' and talk of 'killing swine' and voyaging to Aleppo accompanied by tempest and shipwreck (I.iii.1–32). Once they have encountered Macbeth and Banquo with prophecies, they are said to vanish into 'the air' as if no territory could contain them (ll. 80–1). At their final appearance in Act IV, they speak of dragon, wolf, 'salt-sea shark', 'blaspheming Jew', Turk, Tartar, a 'birth-strangled babe / Ditch-deliver'd by a drab' and, finally, tiger and baboon, all creatures belonging to still wider space. On this occasion Macbeth returns to them of his own volition, determined to enter their world, and he creates a comparable sense of great space, but less remote than theirs. He now foresees the destruction of churches, ships, harvests, trees, castles, palaces, pyramids, and 'the treasure / Of nature's germans' in one overwhelming holocaust. The on-stage actions of the tragic hero are dwarfed by his evocation of this comprehensive vista in sustained and forceful speech: in this imagined world, the consequences of dramatic action assume monstrous proportions and the power to destroy all existence.

Each play has an imaginary context that offsets and extends its on-stage space. At the start of *As You Like It* the action moves between the home of the deceased

Sir Rowland de Boys, the Duke's palace, and the Forest of Arden, each place with different dress, manners, and stage properties. In the forest, an off-stage setting merges frequently with on-stage space. An anonymous 'First Lord' tells of a brook where a 'poor sequestered stag' stood and wept while Jaques looked on and commented on 'worldlings', 'velvet friends', 'fat and greasy citizens', and a 'broken brankrupt' (II.i.29–66). When Jaques enters and holds attention, he extends the view still further, speaking of the 'foul body of th'infected world' where 'the city-woman bears / The cost of princes on unworthy shoulders' (II.vii.60, 74–6) and, later on, to the wars, trial courts, and other settings in which all persons have 'their exits and their entrances' (II.vii.139–66). The play's widest off-stage perspectives are, however, more exotic, occurring in Orlando's verses that range from 'east to western Inde' and 'through all the world' (III.ii.78–85) as he tries to describe Rosalind's many excellencies. When the comedy draws to its close in lovers' meetings and thoughts turn back to the Court, Hymen arrives to speak of the heaven above and to be honoured in a song that celebrates a wedlock that blesses board and bed in 'every town' (V.iv.102–40). A more restricted but less-expected perspective is added with the arrival of Jaques de Boys, Sir Rowland's second son who has not even been mentioned earlier: he tells of 'an old religious man' who lives on the 'skirts of this wild wood' and has so 'converted' the tyrant duke Frederick that he has abandoned the world. Jaques decides to find what can be 'heard and learn'd' in this man's place of solitude; when he refuses to join the dancing and leaves the stage, his demeanour and bearing may briefly lend credence to his off-stage destination.

On-stage Reflection of Off-stage Reality

The plays can also awaken images of the off-stage space in which members of an audience lead their various and often unremarkable lives. On-stage, actors occupy a finite space but the audiences that come to view them belong to a much greater space, potentially an infinite one, and bring with them their very diverse experiences of that real world. While the effectiveness of references to remote or unusual places depends on the knowledge and imagination of individual members of an audience, a play can also awaken visual memories and instinctive responses that every person possesses and can animate whatever ideas and prejudices they bring with them to the theatre. When this happens, an audience is liable to see everything in its own terms and identify directly with one or more persons on-stage as if they shared a common predicament. A play can then engage with the social, moral, and political forces that actually, in real life, control how its audience lives. By reaching out from the stage into the audience's own environment in these ways, a theatrical event can participate in the on-going processes of life, illuminating whatever may be present there and, possibly, revealing hidden and historical conditioning or possibilities for change.

We have already noticed how the words of Shakespeare's texts bring everyday experiences momentarily to mind, making even the most demanding or extreme moments more accessible for an audience (see above, pp. 47–9). Suddenly, as with a more penetrating light, the persons of the drama are revealed in close-up, with pretensions vanished and instinctive feelings exposed. In addition to this recurring openness of the dialogue, the importance of which can scarcely be exaggerated, many specific activities are physically enacted on-stage almost as if they were events happening outside the theatre and independent of the drama. Situations involving both parents and children, brothers and sisters, masters and dependants, the ignorant and the highly educated, native and foreign, male and female, rich and poor, will all give rise to some actions that replicate off-stage behaviour, possibly more closely than words spoken on-stage. Physical actions can be much the same on-stage and off-stage, ranging from how people greet each other or go to sleep, or eat and drink, or work at simple tasks, or how they join together or set off on lone journeys. The basic nature of these activities remains constant and provides a common denominator with events in the plays. Even when persons and circumstances on-stage are exceptional, the drama may have moments or facets which, to the minds of an audience, seem to be happening to persons like themselves in their everyday world.

Inevitably the passing of time has obscured some points of contact between an audience and activity on-stage. When *Macbeth* was first performed, the witches would have provoked specific memories since some people in an audience might have seen witches being publicly executed by hanging; more would have seen someone they thought was a witch, and still more have heard talk of a witch's supernatural power. Such experiences were stirring up controversy: Reginald Scot's *Discovery of Witchcraft* of 1584 demonstrated that their activities were the product of human vindictiveness and fantasy, an argument that King James refuted in *Demonology* of 1597 by drawing on his own experience of a witch's dangerous and evil capability. In 1603, after James's ascension to the English throne, parliament strengthened the law against witchcraft and their trials would become public spectacles. Further topical events surface in *Macbeth* when the drunken Porter speaks of farmers who profit from grain shortage and 'equivocators' who 'committed treason enough for God's sake, yet could not equivocate to heaven' (II.iii.5–14), the latter comment using a form of words taken from the investigations that followed the failure of Guy Fawkes's attempt to kill the king by igniting gunpowder under the Houses of Parliament. When the action of the play moves from Scotland to England, report of King Edward the Confessor's curing of 'strangely-visited people, / All swoln and ulcerous' would have reminded some in an audience that King James was said to have inherited this miraculous ability to cure 'the [King's] evil' by his touch and would sometimes, reluctantly, make public 'assay' of it (IV.iii.141–58).

The slow gestation of playscript, scheduling, and production that is the norm today has destroyed the topicality and closeness to off-stage life that in Shakespeare's day were taken for granted in theatrical events. Only a few weeks had been needed between the players purchasing the outline of a play and performing the completed script, not the six months which would be fast by today's standards.[1] In the absence of newspapers, radio, or television, only sermons, ballads, and occasional pamphlets could compete with theatre performances as public provision of up-to-date opinions, fashions, and news. *The Merchant of Venice* of 1596 or 1597 can be seen as a contribution to a lively and topical debate about borrowing money that was being pursued in the anonymous *Death of Usury* (1594), Miles Mosse's *The Arraignment and Conviction of Usury* (1595), and Thomas Bell's *Speculation of Usury* (1596). On first seeing Antonio, Shylock enters the controversy by calling usury 'usance' and defending it as 'thrift':

> I hate him for he is a Christian;
> But more for that in low simplicity
> He lends out money gratis, and brings down
> The rate of usance here with us in Venice ...
> He hates our sacred nation; and he rails,
> Even there where merchants most do congregate,
> On me, my bargains, and my well-won thrift,
> Which he calls interest.

(I.iii.37–46)

In *Coriolanus*, the election of a consul and the activities of the people's representatives in ancient Rome reflect current issues in the England of King James with regard to membership of official bodies and the right to vote. These matters were likely to have come to Shakespeare's personal attention in a dispute of 1601 about the election of a Warwickshire member of parliament and in another of 1607 about voting rights in the election of churchwardens for St Saviour's, the parish church for London's Bankside. In the same play, demonstrations by citizens reflect the riots of the time in rural areas about the enclosure of common land and scarcity of corn.[2]

Allusions to political and social controversies that are recognized only after academic research into lesser-known publications and surviving documents, will not register with present-day audiences but, when issues of more general interest are involved, performance can reflect the thinking and prejudices of later audiences. For example, in the last years of Elizabeth I, England was poised between great achievements and great uncertainties, with new wealth being enjoyed by some while others suffered from galloping inflation and financial insecurity, a contrast that is not uncommon today. In this situation, lawyers were often criticized, as they can be today, for the practices which allowed them to gain great personal wealth and power. Law was a thriving profession: the Middle Temple, where clients were interviewed and would-be lawyers trained, had grown from a complex with 94 chambers in 1574, to one with 138 in 1586. During the same years, among London's population of some 200,000 to 250,000, the number of lawyers increased by 20 per cent, from 1400 to 1700. Naturally enough, popular opinion was outraged and it was said that 'one of the greatest inconveniences in the land [is] that the number of the lawyers be so great': the profession as a whole was reputed to employ about 4000 persons, plus 'an infinite number' of smaller fry.[3] Lawyers, young and old, had a great deal to celebrate and they did so in a series of regular feasts for their corporate enjoyment during the dark days of winter. On Candlemass day, 2 February 1602, the revelry was topped off with a performance by the Chamberlain's Men of Shakespeare's *Twelfth Night, or What You Will.* This comedy might have been written especially for such an audience and it will have much the same appeal for anyone involved in litigation today.

The play opens with a young nobleman whose wealth is obvious because he is doing absolutely nothing except trying to convince himself that love should be painful and then, in a second short scene, a young heiress arrives, having lost her only brother at sea. She, as any lawyer would be quick to notice, puts her life and fortune

into the hands of a sea Captain whom she knows only by
what he says and by his appearance; she is also free with
her 'gold' as a means of meeting the duke who had been
on stage earlier. A third scene is full of talk about inheritance, hard work, and the regularities of life;

> SIR TOBY   What a plague means my niece to take the
> death of her brother thus? I am sure care's an
> enemy to life.
> MARIA   By my troth, Sir Toby, you must come in
> earlier o'nights; your cousin, my lady, takes great
> exceptions to your ill hours.

Legal phrases are bandied to and fro:

> SIR TOBY   Why, let her except before excepted.
> MARIA   Ay, but you must confine yourself within the
> modest limits of order.
> SIR TOBY   Confine! I'll confine myself no finer than I
> am ...

> (I.iii.1–10)

The play has entered legal territory: class, kinship,
wealth, rules, service, personal liberty are the very stuff of
a lawyer or plaintiff's daily business. Soon a second young
heiress enters in mournful, though more secure, circumstances; she is attended by a steward with ideas above his
station. In the next scene, a young man of good breeding
appears who looks exactly like his sister whom the audience has already seen dressed in the very same manner;
he is now mourning that sister whom he believes to have
been lost at sea. This new arrival is followed on-stage by a
second sea Captain who goes in fear of his life because of
unspecified enemies.

Matters of legal significance multiply as the play proceeds. Service is freely offered and is not accepted;
money is lent without security and taken without apology.
Certifiable madness is shown in various forms and some
care is taken of it. A duel is fought on-stage – at that time
the illegal resort of those impatient of the law[4] – and

another is stopped by the arrival of a person in authority; a third is fought off-stage. Judgements and punishments are both given readily while, at other times, everything seems to be 'Jove's doing' or a matter of 'Fortune'. Wit and quick thinking solve some problems but not all: as Viola says at the beginning of Act II:

> O time, thou must untangle this not I;
> It is too hard a knot for me t'untie.

Twelfth Night is grounded in constant realities of life and yet it is also full of fantastic situations and coincidences: words can be alight with double meanings or accurately strike at flying targets. Illyria, where the action takes place, is a country with sea coast and mountains that knows 'scathful grapple' and the 'smoke of war' (V.i.46–53) and yet it also contains sunlit and gentle countryside, with roses and an orchard, where oxen labour with wainropes and diminutive wrens do as they please. Presented as a Christmas revel, the play's reflection of actual lives could catch the imaginations of its audiences in many ways, many of which are as effective today as they were at first.

While few moments on-stage accurately reproduce the actual happenings and familiar course of every day, each play reaches beyond the stage by arousing personal memories in the minds of its audiences. *King Lear* is a pre-eminent example. Set in ancient Britain and rewriting its history, the play's dialogue and action also deal with issues of its own times in a manner so broadly related to actual experience that its off-stage life continues to be relevant today, even though a moment's thought will remind us of huge differences between the here-and-now and the world shown on the stage. Few kings have absolute power today and in most countries political decisions are made after long and public debate. Time has modified both a man's and a woman's place in society, a parent's and child's relationship to each other, sexual attitudes and behaviour. Change is everywhere, in working and access to money, in fighting wars, in processes of law, means of travel and communication, treatment of physical and mental illness; in language, ways of thinking and causes of laughter. Yet, despite all that is unfamiliar, only a little more thought will show how a performance of this play can cause us, even now, to think of our own lives and so that it seems, in imagination, to take place in our world.

When alone in the storm and speaking as if to the theatre audience, Lear's evocation of the storm can still strike home, despite obsolete phrasing and vocabulary, and awaken an audience's memories however different and varied their lives may be:

> Poor naked wretches, wheresoe'er you are,
> That bide the pelting of this pitiless storm,
> How shall your houseless heads and unfed sides,
> Your loop'd and window'd raggedness, defend you
> From seasons such as these? O, I have ta'en
> Too little care of this! Take physic, pomp,
> Expose thyself to feel what wretches feel, ...
>
> (III.iv.28–34)

Later, on Dover Beach, Lear's talk of sexuality and pain, madness and sanity, age and infancy speaks directly to very ordinary sense-memories derived from watching small creatures copulating:

> Die for adultery? No.
> The wren goes to't, and the small gilded fly
> Does lecher in my sight... .

Even Lear's outrageous hatred and fear of women can so touch our senses by its darkness, burning, stench, and decay that we recoil from the pain as if he had spoken to us:

> But to the girdle do the gods inherit,
> Beneath is all the fiends';
> There's hell, there's darkness, there is the sulphurous
>   pit –
> Burning, scalding, stench, consumption.

Encompassing birth and death in a few assured words, he awakens sensations that everyone watching the stage will have experienced:

> When we are born, we cry that we are come
> To this great stage of fools.
>
> (IV.vi.111–13, 183–4)

Lear's last words and actions, as we have noticed before (see above, p. 24), are so simple that, in a fine performance, they sound as if spoken in absolute truth and we respond to the play's performance as if it were an event taking place in our own lives and in a familiar place.

The off-stage life of a play in the minds of an audience can be at once effective and uncertain. Lear can be considered culpable – he says so himself several times – but in what his fault lies is far from clear. He had been told that he 'was everything', his dependants saying '"ay" and "no" to everything [he] said' (IV.vi.97–105) and yet Kent is an exception to this sycophancy, daring to condemn the king as both mad and old: 'To plainness honour's bound / When majesty falls to folly' (I.i.144–8). But this cannot be all that Kent thinks because he will risk his own life to serve this master, calling him 'the old kind king' (III.i.28).[5] Even the motive for Lear's rejection of Cordelia is not entirely clear since the beloved daughter's first denial of his will is expressed as if she intended to provoke rather than persuade, her words sounding more like obduracy than a caring and filial love. Not one person in the play questions the king's right to 'divide' his kingdom between his daughters or to change the terms of Cordelia's marriage with the result that, from the opening moments of the tragedy onwards, members of an audience are left to judge for themselves how much father, daughter, and loyal earl are to blame for the sequence of anger, bruised feelings, tyrannical and rash judgements, curses, and irrationality. Alternatively, they can take the narrative far less thoughtfully until later

when the action becomes more unremittingly painful
and the mere survival of Lear, Kent, Gloucester, and
Edgar is in doubt. This play draws spectators progressively
towards making judgements as if it were an actual event
in which they are caught up and find themselves person-
ally involved.

If we allow any of Shakespeare's plays to enter the
space of our minds, we are likely to find ourselves in a
world that is our own and not our own, familiar and yet
beyond most other experiences. We are by no means
alone in this open territory because many of the sources
on which Shakespeare drew in presenting the plays are
the common properties of many people in all generations. The more we have read in the literature and histories of the period, the more we will find ourselves to be
among a host of witnesses as we hear echoes of other
writers whose works we know and may recall. A great
stock of varied knowledge, opinion, and philosophy went
into the writing of the plays so that our reponses will
sometimes be shaped by what we half-remember. The
Bible is a notable contributor, especially the Gospels,
Epistles, Genesis, Exodus, Psalms, Proverbs, and the
books of the prophets, together with the book of
Common Prayer. Borrowings from Virgil, Ovid, Plautus,
Seneca, Erasmus, and Machiavelli will not be so recognizable in modern times as they would have been previously
but some in an audience today will catch echoes of
Marlowe, Nashe, Spenser, Sidney and other Elizabethans.

Generations of commentators, editors, and scholars
have added to detailed knowledge of the plays' origins so
that their off-stage existence may now inhabit a territory
that reaches far beyond Shakespeare's England into a
European culture that is world-wide in influence. Tracing
its dimensions becomes an endless task and yet the greatest marvel of this vast intellectual hinterland is that it co-
exists with a close focus on everyday thought and very
ordinary existence: King Lear's 'Who is it that can tell me
who I am?' (I.iv.229) is both a practical observation of
ordinary life and an enduring philosophical question. At
such moments a theatrical event can reach out from the

stage into the furthest reaches and innermost recesses of our consciousness.

Notes

1. See above, pp. 12–14. At the Royal National Theatre in London, the process of production requires some six months between the decision to stage a completed playscript and its opening night.
2. This account of the contemporary background of *Coriolanus* is indebted to the Oxford edition by R. B. Parker (Oxford and New York: Oxford University Press, 1994), pp. 33–43.
3. The opinions are from Thomas Wilson, 'The State of England, Anno Dom. 1600', quoted here from E. W. Ives, 'The Law and the Lawyers', *Shakespeare in His Own Age*, ed. Allardyce Nicoll (Cambridge: Cambridge University Press, 1964), p. 78; the statistics are from documentary sources quoted in the same article.
4. See G. P. V. Akrigg, *Jacobean Pageant, or the Court of King James I* (London: Hamish Hamilton, 1962), pp. 248–63.
5. This phrase is in a passage Shakespeare added to the text after its first performance, being printed in the Folio edition of 1623 and not in the earlier Quarto dated 1608; the addition serves to motivate Kent's loyalty more strongly and offsets adverse judgements made upon the king.

12

Time

A performance of a Shakespeare play can never be what it was in his time. Even if the text could be kept exactly as it was written, it would never be acted or received in the same way. With a great deal of trouble, guesswork, and approximation, theatre buildings and stage management could be replicated today but not their original effect: today, they would strike audiences as antiquated and peculiar. This study has shown that a theatrical event depends on factors that will always be subject to change: the occasion of performance, the composition and disposition of its audience, the individuality and talent of each actor, and the conscious and unconscious decisions that actors make before and during the show. Inevitably, every performance will be both old and new, even when it conscientiously tries to repeat the past. The wonder is that Shakespeare's plays have proved so receptive to change that they continue to be revived and can still draw large audiences after more than 400 years. It seems that the possibility of change has been written into the texts.

Out-of-date Elements in the Plays

Changes in the English language have brought obvious losses. With careful and clear speaking, speeches can retain most of their sense and much of their allusiveness, carrying something like their original charge of thought and feeling, and yet their effect will never be the same as at first, not least because they can never sound so close to ordinary contemporary speech. A few archaic words and arcane references can be changed to bring the dialogue more up to date without too much loss, and some passages that are now obscure can be cut altogether, but still the turns of phrase, management of sentences, and ongoing energy of expression will sound strangely affected to present-day audiences. Even if the dialogue could be made more intelligible, the most convincing modernization is likely to blunt the eloquence and wit for which the plays were praised originally, as much as for their apparent ease and naturalness. Playgoers schooled in Latin would have taken positive enjoyment in his 'hard' words, compound sentences, and rhetorical subtleties, even as they challenged the capabilities of both speakers and hearers.[1]

Many of today's difficulties with the language spring from changes in social manners. We do not respect age and seniority as Elizabethans did in their speech and their ceremonies of greeting and dependence are no longer in use.[2] We do not say *thee, thy,* and *thine* when talking either to intimates or inferiors, and we no longer use *master, father, husband, wife, mistress, son, daughter* when addressing each other in everyday conversation. Even when the choice of words and formation of sentences were much the same as in modern usage, they belonged to ways of living that no longer exist so that *how* they were used would have been different. The way people talked to each other was different too, our approach being less circumscribed, our speech freer in expression. We tend to use the hesitations and punchlines that are effective in the apparently close-to-life media of television and film. Our visual recognition may be swifter because we are accustomed to seeing and speaking of intimacies that were previously strictly guarded.

Shakespeare's society was very different from ours. Early perspective drawings show how churches dominated every town and village; outwardly, their architecture was sometimes amazingly ambitious and their interiors were richly ornamented. They were centres of

communal life as well as the places where almost everyone attended weekly for religious worship and listening
to bible readings and official homilies. At the same time,
unprecedented changes were occurring: Protestants had
challenged the authority of the Roman Church, the
House of Commons was beginning to assert itself against
the Crown. While a person's place in society was still
largely determined by inheritance and birth, grammar
schools, established in earlier Tudor years, were beginning to make self-advancement a possibility for a gifted
few. Changes in the ownership of land after the dissolu-
tion of the monasteries, the arrival of new wealth from
the New World, and the rise of capitalism were beginning
to shift the foundations of business and society.
Inevitably, in great and minute ways, all this influenced
literature, music, visual arts, and, by no means least,
theatre; it did so in ways that not are easy to recognize
and have little force today.

The handling of action can be as easily misunderstood
without knowledge of long-lost and highly significant
aspects of daily life. In *Macbeth*, for example, those who
take hurried journeys on horseback risk considerable
danger. When a 'homely man' breaks unannounced into
the presence of Lady Macduff, the effect of his intrusion
is the greater because it is at once apparent that he
belongs to a lower class; although speaking carefully, he
knows that he will seem 'savage' to the young family he is
trying to save (IV.ii.64–81). The exercise of political
power depends on being watchful and secretive, as it did
in the competitive Jacobean court: 'There's daggers in
men's smiles' ... 'There's not one of them but in his
house/I keep a servant fee'd' (II.iii.139 and III.iv.132).
Irrational behaviour is assumed to be incurable, first
Lady Macbeth's obsessive sleepwalking – 'More needs she
the divine than the physician' – and then Macbeth's
defensive preparations – 'Some say he's mad; others, that
lesser hate him,/Do call it valiant fury' (V.i.72 and
V.ii.13–14). It is against the habits of service when the
previously attentive Seyton loses contact with his master
without a word of explanation, after reporting, 'The

Queen, my lord, is dead' (V.v.16); the mutual silence, indicated by two half-lines, draws attention to his immediate disappearance, that may awaken echoes of the witches' withdrawal in the first Act, refusing to say more after having uttered their prophecies.

References to topical events and to particular individuals who are now unknown will puzzle most present-day spectators. The general relevance of *Twelfth Night* to an audience of lawyers, as noted in the previous chapter, can register today to much the same effect as in early performances, but many details in this text need footnotes to explain them. Any audience will understand and laugh when the ambitious steward produces written evidence that is known to be forged but his earlier citation of 'the Lady of the Strachy [who] married the yeoman of the wardrobe' (II.v.36–8) still awaits a generally accepted explanation. When he fancies himself as 'Count Malvolio' (II.v.32), an early, status-conscious audience would have been quick to remember that marriage to a countess does not confer the title of count on the husband. His charge that Sir Toby and his companions 'make an alehouse of my lady's house' would have struck an audience more harshly when taverns were reputed to be places where lower-class and masterless men resorted and affrays and thieving were common.[3] When Malvolio wishes to 'enjoy my private' (III.iv.85), historical knowledge would be needed today to realize that the right to privacy within a household was the prerogative of its master. In early performances, Malvolio's 'overweening' (II.v.27) would have been evident to an audience whenever he took a position on-stage that was inappropriate for a steward and 'the fellow of servants' (II.v.137–8).

Social behaviour and attitudes to politics, finance, culture, sex, physical and mental well-being, and religion have all been so transformed that a Shakespeare play can cease to be fully acceptable to present-day audiences. Few today will sympathize with Portia when she insists that, as well as forfeiting all his wealth, the defeated Shylock must 'presently become a Christian' (*Merchant of Venice*,

IV.i.382). The treatment given to both Katherine and Bianca in the course of *The Taming of the Shrew* or Helena's willingness to accept Bertram back as her husband at the end of *All's Well that Ends Well* are also hard for present-day audiences to accept. Changes with regard to kingship, class structure, employment, wealth, or divine providence can be so glaringly obvious, especially with regard to the development and resolution of a play's action, that some twentieth-century productions have created an exotic and largely fictional reality onstage by which means consequential issues can be avoided or treated light-heartedly to comic effect. This practice is in keeping with the element of fantasy that is present in all the plays and yet, by removing performances from the ways of thought and lived experience of their audiences, its effect is to limit perception and inoculate against the drama's inherent thrust and excitement.

Another way of circumventing a play's historically conditioned implications is to overlay the text with stage-business appropriate to some later period that is closer in manners and thought to our own, providing scenery and costumes to give an air of reality to the new location. This kind of repositioning has become very common – *Romeo and Juliet* in fashionable, *haute-couture* Italy, *Macbeth* in mainland Europe during the Second World War, *All's Well that Ends Well* in a late nineteenth-century, 'Chekhovian' Russia – these settings can quicken the invention of actors, directors, and designers and the new readings of the text that emerge engage an audience's attention away from the early modern, monarchical, patristic, doctrinaire, and Christian elements of the playtext, besides encouraging publicity and, perhaps, controversy. Unfortunately, the busy detail used to create this disguise is liable to lessen the impact of a play by obscuring the original motives behind its main action.

However spoken and acted, and however provided with settings and costumes, Shakespeare's plays cannot deliver the same effects in later times as they did when they were

first staged and yet, even now, it is the common experience of an audience member to find that moments in a
play seem to be actually happening in the present
moment. Progressively during a performance, archaisms
and scenic inventions tend to fade away and the language
begins to sound more inevitable and immediate. To a
considerable extent, even the morals and beliefs of the
past can become acceptable to audiences. The probable
reason why this happens is that the actors, in themselves,
are not in any way unbelievable or rooted in the past. On
any particular day, as they settle into their roles and grow
more at ease with their audience, the actors change
within themselves and their performances draw more
deeply on their inner resources. The persons presented
become stronger and more convincingly real in consequence; an audience is able to respond more directly as if
to someone like themselves.

This impression of contemporaneity stems from the
actual presence of the actors on-stage and their imaginative involvement in the drama's fiction.[4] Whether the
words belong to Hamlet, Viola, Henry the Fifth, or any
other major role, the actor is responsible for what temporary force they will have, what meaning or meanings,
what suggestions, colours, relevance.[5] There are
moments in a Shakespeare play when all an actor's
resources are called upon and the person performed
seems, in that moment, to take over the very being of the
performer. Or it might be said that, in the course of a
play, actors uncover, or progressively discover, a part of
their own selves by the acting of their roles. No matter
what style a production is given, an impression that it is
taking place in a unique way in the present time is a possibility that Shakespeare has consistently provided for in
the text, as if he had determined that this should
happen. On the other hand, such a transformation may
never take place: although theatre is an art presented by
means of human beings alive in the present time – the
only art form that does so – the sensation of existing in
our time is neither a sure nor a constant feature of a theatrical event. It is a potential that directors, designers,

and every other contributor to the performance, as well as the actors, can encourage or ignore, and audiences can stifle by inattention.

Notes

1. See above, p. 80.
2. See above, pp. 133–5.
3. See Peter Clark, *The English Alehouse: A Social History, 1200–1830* (London and New York: Longman, 1983).
4. In this connection, see Chapter 2, above.
5. For discussion of these opportunities, see pp. 19–21, 45–6, 76, and so on, above.

PART IV: PLAYS IN PRINT

13

Reading

Reading a Shakespeare play is like swimming: however difficult it may seem at first, once started and practised the process becomes entirely natural and readers grow more ambitious. Some will have more difficulty with the language than others and yet, on a first reading, that hardly matters because enough words and images will catch attention and hold it moving forward. For everyone reading will be different as it involves the imagination and brings memories, fantasies, day dreams, and real dreams into play. What we consciously think is also involved, the opinions developed from what we have read and heard and those derived from our own experiences. If we keep an open mind, the plays can quickly become part of that long argument we each have about how and why we live, and what we value most in others. If we are curious and adventurous the plays will start to speak for themselves in unique ways.

Reading any play is not like reading other texts because attention moves on from what is spoken to the persons of the drama, who they are and what they do. With Shakespeare, it is easy to be concerned only with the meanings and wonder of the words and yet if we are to encounter the plays in their proper element they must be seen in the mind's eye as if in performance. This entails more than trying to envisage what actions and movements might take place on-stage in a performance, although that is included. For an audience, the presence of individual actors in their roles is the one factor that contributes constantly to the play and this, too, a reader should try to take into account. Experienced actors and directors read plays in this way as a matter of course and other readers, whether theatre-goers or not, will find that they, too, can begin to imagine the play in performance as they read.

Towards a Theatrical Reading

Although we are all too often left untouched by our reading, the strange truth is that a play can come alive, fitfully and incompletely but with some conviction, as if it were the text's own initiative. This will happen more frequently if we keep at the back of our minds the nature of the theatrical event for which the plays were written. One of the purposes of this book is to help readers of Shakespeare to do just that: to imagine actors performing on the open space of a stage in contact with an audience and interacting with other actors in each moment as it occurs. At times we can become wholly involved when reading, as if we were in an audience: we forget ourselves and gradually become aware of persons in the play as they think and feel, breathe and move, first one taking shape and substance, and then others. No two readers will have the same experience, nor is it likely to happen in the same way twice, or at the same moment. The effect of each reading depends on what we bring to the play, where we have come from and what we have been thinking and doing. Like a sculpture, a performance shows different features and evokes different responses according to the perspective from which it is viewed; and all aspects cannot be seen at any one time.

Some difficulties always stand in the way. One is that the reader is alone and the performance of a play is a social event that unconsciously draws us to be aware of other people, even as we are consciously attuned to our own responses. In this respect, theatre is a provocative medium: we can be drawn along with the sensations and

emotions of many persons whose lives are unknown to us
and whose company we have not chosen. We can either
become part of that crowd or be made keenly aware of
our difference; and between these two extremes, much
else is possible that might never have come to mind while
sitting alone with a book in a quiet room.

Sharing what we have experienced in reading can go
some way towards compensating for the loss of theatre's
sociability. In a preface to the 1623 collected edition of
Shakespeare's plays his fellow actors, John Hemming and
Henry Condell, advised 'the great Variety of Readers' to
read him 'again and again':

> And if then you do not like him, surely you are in some
> manifest danger, not to understand him. And so we leave
> you to other of his friends, whom if you need, can be your
> guides: if you need them not, you can lead your selves,
> and others. And such readers we wish him.

In the days before radio and television arrived to fill an
evening's leisure, groups of friends would meet regularly
to read the plays together and, today, students often do
the same as a means of becoming familiar with a text.
Occasions like these are a step towards the social context
proper to theatre and something of a play's performative
qualities can be experienced in varied voices and the
beginnings of impersonation, however stumbling and
inexpert the participants may be.

One of the pleasures of reading is the ability to stop
and, as it were, soak up all that a moment offers but,
compared with being at a theatre, great losses are
entailed in this gain. A reader is less likely to be caught
up in the on-going action or to experience the continual
exchange between waiting for the narrative to move
forward and being impelled to stretch one's mind to
keep track of multiple happenings. Conflicting ideas or
warring factions are not likely to be realized indepen-
dently, on their own terms and with equal force. A sense
of progression leading towards climax or completion, or
from uncertainty to clarification, can hardly survive if

other business interrupts the reading or another person enters the room. In the theatre, as a Shakespeare play holds attention, a more penetrating view of the dramatic action is slowly developed: the viewer begins to feel closer to what is happening on-stage; emotions and sensations become stronger and the consequences of action more evident. These responses a reader's personal freedom is likely to lessen.

And yet in one way, if all goes well, a reader may sometimes enjoy a play with greater freedom and personal satisfaction than most audience members. This pleasure is a little like that of a dramatist in the process of writing and before starting to correct what has come in a first flight of invention and imagination. In the days of his early successes, John Osborne admitted that 'Of course, when I'm writing [my plays] I see all the parts being played beautifully by me, to perfection':[1] and something like this spirited and egotistical identification can be a reader's if the full theatrical event is kept in mind. By letting each person in the play respond freely to the text, an imaginative reading can set a play in action without being limited by what a production is able to achieve: the experience is very much our own. More thought and careful study can then take the experience further.

Notes

1.   'That Awful Museum' (a conversation with Richard Findlater), *Twentieth Century*, clxix (1961), 216.

14

Study and Criticism

Trying to understanding how Shakespeare's plays function in a theatrical event is an undertaking that will never be complete.[1] All the difficulties experienced by a reader are met in greater force when setting out to discover what is dominant or constant in a play's theatrical life. As this study has shown, any one production is never the same as another because it relies on the presence and achievements of individual actors and the skills of managers, directors and designers. And the experience it gives is never easy to understand because it reflects the culture of the time and the response of each audience is influenced by the place and occasion of each performance. This ever-changing set of circumstances affects the presentation of speech, argument, narrative, and the persons of the play. Nothing exists in theatre except as a part of a re-creation of life that cannot be closely or permanently defined and is not limited in its effect to what can be readily described. It follows that any account of performance will have to be, in part at least, impressionistic and must draw upon a very personal response. Nor will it ever be sufficient to quote the words of the text as if they provided sufficient or accurate evidence about any one moment. Nor can any one moment be considered apart from others; each second of a performance depends on what has gone before and, to some extent, carries its own contribution forward. The study of Shakespeare's plays in a theatrical context is bound to be incomplete and tentative: and yet there is no more revealing way of trying to understand the achievements of these texts.

Seeing a play in a theatre opens a wide door through which the most inexperienced student can begin a critical adventure and the most experienced find questions to pursue. Everyone present is likely to have something to say about the performance, having been drawn to what interests them most and noticing some effect that others have missed; they are likely to give praise and blame with equal enthusiasm. Expressing an opinion in these matters is almost always enjoyable because sense memories and imagination will have been awakened before any meanings began to occupy and, possibly, confuse the mind. Imperfectly and, perhaps, excentrically the play has been palpably there, in front of the viewer, to be seen and heard in company with other viewers, all of whom will be ready to make judgements. But while the wish to make sense of a play in performance is instinctive, taking a responsible part in critical debate about the experience is a complex business. Because the plays were written for performance with all its vagaries and complications, they need to be studied in detail and with patience.

Studying a Play in Performance

Shakespeare's imagination was caught and his invention driven by images of men and women in action, not merely by words and speeches. He could neither foresee nor control how the actors would perform these persons on any occasion but his art was to write down what they should speak while impersonating the persons he had seen in his mind, according their own individual talents and imagination. Faced with describing such complex and unstable phenomena, a critic must first decide which performances to consider and then which incidents and impressions should be given most attention. Because personal history and background will influence these choices and the reactions that follow, the best person for the task might be someone of strong sensibilities and wide experience but with no predilections concerning the play or foreknowledge of its stage history; such a critic might give attention to a performance entirely and openly as it evolves moment by moment, seeing clearly and responding imaginatively in company with others in the audience. On the other hand, a person experienced enough in theatre to be on the lookout for what is new and for what has been achieved with special power or in closest accord with Shakespeare's words, might be the more useful critic, although a more biased one.

Despite its many difficulties, the study of 'Shakespeare in Performance' has become a distinct and thriving species of Shakespeare criticism, a tree with many branches of varied value and reach. Numerous books of reflective criticism have been based on the observation of numerous productions staged over the course of many years and in several countries. Other studies, whose purpose is mainly literary, will refer to productions incidentally when what an actor or director has done supports a particular judgement or can open to a new line of argument. In practice, most critics restrict their attention to what happened on-stage in a small number of performances and occasionally an entire book will deal with a single performance rather than the play's wider potential. Study is often narrowed still further by concentrating attention on how the text of a play has been used, disregarding other elements of a production. Critics trained in literary studies may not wish to describe physical images and fleeting effects and therefore they concentrate on what the play *says* rather than what it *does* or what it might *be* in its entirety. Not attempting to assess what happens on stage, they describe how the words are spoken and with what gestures; they then proceed to explicate what, in their opinion, the speaker had meant. This usually involves a further narrowing of attention since a play is performed for an entire audience, not one individual critic, and the nature of a performance is affected by the composition and response of that audience: the culture in which a theatre is located also has its place in study and criticism.

What has been achieved can be conveniently illustrated by recent scholarly editions of single plays. When two editions of the same play are published simultaneously, as happened with *Measure for Measure* in 1991, comparison reveals some of the different uses that can be made of the same evidence. In the Introduction to N. W. Bawcutt's Oxford edition, a section on 'The Play in Performance' precedes one on 'The Play', as if theatrical matters should be dealt with before proceeding to the main task in hand. In Brian Gibbon's edition for Cambridge, 'The play on the stage' is the concluding section of the Introduction and develops many earlier issues. Both editions recount numerous undebatable facts about the various cuts and additions that have, at various times, been made to the text but they are very different when concerned with acting. Naming the actors in principal roles or describing pieces of stage business is usually as much as the Oxford provides although, for no specified reason, the 'real, sombre splendour' of John Emery's 'depraved, abandoned' Barnardine in a production of 1846 is represented by a lengthy quotation (p. 29). The Cambridge edition seldom cites any actor without describing some detail of the performance and attempting to characterize its style. While N. W. Bawcutt reports that Sarah Siddons was 40 years of age in 1795 when playing Isabella (p. 29), Brian Gibbons notes that in 1811–12 at Covent Garden, she was 'so weakened by age that when she knelt in the last scene before the Duke she could only get up again with his help' (p. 56). However, neither editor draws any critical deduction or gives any reason for mentioning this oddity.

The Cambridge edition is the more ambitious in suggesting the context for a piece of information. While both editors tell the story of William Poel placing an 'Elizabethan stage' within a picture-frame stage, it is Brian Gibbons who notes that, in 1908 at Stratford-upon-Avon, Poel's actors played 'constantly to the front' and that the stage projected 'beyond its usual limits' (p. 59).

While both note that in his production of 1950 Peter Brook asked Isabella to hold a long silence before pleading for Angelo's life, only Gibbons tells how, afterwards, her 'words came quiet and level, and as their full import of mercy reached Angelo, a sob broke from him' (p. 64). Of Keith Hack's production at Stratford in 1974, the Oxford edition notes that, at the beginning of Act V, the Duke 'descended from the flies on a bar labelled "Deus ex machina"' (p. 40) while the Cambridge explains that the director was an admirer of Brecht and had conceived the play as a 'fable of social oppression'; his Duke was the actor-manager of a jaded and underpaid company of actors and yet:

> For the final scene the Duke with golden hair descended on a ramp labelled 'deus ex machina'; his over-acting was intended to undermine the audience's belief in the happy ending.
>
> (p. 70)

'It was ironic', the editor adds, 'that this production failed to give the low-life characters substance: [they] were mere caricatures without conviction.' It is also ironic that a critic concerned with 'the play on the stage' does not consider whether the scenic marvel he describes contributes to an understanding of Shakespeare's play.

The small scale of both these accounts of a play in performance accentuates the dangers of any study that only pays attention to specific moments, but Marvin Rosenberg's four lengthy books on the major tragedies in performance, published between 1961 and 1992, are similarly incomplete. Although Rosenberg wrote at increasing length from book to book, he never had enough words for all the moments he wished to record. Of the many star actors from the sixteenth century onwards and from many countries that are represented here, not one is followed throughout the entire action of a play and so the overall shape and impact of a performance is scarcely considered – a serious shortcoming in view of the progressive nature of all theatrical events. By recording how actors spoke Shakespeare's words and what they did while doing so, this study is a patchwork of small observations that allows almost no scope for considering the whole substance, shape, style, or effect of any one production. In Rosenberg's latest volume, *The Masks of Hamlet* (Cranbury, NJ, and London: Associated University Presses, 1992), thousands of words are spent on how various Hamlets have, or might have, said 'The rest is silence' and, sometimes, the Folio's additional 'O, o, o, o.' as well. An earlier section considers other figures on-stage in this scene but very briefly and mostly in their relationship to Hamlet. The verbal and momentary focus of the book is unmistakable: 'What may Hamlet be trying to convey?' is the persistent question and one that Rosenberg cannot answer with any certainty, as he tells his readers several times; for example: 'All the words about Hamlet, almost three centuries of words, and as many of stagings, and the adventure into the depths of the play has hardly begun' (p. 924). An indigestible mass of information is not the only shortcoming of this method because the play has width, as well as 'depth', and in that broad perspective is reflected much of the life that Shakespeare shared with other people of his time. The play's social, political, and philosophical content is expressed in argument, narrative, dramatic structure, interactions, and the more elaborate stage-images, all of which involve large numbers of actors and supernumeraries and cannot be fairly represented in accounts of individual star performers.

Reliance on momentary observations has further shortcomings. In performance, how any one moment has been reached will always help to define that moment, the past leaving indelible marks on the minds and bodies of performers and so modifying the attitudes and expectations of the persons they play. An audience's attention also changes with time and this influences both performance and perception of it. While all this is slipping through the net of this form of study, a still greater limitation is a dependence on the choice of moments to consider. Very often they are ones that can be easily described and these do not always represent the full force of a production or the reason for its success or failure with an audience.

Increasing the Range of Criticism

That study should reach out from textual concerns to consider a play's total theatrical effect is clear enough but how to achieve this within reasonable length is not. By writing about a single 1955 production in '*Macbeth*' *Onstage* (Columbia, Missouri, and London: University of Missouri Press, 1976), Michael Mullin was able to include a facsimile of the text annotated by Glen Byam Shaw, the play's director. He also reproduced numerous production documents, photographs, and design sketches and quoted from press reviews and interviews with actors (but not, unfortunately, with Laurence Olivier or Vivien Leigh, the two stars of the production). For students this large and handsome book is a treasure trove of material for investigating the play in the process of preparation and rehearsal, as well as in performance. The drawbacks of this kind of study are that little room is left for analytical or comparative criticism and that finance for such a book would face stiff competition today.

Critics writing a book-length stage-history of a single play are able to move more slowly through its action than an editor in the Introduction to a text and therefore give a better sense of the overall achievement of productions and their impact on audiences. Gary Jay Williams's '*Our Midnight Revels*': '*A Midsummer Night's Dream*' *in the Theatre* (Iowa City: University of Iowa Press, 1997), for example, considers every major role and the effects of contrast, spectacle, crowd scenes, scenic invention, music, sound, and other stage devices. A synoptic view of the text's theatrical potential is given, identifying both recurrent and unusual strategies in production. As an account of theatrical events, however, it is less informative about the preparation for performance or back-stage complexities than Mullin's documentation.

Two series, designed for student use, have established contrasting ways of studying a single play. After a wide-ranging introduction, Robert Hapgood's book on *Hamlet* (Cambridge: Cambridge University Press, 1999) follows the format of the *Shakespeare in Production* series by reprinting the entire text and supplying footnotes that describe the interpretive line-readings of well-known actors and the accompanying gestures and stage-business. Although readers can follow the play's on-going action in the text, the commentary has space for noting only momentary and word-based effects from particular performances and can give no actor continuous attention. Books in the series *Shakespeare in Performance* do not reproduce the text and so their authors take what space they need for any one moment and can make occasion to assess a production's longer term effects and its overall style, shape, and emphasis. Within this less restrictive format, a student is generously served but the size of a critic's task becomes still more evident. If Anthony D. Dawson were to have all the scope he wanted for his volume on *Hamlet* (Manchester and New York: Manchester University Press, 1995), he would have filled three or four separate books small enough to be as reasonably priced as this.

One of Dawson's books would have considered how leading actors, directors, and designers have responded to the texts of the Folio and the two earlier Quartos. It might well run to many hundreds of pages because he is concerned with developments in theatre technology and changing styles of performance as well as the speaking of dialogue and accompanying actions. Another volume, perhaps equally large, would be about audiences or, as this critic would say, the cultural contexts of productions:

> One thing I try to do in this book is to suggest, however tentatively, some of the links that may exist between how the theatre gives *Hamlet* meaning and produces Hamlet's subjectivity and how the culture generally approaches problems of meaning, value, and selfhood.

(p. 22)

A third book would be about *Hamlet* produced for film and television. The disparate nature of this material has been recognized in Dawson's single volume by setting it apart in two chapters on '*Hamlet* at the movies: Olivier and Kozintsev', and 'Through the looking glass: Zeffirelli and the BBC'. The difficulty here is not that of dealing with many productions, but of sampling the huge number of visual images that are available for study and, as the chapter titles indicate, responding to the very different effects of lens-media.

Because Dawson is mindful of both culture and theatre, his fourth book would be about productions of *Hamlet* elsewhere than in Britain and North America: English-language productions in Australia, South Africa, and New Zealand, for instance, and productions in other languages in many countries around the world, especially in India and Japan where distinctive theatre traditions have been maintained from earlier times. In his single volume, few examples had to stand in for a great mass of material:

> Throughout the writing of this book I have been conscious that I have for the most part confined myself to the Anglo-American tradition of *Hamlet* performance, concentrating on those canonized performers who have a legendary relationship to Shakespeare's most famous role. In some ways this has been inevitable, given the nature of my own training and native language, the available evidence, the series of which this book forms a part, and the daunting breadth of the task of coming to terms with even the British stage tradition, let alone performances in other languages and media.
>
> (p. 224)

Most critics recognize limitations and establish their own priorities for studying Shakespeare's plays in performance. Dawson's book suggests that restriction to one play is insufficient for many purposes. His treatment of film and television makes little reference to theatre performances and could be off-loaded into a separate

volume without affecting the rest of the book; its removal
would make space to lessen overcrowding elsewhere. The
cultural background to productions is the cuckoo in this
nest, with an appetite that demands almost constant
feeding to be healthy. At the end of Dawson's chapter on
two *Hamlet* productions by John Barton and Richard Eyre
the reader is offered just two paragraphs of cultural generalities. Struggling to define a 'single vision' for the productions, the author knows that 'such a chimera' may not
exist but combines features from both as he tries to
define the influence of their cultural context. He points
to various oppositions and accumulations of 'sense' and
'awareness', noticing:

> perhaps most of all a conviction of the theatrical con-
> struction of selfhood interwoven with an equally com-
> pelling sense of the truth of the self's vision of things.
> Such perhaps were some of the contradictions of the
> 'time' and its multiplex forms and pressures.
>
> (p.169)

He is not a happy critic who has to introduce *perhaps* so
often in the concluding paragraph of his last chapter
on contemporary stagings of a Shakespeare play, especially when he is writing about 'conviction' and a 'compelling sense of the truth'. A consideration of the
cultural context of theatrical events calls for wide experience and sufficient space to handle the subject with
confidence.

Strict limitations have produced some of the most
responsible and illuminating studies. By considering the
work of only one or two actors a critic can make a well-
documented appraisal with reference to several plays.
Examples are Alan Hughes's account of an actor's long
career in *Henry Irving, Shakespearean* (Cambridge:
Cambridge University Press, 1981) and David Wiles's
*Shakespeare's Clown: Actor and Text in the Elizabethan
Playhouse* (Cambridge: Cambridge University Press, 1987)
which contrasts William Kemp with Richard Tarlton and
Robert Armin. Both these authors are concerned with

popular successes and, to some extent, failures and are therefore very aware of audience reactions and the contexts of performance. For theatre nearer to our own time, some actors and directors have assessed their own work with comparable thoroughness. Harley Granville-Barker's *Prefaces to Shakespeare*, written between 1927 and 1947, fulfil many of a student's needs and some of a critic's tasks. These accounts of individual plays grew more lengthy over the years as their grasp on theatrical events became more comprehensive. The preface for *Antony and Cleopatra* (London: Batsford, 1930) has sections on the performative consequences of the play's construction and the challenges facing the principal actors; others deal with staging, costume, speaking of the verse, and the contributions of smaller roles. Barker was also aware of the effect made on an audience, sometimes leading to impressionistic comment, as in: 'the vibrations of emotion that the sound of the poetry sets up seem to enlarge its sense, and break the bounds of the theatre to carry us into the lost world of romantic history' (p. 127). He was more precise when dealing with exposition, narrative, or dramatic conflict and when comparing an audience's expectations with what subsequently happens on stage.

Among later directors who have worked extensively on Shakespeare, Peter Brook stands out in maintaining a critical perspective on his productions and sharing the development of his thought in books, lectures, and workshops. In *The Empty Space* (London: MacGibbon & Kee, 1968) and *The Shifting Point: Theatre, Film, Opera, 1948–1987* (New York: Harper and Row, 1987) Brook combined theoretical considerations with accounts of his own practice and so was able to deal with aspects of the theatrical event that other critics miss: varieties of audience response and a director's manipulation of them; the effect of the place and occasion of performance; an actor's means of rehearsal and the demands of performance. In recent years, these very personal and thoughtful books have been joined by many others based on practical experience that have greatly assisted the study and

criticism of Shakespeare. Some are collections of interviews and essays by actors and directors,[2] others are auto-
biographies or commemorative histories of theatre
companies; some are training manuals that share their
author's expertise.[3] From the viewpoint of a student of
Shakespeare in performance, these books contain valu-
able information about the workings of theatre: how
various options arise in rehearsal, in what ways an actor
interacts with other actors, the characteristic excitements
and discoveries of performance, and much more. These
are essential ingredients of a theatrical event that are
often missing in the cooler, less biased accounts written
by scholars and critics.

A productive limitation of study has been to consider
only one aspect of production. By concentrating on sets
and costumes, Dennis Kennedy's *Looking at Shakespeare:
a Visual History of Twentieth-century Performance*
(Cambridge: Cambridge University Press, 1993; 2nd
edition, 2001) was able to advance a 'visual criticism' of
the plays in performance and, at the same time, establish a wide view of a production's cultural and political
contexts. The historical and European range of this
study, together with its illuminating use of the terminology and sensibility of art criticism, rapidly gave this
book a classic status. For many, the information and
pleasure given by its 150 illustrations made this a valu-
able book. By encouraging a wider perspective for criticism, the effect of this limited approach to the plays in
performance has been far from narrow. Taking a very
different restriction of view, M. M. Mahood's *Playing Bit
Parts in Shakespeare* analysed some 500 minor roles and
demonstrated how they contribute to the main action
of a play and its effect in performance (1992; second
edition, London and New York: Routledge, 1998).
Mahood's close focus and concern for practical stagecraft revealed many details about what Shakespeare
expected from performance that had previously lain
hidden in the texts.

Books and articles on film and television versions of
Shakespeare's plays represent a specialization in criti-

cism, rather than a limitation. Easy recourse to videos and films means that reference to enactment can be uncommonly accurate and detailed but these media are significantly different from theatre. How the plays are 'seen' today and some aspects of the demands they make upon actors can all be studied in films and videos but what is potent on a screen does not operate in the same way in a theatre and taking part in a theatrical event is not equivalent to the private enjoyment of a recorded and edited performance. While film and television have enhanced our understanding of the playtexts by giving them a new and often close-up semblance of life and by placing them in immediately recognizable settings, study of these media productions has little direct bearing on 'performance criticism' of the plays themselves.

Evoking Elizabethan Theatre Practice

Many critics refer neither to records of specific productions nor to their own experience of the plays in a theatre when they try to deduce what performances Shakespeare's plays were originally given. To avoid the difficulty of studying plays written for a theatre that no longer exists, they devise an imaginary theatre that, in their view, is closer to Elizabethan models and there, in their minds, envisage the plays in performance. The obvious drawbacks of this criticism are reliance on hypothetical reconstructions and the absence of those actors who were prominent ingredients in Elizabethan performances and a principal cause of their success.[4] However this work is supported by many works of scholarship of which Bernard Beckerman's examination of the staging procedures and repertoire of the King's Men in *Shakespeare at the Globe, 1599–1609* (New York: Macmillan,1962) is an early example which is still useful today for its detailed and practical assessment of dramatic construction and management procedures. Constant re-examination of documents, literary references to theatres, playtexts, and the few extant drawings of theatre buildings has slowly refined earlier perceptions of the Globe and other theatres of Shakespeare's time. Encouraged by this, critics have renewed earlier efforts to work out how the action of the plays might have been staged originally and the consequences of this on performance and reception. For example, in a series of *Theatre Production Studies* published by Routledge in London and New York, Michael Hattaway's *Elizabethan Popular Theatre* (1982), Peter Thomson's *Shakespeare's Theatre* (1983; second edition, 1992), and Alexander Leggatt's *Jacobean Public Theatre* (1992) have combined hypothetical reconstructions of original productions with critical reassessment of individual plays. Alan C. Dessen's *Recovering Shakespeare's Theatrical Vocabulary* (Cambridge: Cambridge University Press, 1995) is based on a meticulous examination of stage-directions in printed texts of the period and attempts to deduce their practical implications for Shakespeare's plays.

Recent excavations of the remains of the Globe and Rose theatres on the South Bank of the Thames and the building of a reproduction of the Globe close to the original site have brought more stimulus to critical and scholarly debate. The large audiences attracted to the new theatre ever since its first regular season of 1997 have given further interest to critical enquiry. The turn of the century saw the publication of C. Walter Hodges, *Enter the Whole Army: a Pictorial Study of Shakespearean Staging, 1576–1616* (Cambridge: Cambridge University Press, 1997), J. L. Styan, *Perspectives on Shakespeare in Performance* (New York: Peter Lang, 2000), and Andrew Gurr and Mariko Ichikawa, *Staging in Shakespeare's Theatres* (Oxford: Oxford University Press, 2000). While these studies are not based directly on the modern Globe's productions – recognizing that neither the Elizabethan actors and audience, nor the original production conditions, can ever be reconstructed along with the theatre – the actual building of that theatre has helped to give sharper lines to what must remain hypothetical conjectures about the plays' original productions. More attention is given now to 'staging' – that is gesture, stage-business, and on-stage

movement – than to speech-acts and individual performance but other, earlier critics had tackled these. With
little reference to an imaginary Globe, Michael
Goldman's *Acting and Action in Shakespearean Tragedy*
(Princeton, NJ: Princeton University Press, 1985) is a
careful discussion of the demands made upon actors by
the plays' language. Since the mid-twentieth century, con-
jectural reconstructions of both staging and performance, coupled with critical discussion of the playtexts,
have been the subject of very many books, including
several by the writer of this one. Robert Weimann's
*Author's Pen and Actor's Voice; Playing and Writing in
Shakespeare's Theatre* (Cambridge: Cambridge University
Press, 2000) marks a more recent development, being as
much concerned with cultural context and theories of
performance as with dramaturgy and the original staging.

Many recent books that are relevant to the theatrical
events of Shakespeare's own day scarcely mention either
the stage or theatre. The end of the twentieth century
saw a great increase in cultural studies by sociologists, his-
torians, philosophers, linguists and psychologists, as well
as literary critics, and this has immeasurably added to our
understanding of the original reception of the plays.
Cultural and theatrical interests did come together
profitably in some books, as in Steven Mullaney's *The
Place of the Stage* (Chicago: University of Chicago Press,
1988), Jean Howard's *The Stage and Social Struggle in Early
Modern England* (London and New York: Routledge,
1993), and *The Culture of Playgoing in Shakespeare's
England; a Collaborative Debate* by Anthony B. Dawson and
Paul Yachnin (Cambridge: Cambridge University Press,
2001). The endless quantity of original sources and their
possibilities for misinterpretation ensure that cultural
research is no more likely to yield certainties about how
Shakespeare's plays were received by contemporary audiences than the study of present-day performances or
hypothetical reconstructions of early ones are able to
describe with confidence the play's life on the stage.
Cultural scholars tend to fasten on what they find the
most surprising or peculiar in their reading of early

modern literature and documents, or on what appeals most directly to their personal tastes in contemporary texts, and then reinterpret Shakespeare's texts as if they had found significant strands in their composition. Their evidence will sometimes have only tenuous verbal echoes in the plays and even their most authenticated discoveries are likely to cast only accidental light on performance. Without a wide sampling and careful assessment of evidence, cultural studies can be wayward in their conclusions and yet constantly provocative with regard to perceived meanings, topicality, enthusiasms, puzzlement, doubts, and other ingredients of audience response. Perhaps their most lasting effect so far has been to establish how varied individual responses have always been and how different Elizabethan audiences were from those of today.

Audience response has long been a subject for specialist research in other ways. Ernst Honigmann's *Shakespeare: Seven Tragedies* (London and Basingstoke; Macmillan Press – now Palgrave Macmillan, 1976), which carries a subtitle, 'The dramatist's manipulation of response', is an early example, based primarily on textual analysis. Andrew Gurr's *Playgoing in Shakespeare's London* (1987; second edition, Cambridge: Cambridge University Press, 1997) deals with the audience's behaviour and predilections. Susan Bennett's *Theatre Audiences: a Theory of Production and Reception* (London and New York: Routledge, 1990) widened the scope of enquiry still further by referring to the plays, audiences, and theatres of many different times, including our own. The cultural context of the processes of production has also been studied, for example in Muriel Bradbrook's *The Rise of the Common Player: a Study of Actor and Society in Shakespeare's England* (London: Chatto and Windus, 1962) and Robert Shaughnessy's *The Shakespeare Effect* (London and New York: Palgrave – now Palgrave Macmillan, 2002), which is concerned with the cultural and political background of innovative twentieth-century productions.

Studying Live Theatre

Whatever aspect of Shakespeare's plays in performance is being investigated, most students and critics have an instinctive need to see for themselves. Film and television offer ready access to their versions, but live theatre is irreplaceable for demonstrating the plays' theatrical potential even though productions are geared to present-day interests and often disguise the implications of the texts. Theatre-going can sometimes be of most use as an opportunity of becoming more aware of the kind of attention we give to a play and the uncertainties of any theatrical event. If we are able to see the same production a number of times, we may also begin to recognize the constant features of that text in performance, distinguishing them from what is accidental or solely the invention and introduction of actor, director, producer, or designer. The modern practice of opening a production with public previews offers the further chance of seeing the results of rehearsals when actors are still exploring a text and the roles they are to play, and are not yet fully settled into a more or less final form.

Faced with the impossibility of converting oneself into a member of an Elizabethan or Jacobean audience and the difficulty of seeing beyond the current styles and fashions of theatre, some scholars have travelled to countries where both productions and audiences are more in keeping with what is known of those in Shakespeare's time. In parts of Asia, Africa and South America, some audiences are still truly popular and going to the theatre is an inexpensive holiday occasion. Actors sometimes perform on an open stage in the same light as their audience, developing close contact with them, and sometimes they are greeted in return with vocal acclaim or advice. Plays can be highly topical and local in reference and are often performed in a repertoire that changes daily. Theatre companies are often run by leading actors, their members belonging to an independent and largely permanent company. Productions may use expensive costumes but very little in the way of stage-properties or

changeable scenery. Male actors will sometimes play
female roles. All these features were common in
Shakespeare's theatre and are therefore of interest to students used to other forms of theatres. Even when these
similarities are missing, the very fact of sitting among an
audience of whose language and culture one is almost
wholly ignorant draws attention to what is unfamiliar in
an audience's behaviour and, consequently, to the part it
is playing in the performance.

Another way of rolling back time and experiencing elements of an Elizabethan theatrical event is to visit small
theatres and experimental productions. These can
provide a substitute for travel to distant places and in
some ways are the better alternative because they do not
involve alien and largely unknown cultures. In these
financially stringent times, small companies often have
no option but to use very simple staging and learn how to
use actors as the chief attraction of their productions.
Doubling of roles and casting against type are increasingly common and ensembles are formed in ways not dissimilar to the earlier family-based touring companies.
Theatres develop their own kinds of 'physical theatre',
'music theatre', 'total theatre', or, even, 'silent theatre'.
Improvisation is a common and, sometimes, a featured
attraction of the performance. While the technically elaborate productions of Shakespeare in well-subsidized theatres are often predictable, not least in their fashionable
novelties, forgotten kinds of theatre experience can be
found among poorer, less established companies. Some
of the work will be unskilled and carelessly produced, but
a growing number of alternative, fringe, experimental, or
studio theatres are extending the spectrum of current
theatre in their search for new and economical modes of
production. Companies like Théâtre de Complicité in
Britain and the Wooster Group in the United States have
produced a considerable body of innovative work and
their productions often suggest how some features of
Shakespeare's plays might have been handled, using the
strengths of ensemble acting and an open engagement
with their audiences.[5]

Studying a Play as Part of a Theatrical Event

In all this theatre-going, study, and criticism, one question keeps recurring in different forms – 'Is it possible to identify the permanent theatrical potential of a particular text?' Shakespeare's writing for the stage allows such ample scope to actors and directors and is able to support so many different interpretations, that the plays in performance continue to change with each generation and each theatre company. Obviously some performances are of trivial importance, being hastily conceived and poorly executed, or staged in unsuitable and impoverished circumstances. Even the most imaginative and skilled performances are likely to be remarkable for temporary and individual achievements rather than the discovery of what is inherent and permanent in the theatrical life of a play. Criticism of a production is usually content to fasten on a few details of textual interpretation, one or two characters, a single theme, or one particular aspect of the context in which the text was written or performed.

A more comprehensive understanding may be obtained through the research into Performance and Theatre Theory that has been conducted at numerous universities during recent years. We now have terms for describing and analysing role-playing, ritual, ceremony, sign and signifier, simultaneity and co-existence, transgression, foregrounding, presence, transformation, and much more.[6] Unfortunately, the application of this work to the study of Shakespeare has barely begun and, necessarily, little certain evidence is available about stage-practices in his time on which to base performance analysis. But advances have been made and a theatrical study of the plays can now reach beyond what happens to the text: the persons and training of performers, the physical and visual effects of staging, and the response of audiences can all be taken into account. Performance may be judged as part of an entire theatrical event to which theatre building and stage, location and occasion, and the response of spectators will all contribute. What

happens on-stage is not an isolated and constant phenomenon; it can be distinguished from life but is quite as
difficult to comprehend and to assess in its social, moral,
political, historical, and cultural context.

Much simpler and available to every student are very
basic practical exercises that explore the performative
qualities of a text. Examples include speaking aloud all
the lines of one particular person in a play, noticing repetitions, complications, silences, and reactions to what has
been said by others; or repeating a single speech of some
10 or 15 lines and charging it with different emotions
and intentions, taking one at a time, working slowly, and
then questioning which rendering fits the situation best;
or, having chosen a scene and represented each person
in it with a coin or other small object, place these tokens
in meaningful relation to each other and then change
their positions in response to a reading of the text aloud,
from beginning to end. Because they engage the imagination and respect the nature of a theatrical event, these
elementary explorations can give substance to other
investigations and lead to a practical understanding of
what could happen in performance. Nothing very surprising may be discovered, certainly nothing unquestion-
able, but involvement in these practical and mental
experiments leads to a fuller awareness of Shakespeare's
stagecraft and a heightened enjoyment when reading and
re-reading the text. Within a small compass, they demonstrate what a particular play needs from its performers
and what it offers to an audience.

No study of Shakespeare's plays in performance is likely
to bring absolute certainty and no criticism to find widespread agreement because neither result would accord
with the nature of theatre as an art. Our approach to the
texts needs to be exploratory and experiential, involving
imagination and sensation as well as observation, analysis,
and critical judgement. Any conclusions will be open to
challenge because, whether we are readers, students,
players, or audience members, these texts invite us to
take possession of them as plays, making them fully, and

quite singularly, our own. While this book has examined the life of these plays as they become part of a theatrical event, the need for this kind of study and criticism has become increasingly clear. It will pay attention to permanent and characteristic features of their texts, and not least the many opportunities they offer to actors and the varied appeal they can have for audiences.

Notes

1. This chapter develops earlier accounts in 'Shakespeare in Performance', *The Shakespearean International Yearbook, 1: Where are we now in Shakespearean Studies*, ed. W. R. Elton and John M. Mucciolo (Aldershot and Brookfield, USA: Ashgate, 1999), pp. 108–17, and 'Writing about Shakespeare's Plays in Performance', *Shakespeare Performed: Essays in Honor of R. A. Foakes*, ed. Grace Ioppolo (Newark and London: Associated University Presses, 2000), pp. 151–63.

2. Books in a series called *Players of Shakespeare* (Cambridge: Cambridge University Press, 1985 etc.) contain essays by actors of the Royal Shakespeare Company, recounting the experience of preparing and playing individual roles; these are geared to the interests of students and have also proved useful to critics and scholars.

3. John Barton's *Playing Shakespeare* (London and New York: Methuen, 1984) has been reprinted many times and is widely influential.

4. See above, pp. 85, 106–7, and 112.

5. See, for instance, pp. 52–6 above.

6. For example, Manfred Pfister, *The Theory and Analysis of Drama* (Cambridge: Cambridge University Press, 1988), Richard Schechner, *Performance Theory*, revised edition (London and New York: Routledge, 1992), Marvin Carlson, *Performance: A Critical Introduction* (London and New York: Routledge, 1996), and a book to which the present study is particularly indebted, Willmar Sauter, *The Theatrical Event: Dynamics of Performance and Perception* (Iowa City: University of Iowa Press, 2000).

   See, also, *Shakespeare, Theory, and Performance*, ed. James C. Bulman (London and New York: Routledge, 1996).

Index

Actors, 30–2, 36, 39, 42, 60–1,
    65–82, 84, 90–2, 100, 106–7,
    112–15, 117, 130, 150–1,
    155–60, 165, 166–71, 179,
    180, 202–3, 212, 222,
    227–8
'boy actors', 42–3, 49–50, 56,
    61, 76, 228
companies, *see also* King's Men,
    55–6, 60–1, 78–8, 138,
    155–6, 168–9, 227–8
actresses, 60
Akrigg, G. P. V., *Jacobean Pageant*,
    196 n.4
All's Well That Ends Well, 37, 62
    n.5, 201
Antony and Cleopatra, 43, 48–9,
    89, 98–9, 221
Aristotle, 87
    Rhetoric, 92
Armin, Robert, 221
Arnheim, Rudolf, 149
    Visual Thinking and *Power of the
    Center*, 121, 149
Arratia, Euridice, 55
Artaud, Antonin, 118–19, 136
    n.2, 159
As You Like It, 36–7, 43, 44, 46,
    47, 89, 131, 157–9, 167,
    185–6
Ascham, Robert, *Schoolmaster*, 83
    n.4
Asides, 19
Audiences, 2, **7–28**, 30–3, 39,
    42, 44–53, 56–8, 61–2, 71–8,
    84, 90, 106–7, 112–15, 118,
    130, 133, 135–6, **137–49**,
    150–1, 153, 156–7, 160–1,
    180, 182–4, 186–8, 192,
    197–8, 200–3, 211–13, 226,
    227–8
auditorium, darkened, 10, 12

BBC, 219
Baker, Sir Richard, 62 n. 3
ballads, 13, 189
Barton, John, 220
    Playing Shakespeare, 78, 231 n.3
Bawcutt, N. W., 214
Beaumont, Francis and John
    Fletcher, 29 n.10
    King and No King, 85
Becker, Boris, 25–6
Beckermann, Bernard,
    Shakespeare at the Globe, 223
Bell, Thomas, *Speculation of
    Usury*, 189
Bennett, Susan, *Theatre Audiences*,
    226
Berry, Cicely, *Actor and his Text*,
    66–7, 82
Bible, the, 195
Blackfriars Theatre, 25
Boar's Head Theatre, 8
'boy actors', *see* actors
Bradbrook, Muriel, *Rise of the
    Common Player*, 226
Brantley, Ben, 54
Brecht, Bertolt, 215
Bremer Shakespeare Company,
    62 n.10, 179 n. 4
Brook, Peter, 68–70, 214–15
    Empty Space and *Shifting Point*,
    221
Brown, John Russell, 225
    New Sites, 62 n.6
Bullough, Geoffrey, *Sources of
    Shakespeare*, 40 n.5
Burton, Robert, *Anatomy of
    Melancholy*, 35–6

Carlson, Marvin, *Performance*, 231
    n.6
celebrations, 153, 167, 169, 184,
    190, 192

ceremonies, 133–5, 143, 198
Chamberlain's Men, *see* actors,
    acting companies
characters *see* persons in a play,
    84–95
choreography, 60, 118–20,
    122–30, 135–6, 41
Christianity, 183–4, 199, 200–1
Cicero, 92
Clark, Peter, *English Alehouse*, 203
    n.3
Clode, Charles M., *History of …*
    Merchant Taylors, 29 n.14
Coleridge, Samuel Taylor, 34,
    36
commedia dell'arte, 151–2
Commons, House of, 188, 189, 199
Condell, Henry, 40 n.8, 209
Coriolanus, 82, 86–7, 97, 169, 189
costumes, 123–4, 126, 133, 166,
    168, 169, 171, 201
Coult, Tony and Baz Kershaw
    (eds), *Engineers of the*
    Imagination, 29 n.15
countryside, 192
    Warwickshire, 184–5
Craig, Gordon, 117–18, 119
criticism, **211–30**
Cymbeline, 167

Daily News, 54, 56
Damon and Pythias, 31
dance, 51, 55, 60, 127, 129
Dawson, Anthony D., *Hamlet*,
    218–20
    Culture of Playgoing (with Paul
    Yachin), 225
Death of Usury (Anon.), 189
Dekker, Thomas, 11
    If It Be Not Good, 29 n.9
Dessen, Alan C., *Shakespeare's*
    Theatrical Vocabulary, 224
directors, 27, 119, 136, 175, 179,
    221–2
Donne, John, 43
    Songs and Sonnets, 38
Drayton, Michael, 11, 29 n.8
duelling, *see* fighting

Elizabeth I, 190
Emery, John, 214
Erasmus, Desiderius, 195
    Praise of Folly, 96
Eyre, Sir Richard, 220

Fawkes, Guy, 188
Feingold, Michael, 54
Ferrara, 176
fighting, 27, 121, 131–2, 191–2
film, 10, 61, 219, 223, 227
Fletcher, John, *see* Francis
    Beaumont
folio edn of Shakespeare's *Works*
    (1623), 40 n.8, 209
fools, 22, 129, 143, 153
Frazer, Winifred, 29 n.11

Gargi, Balwant, *Folk Theater of*
    India, 62
Garrick, David, 28 n.8
Gibbon, Brian, 214
Globe Theatre, 8, 13, 25, 53, 56,
    155, 224
    hypothetical reconstructions,
    223–5
Globe, the New, 12–13, 224
gods, 167–8, 176–7, 186, 192
Goldman, Michael, *Acting and*
    Action, 225
Granville-Barker, Harley, *Prefaces*,
    221
Greek theatre, 152–3
groundlings, 13
Gurr, Andrew, *Playgoing*, 28 n.1,
    226
    Staging (with Mariko
    Ichikawa), 224

Hack, Keith, 215
Hall, Joseph, *Virgidemiarum*, 79
Hamlet, 1–2, 9, 14, 15, 19–21, 35,
    36, 43, 45–6, 47, 51, 79, 81,
    82, 85–6, 89, 98–9, 114–15,
    131–2, 134–5, 143, 151, 153,
    166–7, 171, 172, 183–5, 216
    quarto and folio texts, 135,
    216, 218

Hapgood, Robert, *Hamlet*, 218
Hattaway, Michael, *Elizabethan Popular Theatre*, 224
Hemming, John, 40 n.8, 209
Henry IV, Part One, 93, 171, 168
Henry IV, Part Two, 47, 80, 93, 171, 179 n.2
Henry V, 44, 112–14, 169, 171
Chorus, 31–2, 81, 99, 166
Henry VI, Part One, 43–4
Henry VI, Part Two, 48
Henslowe, Richard, 29 n.11
Heywood, Thomas, 12, 29 n.12
Hodges, Walter C., *Enter the Whole Army*, 224
Holinshed, Raphael, *Chronicles*, 96, 107, 109–11, 116 n.2
Honigmann, Ernst, *Seven Tragedies*, 226
Howard, Jean, *Stage and Social Struggle*, 225
Howard, Pamela, *What is Scenography?*, 175
Hughes, Alan, *Henry Irving*, 220
Hunter, G.K., *King Lear* (ed.), 145, 149 n.2

Ibsen, Henrik, *Peer Gynt*, 52
Ichikawa, Mariko, *see* Andrew Gurr
imaginary spaces, *see also* off-stage space, 171–5
imagination, **31–9**, 41–2, **46–53**, 56–8, 61–2, 81, 179, 180–2, 187, 192–3, 212
improvisation, 27, 91, 148, **150–61**
innovation, theatrical, 53
Irving, Henry, 9
Irving, Lawrence, *Henry Irving*, 29 n.6
Ives, E. W., 'Law and the Lawyers', 196 n.3

James I, 188, 189
Jatra theatres, 18, 50
jigs, 8
Jonson, Al, 54

Jonson, Ben, 40 n.8, 85, 94–5, 97, 178
Every Man, 94–5
Julius Caesar, 21–2, 35, 114, 168, 169

Kabuki theatre, 50
Bone Gathering, 51
Kane, John, 68
Kathakali performances, 154
Kemp, William, 221
Kennedy, Dennis, *Looking at Shakespeare*, 222
Kershaw, Baz *see* Tony Coult
King John, 169
King Lear, 22–4, 43, 44, 74–6, 81, 89–90, **137–49**, 171, 192–5
quarto and folio texts, 24, 76, 97, 145–6, 196 n.5
King's Men, *see also* actors, companies, 26, 153, 155
Kozintsev, Grigori, 219
Kuttiyattam performances, 154

Laban, Rudolph von, *Mastery of Movement*, 119–20
Latin, 70, 85, 165, 198
law, 190–2
Le Compte, Elizabeth, 55
Leggatt, Alexander, *Jacobean Popular Theatre*, 224
Leigh, Vivien, 217
lights, stage, 12, 54, 60, 130, 153, 169, 174
Love's Labours Lost, 81, 179 n.1
Luther, Martin, 184

McCarthy, Gerry, *Molière's Theatres*, 161 n.1
McGrath, John, 17
Good Night Out, 29 n.16
Macbeth, 9, 35, 38, 43, 90, 97–9, 131, 160–1, 171, 172–3, 185, 188, 199–200, 201, 217
Machiavelli, Niccolò, 195
Macready, William Charles, 9

Mahood, M.M., *Playing Bit Parts*, 222
Mankind (Anon.), 92
Marathi theatre, 18
Markham, Pigmeat, 54
Marlowe, Christopher, 195
Marston, John, 11
masks, 51
Mason, Bim, 17–18
  Street Theatre, 29 n.17
masques, 34, 85, 167–8
Massinger, Philip, *Roman Actor*, 85
Measure for Measure, 43, 44–5, 94, 168, 214–15
  modern editions, 214–15
Mee, Susie, 62 n.8
Merchant of Venice, 15, 167, 177–8, 189, 200
Merchant Taylors' Company, 14
Merry Wives, 70, 95
metre, **69–76**, 103
Middle Temple, 190
Middleton, Thomas, 29 n.7
Midsummer Night's Dream, 30–3, 36, 46, 51, 68, 82, 85, 179 n.2, 217
Miller, David, 25–6
Molière, 151–2, 161 nn. 1, 2
  Dom Juan, 152
Montaigne, Michel de, *Essays*, 96
morality plays, 128
Mosse, Miles, *Arraignment … of Usury*, 189
Mullaney, Steven, *Place of the Stage*, 225
Mullin, Michael, '*Macbeth*' *Onstage*, 217
music, 51, 56, 60, 127–30, 168, 175
Much Ado About Nothing, 41, 47, 51, 81, 82, 89, 98, 131, 167, 169
mystery plays, 153
myths, 175–8

Nashe, Thomas, 195
National Theatre, Royal, 157, 196 n.1

Nehru Centre London, 62 n.10
New Characters (anon., 1615), 71, 80, 87, 165
New English Dictionary, 165
New World, the, 49, 199
New York Times, 53–4
Newington Butts theatre, 29 n.11
Nicoll, Allardyce, *Garrick Stage*, 28 n.4
Nordern, John, 165
North, Sir Thomas, 35

off-stage space, **180–96**
Olivier, Laurence, 217, 219
O'Neill, Eugene, *Emperor Jones*, 53–6, 61
Osborne, John, 210
Othello, 22, 43, 46, 51, 89, 97, 99, 122, 132–3, 167, 168, 170–1
O'Toole, Fintan, 54, 56
Overbury, Sir Thomas, *A Wife*, 87
Ovid, 195

Parker, R. B., 196
parliament, *see* House of Commons
Parnassus, Part Two, 62
Patterson, Michael, *Peter Stein*, 62
Pericles, 167
persons (in a play), **84–99**, 208–9
Pfister, Manfred, *Theory and Analysis of Drama*, 231 n.6
Pisk, Litz, *Actor and His Body*, 120
Plautus, 195
Players of Shakespeare (series), 231 n.2
playhouses *see* theatres
plays as literature, 3, 27, 213
plays, new, 12, 29 n.11
Plutarch, *Lives of … Grecians and Romans* (tr. Thomas North), 35–6, 96
Poel, William, 214
production, theatre, 27–8, 30, 41, 52–3, 55–6, 60, 77, 92, 130, 150–1, 153, 160, 169–70, 175, 201–3, 211–12, 215–18, 224, 226, 227–8, 229

prompt books, 119
properties, stage, 131–3, 166–7
publication, 13
puppets, 51, 169

Quintillian, 92

radio, 13, 189
Ralph Roister Doister, 93
readers, 49, 179, 207–10
realism, 52–3, 56, 60–2, 186–94
rehearsals, 30, 77, 90–2, 221–2
repertoire, 13, 155, 227
research, vii, 2–3, 51, 153, 178,
    195–6, **211–30**
reviewing, 10, 150
Richard II, 107–12, 116, 171, 177
    quarto and folio texts, 116 n.2
Richard III, 22, 44, **100–7**, 133–4,
    169
Robeson, Paul, 54
Romeo and Juliet, 43, **56–61**, 122,
    131, 171, 180–3, 201
    quarto text, 57
Rose Theatre, 12, 29 n.11, 165, 224
Rosenberg, Marvin, *Masks of
    Hamlet*, 215–16
Royal Shakespeare Company, 77,
    78

Saint-Denis, Michel, *Training for
    the Theatre*, 67
St Saviour's Bankside, 189
Sauter, Willmar, *The Theatrical
    Event*, 4 n.2, 231 n.6
Saxo Grammaticus, 183
scenography, *see* stage design
Schechner, Richard, *Performance
    Theory*, 231
scholarship, *see* research
Scot, Reginald, 188
Seneca, Lucius Annaeus, 195
sermons, 13, 189
sexuality, representation of, 39,
    42–50, 60, 192, 193
Shakespeare, William, *see under
    individual works*
    member of acting company, 2

Shaughnessy, Robert, *Shakespeare
    Effect*, 226
Shaw, Glen Byam, 217
Sher, Antony, 77–8
Shergold, N. D., *History of Spanish
    Theatre*, 28 n.3
Siddons, Sarah, 214
Sidney, Sir Philip, *Apology for
    Poetry*, 69
Sisson, C. J., *Boar's Head*, 28 n.2
soliloquies, 19–21, 100–6, 108–9,
    112–15, 140–1, 147–8
Sonnets, 33, 179 n.2
sound effects, 11, 130, 153, 169,
    174
Spanish theatres, performance
    times in, 8
spectator sports, 25–6, 154
spectators, *see* audiences
speech, 2, 59, **72–81**, 149, 198,
    225, 230
Spenser, Edmund, 195
    Faerie Queen, 38
stage business, 119, 131–3, 142,
    151, 155, 168–9, 188–9, 207
stage design, 41, 130, 136, 173–5,
    179, 201
stage directions, 19, 119
Stein, Peter, 52
Stich, Michael, 25–6
Stratford-upon-Avon, 70
Styan, J. L., *Perspective on …
    Performance*, 224
syntax, 21, 70–5, 104–5

Taming of the Shrew, 47, 201
Tarlton, Richard, 221
taverns, 200
television, 10, 13, 189, 219–20,
    222, 227
Tempest, 34, 44, 51, 85, 93–4,
    159–60, 168
tennis, 25–6
texts of plays, 2–3, 19, 30, 39, 42,
    52, 61–2, **65–82**, 90, 119, 149,
    159, 187, 197–8, 201–3,
    207–9
Théâtre de Complicité, 228

theatres, Elizabethan, 11–12, 16, 44, 121, 123, 130–1, 165, 223–4
Theophrastus, *Characters*, 87
Thomson, Peter, *Shakespeare's Theatre*, 29 n.11, 224
Times (London), 25–6, 77–8
Timon, 169
Titus Andronicus, 83 n.6, 169
touring, 79, 155, 156, 166, 228
Tourneur, Cyril, *Revenger's Tragedy*, 93
Trewin, J. C. (ed.), Macready, *Journal*, 28 n.5
Troilus and Cressida, 49, 79, 168, 169
Twelfth Night, 34, 46–7, 48, 72–4, 80, 82, 89, 96–7, **122–30**, 143, 151, 170, 200
Two Gentlemen, 93

Ullmann, Lisa, 119

Valk, Kate, 53–5, 57, 61
Venus and Adonis, 36
verse, *see* metre
video cassettes, 10, 223

Village Voice, 54
Virgil, 195
voice training, 65–7, 78, 80

Webster, John, *Duchess of Malfi*, 85
White Devil, 87–8
Works, ed. F. L. Lucas, 83
Wedding, The, 85
Weimann, Robert, *Author's Pen and Actor's Voice*, 225
Welfare State theatre company, 16–17, 19
Wiles, David, *Shakespeare's Clown*, 220
Williams, Gary Jay, '*Our Midnight Revels*', 217
Wilson, Thomas, *Art of Rhetoric*, 92
'State of England', 196 n.3
Winter's Tale, 47, 167–8
Wooster Group, 53–6, 60, 228
wordplay, 47, 101, 103

Yachnin, Paul, *see* Anthony B. Dawson

Zeffirelli, Franco, 219